"Marie Trout has done something quite unique. Many can write about the *business* of the blues, but not many can speak personally about the tribulations along the way. Although she may not play or sing blues for a living, there's *no* question about her personal contact with The blues. I recommend you read this unique perspective."
- Joe Louis Walker, Grammy Award winning blues musician, Blues Hall of Fame inductee

"Marie Trout's, *The Blues,* is a fascinating work of social history about fans of blues music. Her insightful analysis also sheds new light on events in the broader society and her findings will be of great interest to sociologists and social psychologists."
- Raymond Moody MD, PhD, world-renowned scholar and researcher, award-winning author of *Life After Life*

"From where the blues came to where the blues are going, a fascinating journey of a universal genre. Wonderfully written and totally relevant."
- Sandy Carrol, Memphis-based contemporary blues singer/songwriter

"Standing on deep inquiry, this book is a landmark… a must read for anyone with even a passing interest in the blues. Phenomenal."
- Stephen Dale Petit, Musician, New Blues Ambassador and writer

"*The Blues - Why It Still Hurts So Good* is a breathtakingly complex and beautiful exploration of a musical genre that embodies powerful healing potential for the world. In part, because through Trout's study of current blues fans, she demonstrates how blues contains a universal language capable of expressing our shared experience and connectedness. *The Blues* is both groundbreaking and paradigm-shifting in its complexity! She employs a lens that ranges from blues

history and blues legends to blues wisdom and the neuroscience of feelings, and how we are affected by a genre that insists on "telling it like it is!" A truly extraordinary musical journey and an important historical, intellectual, and creative contribution to an important genre."
- Belvie Rooks, essayist, educator, and producer

"While there are many good blues artist biographies, we have lacked a concise empirical study of why so many people love the blues. Until now. Marie Trout's groundbreaking book fills that sorely missing gap, and does so in an enlightening and entertaining manner. This is an important book, and an enjoyable read. Anyone who wonders why so many people love the blues, will not only want to own, but to share Marie Trout's *The Blues*."
- Jesse Finkelstein, author, attorney at law, and broadcaster of Blues Radio International

"In her book, *The Blues - Why It Still Hurts So Good*, Marie Trout adeptly explains to the reader how the music of the blues captivates and then emotionally impacts the listener. Her work is grounded in academic research yet accessible to all, and her theses are made even more impactful by the manner in which she weaves her personal story, as well as that of other blues fans, artists, and professionals, into the narrative. This book is the perfect read for the blues lover who wants to better understand his or her own connection to the music. But I would also strongly recommend it to the music fan who is confused by the passion with which blues lovers are drawn to this specific genre. If each of us could connect to the stirring power of the blues of which she speaks, perhaps we might better identify with each other, or even more, connect with our inner selves to find that peace and healing which we ultimately seek."
- Barbara B. Newman, President and CEO of the Blues Foundation

THE BLUES

-Why It Still Hurts So Good

By Marie B. Trout, PhD

To my dear friend, Lynda, who knows the blues.

(signature)

Keep believing!

 Feb 2017

YAKKABIZ
— PUBLISHERS —

- A division of Fish-Net Productions, Inc.
Las Vegas, NV

For information about permission to reproduce selections from this book, or to contact the author, please write to: Yakkabiz Publishers, P.O. Box 108, Huntington Beach, CA 92648, United States of America.
To contact the author via e-mail: marie@marietrout.com
www.MarieTrout.com

LIBRARY OF CONGRESS CATALOGING-IN-PUBLICATION DATA

Trout, Marie B.
Library of Congress Control Number: 2016914073
The Blues - why it still hurts so good / Marie B. Trout.—First Edition
Includes bibliographical references and all contents.
ISBN: 978-0-9979983-0-6
MUS003000 Music / Genres & Styles / Blues
SOC026000 Social Science / Sociology / General

Formatting: Theresa Matthews and Scott Pantall
Interior book design: Vince Pannullo
Cover design: Cathi Stevenson
Cover (and Part IV) Photograph: Aigars Lapsa
Photo of Author on back cover: Denise Truscello
Dedication illustration: iStock.com/9george
Part I illustration: iStock.com/mj0007
Part II photography: iStock.com/cyano66
Part III art: iStock.com/bestdesigns
Epilogue Illustration: Jared Shomo
Graphical illustrations designed by: Theresa Matthews
Charts and graphs by:Vizzlo

Printed in the United States of America by RJ Communications.

This book is dedicated with love
To anyone
Who has lived with an inner, silent scream
Of grief, heartache, despair, and desperation
And who has longed
To understand, explain, and express
That which cannot
Be put into
Words

Contents

Part I - Blues Fans in the 21st Century

Part II - Blues Boomers: Wired for the Blues

Part III - The Transformative Power of Blues

Part IV - Blues Healing: Now and in the Future

Preface

The material in this book is based on findings from a Grounded Theory research study of modern blues fans. A combined survey and interview process was used. The survey was distributed anonymously on third-party websites, and was taken by over 1,000 blues fans who were asked 62 wide-ranging questions about their relationship with the blues. In addition, in-depth interviews with fans and industry professionals were conducted using open-ended questions. The interview process continued past the point when new themes or "new types of statements" appeared. Theoretical saturation was thoroughly reached. The interviews confirmed and deepened the themes that emerged in the survey - and the two instruments combined gave a very clear picture: a look at the relevance of blues music today for its current main audience, and how this audience, in turn, shapes the continuing trajectory of the music.

This is consequently a book about the history of those who are blues *fans* today (whether they play the blues themselves or not). This book explores why these 21st century fans are primarily white baby boomers and what has "wired" them to resonate so powerfully with the genre. It contains an investigation of what blues music means to those who embraced it after the 1960s, when African American blues fans largely left it to explore other realms of musical expression. There is a great deal of danger of being misunderstood when writing about the blues from this vantage point, since African Americans created and originated this expressive musical art form.

The exploration in this book thus starts where a study of the blues normally ends. It is written with the assumption that the reader has an interest in, and is well aware of, the history of the blues and those who created it. This book you hold in your hands is intended as a heartfelt tribute to these blues masters who created such enduring, powerful, and enigmatic music under unbearable circumstances. They gave a musical gift of immense beauty, renewal, restoration and healing to our world, which cannot be appreciated and venerated enough. And as racial tension is continuing in our world, studying blues history helps those of us who are 21st century blues fans come to terms with the fact that while many share our joys and pains, there are many more who have it much worse.

Without African American blues masters of times gone by; much of our musical landscape would not be the same. This book seeks to investigate the power of this musical art form they created, because it changed how we see ourselves, and how we approach and understand music and each other. As you read, please keep in mind that the perspectives in this book are an expression of collected data from a study of current blues fans. This is the first time their perspective has been compiled and explored as a group. There are findings and perspectives in this book I do not agree with or share. I have simply sought to compile data, present it, analyze it, illustrate it, and provide background for it.

Ultimately this book is a tribute to blues music and to those who birthed it out of the Mississippi mud. This book shows that the blues contains wisdom that seeks to express rather than suppress, to heal rather than hate, and to connect rather than isolate. It is in the spirit of being its servant that I have entered into this exploration.

Acknowledgements

I want to thank each and every one of the more than one thousand blues fans who responded to an extensive online survey about their experiences with blues music today for their honest, direct—and often comprehensive—answers to the many questions. I owe a particular debt of gratitude to the fans and industry professionals who, in addition, allowed me to interview them—sometimes for many hours— and who thus helped deepen the story of the relevance of this art form in the 21st century. Of these I particularly want to thank: Chris Barber, Bruce Iglauer, Joe Louis Walker, Jon Brewer, Stephen Dale Petit, Jay Sieleman, Janiva Magness, Thomas Ruf, Art Tipaldi, and Ted Drozdowski, Peter Morley, David Tannen, Mark S. Webb, Geri Geasland, Ross Weiss, Robert Kintner, Barry Moon, Joyce Papania, Scott Sparks, Barry B. Shanks, Larry C. Brown, Jimi Patricola, Jay Summers, Kate Del Corpo, as well as those who wished to partake anonymously. Thank you all from the bottom of my heart.

Walter: you are my life, my love, and my main connection to the blues. Without you in my life, nothing makes sense. You have provided me steady support, space, understanding, feedback, and encouragement, when I decided to jump into this crazy endeavor of studying, researching, and writing about the role of the blues music today. You are my rock, my inspiration— and along with our three sons, Jonathan, Michael and Dylan—my endless inspiration and joy.

Throughout the research and dissertation-writing phase of this project, I was aided immensely by my Major Advisor, Mark Ryan, whose academic discipline and insights, including his 20 years of experience as a Dean at Yale University, provided vital support for this project. Mark's presence and involvement in this project offered a firm, structured guidance at a time in my life when so much was falling apart. I cannot adequately express my gratitude for his time, insights, encouragement, and patience.

A warm thank you to the websites that allowed me to post links to the survey anonymously: AmericanBluesScene.com, Blues411.com, Blues-e-news.com, and DannyBryant.com

In order to accurately compile data from the interviews, I was aided by my collaborator, Scott Pantall. Scott is not a blues fan, and was able to provide a cool, clear, outside perspective. He was a great help in uncovering this collective voice of blues fans as he and I discussed the meanings of the data (for weeks on end) by asking: "What is the interviewee *really* saying here?" Scott is professionally trained in decidedly ascertaining meaning from statements, and his overall help in this project was invaluable to me.

And then there is my dear friend and formative teacher, Adjunct Mogens Kjær, who has, what must be, the largest privately held blues collection in my native country of Denmark, and who possesses a deep knowledge of, and love for, the blues. Mogens and his wife Karen Lemming have hosted countless dinners, and spent many nights with me in front of the fire (for some reason mostly during blizzards), discussing the direction of my work from its inception to its final form. Mogens' help, support, and critique have played a pivotal role in my life, my research, and my writing.

To my mentors and teachers: Stanislav Grof, Raymond Moody, Jean Houston, and Bruce D Schneider, you have all helped change the world in profoundly meaningful ways, and certainly *my* world. To Jim Hickman, Will Taegel and Judith Yost: you have been a well of profound wisdom in my studies and in my life. Thank you also to Carolyn Atkinson, who helped me identify the topic for my research. Conducting a Grounded Theory Study on the relevance of the blues for its core audience was a gargantuan task, and without the support, know-how and advice from Jim Van Overschelde, who is an assistant research professor at Texas State University, my efforts would surely not have been successful.

I want to also give a warm thank you to my friend, Theresa Matthews, for her keen eye with regard to text formatting, illustrations and continuous feedback and editorial assistance through my entire process of research and writing. To Jesse Finkelstein: thank you for all you do for the blues in our world, and for your encouragement and suggestions with regard to parts of this material. I also want to thank President and CEO, Barbara B. Newman, Board Chairman Paul E. Benjamin, the Board of Directors, and the many contributing members of the Blues Foundation for their endless work to prioritize, preserve, and promote blues music, its history, and its continuing relevance. A heartfelt thank you to my editor and friend, Nina Blum, who has helped me make this book more cohesive through several of the interim versions of this material.

There are many others—too many to name—who have offered support, critique and input throughout this project: you know who you are, and please know that I do too! Each one of you, whether named or not, have helped to birth this testimony to the relevance of blues music as an art form with a continuing potential to change lives, while providing gratifying musical experiences for those who are able to momentarily let go and let the blues take over.

With deep appreciation,

Marie Trout

Introduction

Does the blues have a multiple personality disorder?

Why do we call it "the blues"?

There are several possible origins of this term: a direct link comes from the British Isles. Prior to the 20th century, the English used the phrase: *blue devils.* The term described a state of suffering from feelings of shame or sadness. It might also have been used to describe the state of delirium tremens in someone who had imbibed alcoholic beverages too excessively for too long and suffered the effects of severe alcohol withdrawal. The first literary reference to *feeling blue,* with the connotation of feeling sad or depressed, is likely from 1741, when an English actor named David Garrick wrote in a letter:

I am far from being quite well, tho not troubled wth ye Blews as I have been.

But there is another component to the creation story of the term. In certain West African cultures, notably the Yoruba, the term, *itutu* translates as "mystic coolness" or awareness. It is associated with being calm, collected, in emotional balance and with a potential to sense the sacred. The color blue was associated with the concept of itutu. Blue is, of course, also the color of the sky and the oceans. It confers depth, stability, endurance, and eternity.

When European and African influences merged on the North American continent, it is likely that the staying power of a phrase or a word like *the blues* to describe a musical expression was partially helped by the fact that it resonated bilaterally. Certain linguistic and symbolic transfers might have taken place differently due to cultural variances where the color blue—with its African symbolic meaning of "mystic coolness"—and the European American understanding of "feeling blue" as "being out of it, depressed, or sad" combined. A multi-faceted potential thus was born into the term from the beginning. It is certainly indisputable that the united, bi-cultural connotations, interpretations, and practices of the blues at various times, to an assortment of interpreters, have straddled the realms of the sacred and the profane; the playful and the reverent; the rebellious and the cathartic; the repressive and the rebellious. It has manifested in those who approached it with wild, reckless abandon, and it has accompanied those who sat in quiet, musical contemplation. All of it became an integral part of the blues. It was about the emotions felt right here and now.

Today, the blues remains a paradoxical, brilliant, and in many ways indefinable entity. Depending on who describes it, and the definitions and interpretations they use, it can be seen as a historical, exclusively African American manifestation of a musical art form, a simple description of a specific musical structure, or it can have more elaborate or diffuse associations. It is clear however that both the term and the music are born at the crossroads of intersecting cultural hurts, traits, trends, and influences. They are birthed out of intersecting environments fraught with an appalling cocktail of historical denial, shame, anger, resentment, double-standards, misrepresentation and appropriation. In spite of it all, like a flowering lotus that can only thrive in murky water, the blues continues to grow immense beauty. It offers many gifts to those who create it and those who listen to it. It reaches those of us who listen and partake in it wherever we are, whoever we are, whenever we are ready. It offers a potential for identification and understanding with those who came before us, those who suffer, and those who let go of worry and dance in the rain. And once enveloped in the blues, it can give us experiences that make us feel so very alive.

Part I

Blues Fans in the 21ˢᵗ Century

Chapter 1:

Why I Wrote this Book

Having worked for 25 years as artist manager—and wife—of blues rock artist Walter Trout, I often wondered about what constitutes the magnetic pull that keeps blues fans engaged with all kinds of blues and blues-inspired music. Why do these devoted groups of blues fans feel such a strong connection to this musical art form in the second decade of the 21st century? Ultimately the question was also my own: what is it about this music that hooks me so strongly? Why does it feel so good?

After engaging with, interviewing, and surveying blues fans for years, I am in awe of the enduring power of the blues as it still manifests here and now, in the 21st century. I am also, more than ever, a blues fan myself. I understand completely why fans come home from work, throw everything aside and start playing the guitar, harmonica or simply tap their foot in time to a favorite record. I get how blues fans live for the weekends, when they go out to hear music in clubs, watch a blues jam at the local bar, or play gigs themselves—often for little or no compensation. It makes sense that a couple spends their vacations traveling on blues cruises, going to festivals with friends, or following around favorite bands. And why someone might spend hours every week volunteering for the local blues society or for the blues foundation. It is clear why someone depends on their morning ritual of listening to a blues station when they drive to work. And this picture also fits in with why so many of us do whatever we can to work for the blues: as volunteers, musicians, agents, managers, record label people, promoters, radio DJ's, writers, photographers, etc.

It has become clear to me that the blues fills needs that our current culture doesn't. And therefore it also makes great sense that many of us want to make sure that the blues survives, thrives, and continually reaches new people. Blues fans all know what they get out of it (although it is really not easy to give a quick elevator speech about). The vast majority of us desperately want to convey this to those who are not fans of the genre, and particularly to younger generations. Many of us work tirelessly to promote blues music and find ourselves repeatedly preaching to the choir. We celebrate the few times we manage to reach beyond the small, current audience of the blues today, but honestly—we rarely succeed.

And how do we change that? How do we help others discover the transformative power of the blues when it is so difficult to even explain what it is? We might bring uninitiated blues fans to a concert who often, then, stand kind of unaffected and listen politely—but we can sense that the music doesn't get to them like it does to us. We play a cut from a blues master that to us is revelatory, and they say that they just don't get it. How come they don't hear it? What is it that makes them unable to understand the brilliance of this music? And when it just doesn't seem to translate to people we otherwise respect and love, we feel a sense of disbelief and disappointment, or we get tempted to point the finger at them: they are simply not as cool, as deep, or as hip as we initially took them to be.

The above was certainly a part of my own frustration. Since I often meet people, who like me "know" what blues music is and does, but who also find it frustratingly difficult to convey this knowledge, I decided to look for explanations in literature. What does blues music do to modern blues fans? I found that there is a great deal of information about the blues. The available literature falls in two main groups:

- Academic literature—musicological, ethnomusicological, historical, sociological, psychological, philosophical, as well as many individual analyses of blues music.
- Artist biographies or historical explorations of the lives of blues artists.

Combined, existing literature provides an insightful view of what blues is and where it comes from. But it does not explain, beyond individually felt experiences, what blues *does* to us, how it affects us, and how it changes the lives of those who are far removed from the historical origins of the blues: those who are blues fans today. Each of us has our personal explanations of why blues is awesome, but to individually try to convey our experiences is similar to a devoted fan of spinach seeking to explain its wonders to someone who can't stand it: "It tastes so good, it's good for you, it heals, it is the best..." It just doesn't work: no matter how much we preach, proselytize, and pontificate, it remains as meaningless to the spinach hater, as it usually does to the uninitiated blues fan.

I set out simply to ask questions. The answers began to appear as the data were compiled from the large group of blues fans. And the answers provided a moving tribute to the power of blues music. On my journey to explore the role of blues music to those who love it today, I explored questions such as:

- Why is the preponderance of blues fans today white and middle-aged?

- Did historical events, societal conditions (including being raised in 1950s and 60s suburbia) help to set the stage for the popularity of the blues for this population group?

- Why were British musicians instrumental in creating attention for the blues in the 1950s and '60s?

- Why did broader appeal of blues music to Caucasians only happen in earnest after the blues was adopted and played by white musicians?

- Why did African Americans generally leave the blues when Caucasians found it?

- Are all human beings born with innate preferences for those who look and sound like themselves, and if so, can blues music help provide a universal "language"?

- Does the blues, even when related to "sad" topics, makes us feel better, and if so why?
- How can we define the concept of "authentic" blues without closing the door to current and future interpretations of it?
- Is it appropriate, at the same time, to talk about "authentic" blues as something that only exists in a bygone era, performed by African Americans? And if so, what the heck is the concept of "authenticity" *really* when we talk about the blues?
- What is it about blues music that gives it the potential to be so expressive?
- Why is it so difficult to make the notes "speak"?
- Why does the same piece of blues music mean something different to the same person at different times?
- What is the role of improvisation, immediacy, involvement, immersion and spontaneity in blues music?
- What is a groove? Why does blues music need to groove – and can we conceptually define it – or does it disappear like dew at first morning sun, if we try to shine the light of analysis on it?
- Does the blues have the potential to activate emotional awareness and make us more attentive and compassionate?
- Why is the blues still alive? Why hasn't it gone the way of disco?
- Can playing or listening to the blues temporarily change our state of consciousness?
- Why does the blues affect us differently, and why do some people just not get it?
- Why is it so important to current blues fans that the genre lives, and to share their love of it with others? It is obviously because they get something extraordinary out of their love affair with the blues, but what exactly is it?
- Are there common denominators for what blues is and does for contemporary blues fans?

- Is there a common narrative that contemporary blues fans connect to?

After starting the research, the data quickly confirmed what many have observed: that blues music today attracts mainly a group of people who are not typically oppressed, marginalized, or poor. In fact, most blues fans today are white and middle-aged. I call this segment of blues fans today *blues boomers*. They collectively told me a poignant love story of their relationship with the blues: their story is about how music and fans mutually inspire and reflect each other. In order to understand why the blues speak to this group in particular, I decided to primarily focus on *their* particular set of sociological circumstances in order for me to dig in and begin to understand their attraction to the genre. I was curious to explore what this group of people, who grew up in times of unprecedented wealth, finds so powerful about a musical art form that was created under the harshest of circumstances over a hundred years ago. When referring to "fans" or "blues fans" in the following, it is this main group of the current blues audience that I am referring to.

Today, blues music is considered a "niche genre," and is often regarded by popular culture as somewhat of a museum piece along with the cotton gin, steam traction engines, and wood-burning stoves. It is not really commercially successful—at the Grammy's the blues barely gets a mention when awards are handed out. At the same time, for those who are fans of it today, it has a power that is undeniable: it captures and expresses our humanity in ways that are deceptively simple, subtly complex, and ingeniously elegant. It has merged with many other influences that have shaped our culture and therefore, it exists as a constant undercurrent of our musical awareness. It has an undeniable capacity to express human emotions, and for this reason Blind Willie Johnson was chosen as an inter-stellar blues ambassador on the Voyager spacecraft with a recorded track of "Dark Was the Night, Cold Was the Ground"[1-1]. In 3 minutes and 15 seconds, Blind Willie and his guitar nonverbally communicate to whomever the spacecraft might eventually encounter the essence of the human soul—its suffering, its beauty, and its gentleness. Brilliantly, powerfully, and simply.

As I conducted the study of blues fans in 2013 and 2014, my personal life was falling apart; I was watching the love of my life, who is also my business and blues partner, fade away from end-stage liver disease caused by Hepatitis C and repeatedly come close to death. As I was faced with uncertainty and the inability to plan more than an hour—or sometimes only minutes—into the future due to the all-consuming, chaotic dictates of a life-threatening illness, the structure and discipline of a methodical research framework provided an island of calm in the stormy seas of ever-changing circumstances. At the same time, as the results from the study emerged, I found a new perspective: objective results from the collective stories of blues fans danced a tango in my subjective awareness and helped to change the perspective from which I understood myself, my work, and the role of blues music in our culture. Since the findings of this research impacted me so powerfully, I decided that this information ought to be available to others as well. And this is the raison d'être for the book you now hold in your hands.

This story of the compiled, sorted, and analyzed data about the role of blues music to those of us who are fans of the genre today frankly took me by surprise. It was a story about the blues that goes far beyond the parameters of the people I studied. It is the story of an art form that connects us to blues ancestors who continually teach blues disciples of all colors how to *walk through* our blues rather than getting stuck in it. It is a story about how human beings need to feel authentically and meaningfully connected to others. It is a story of how the genius of blues music injected improvisation, spontaneity, immediacy, mystery, play, and powerfully healing elements into a relatively formal and formulaic postwar culture. It is a story of contemporary blues fans' gratitude for, and ever-important need to honor, the originators of the blues who gave such (still) underappreciated gifts to the culture into which they found themselves forcibly injected, and by which they were historically abused. It is a story that cannot be told without also exploring the deep wounds in our culture caused by racist mindsets—the effects of which might have been ameliorated—but that are still open or in various stages of healing.

We now move into the story that was told to me by blues fans today. It contains four parts forming the skeleton of this book:

- In Part I, we will begin to explore 21st century blues as entertainment, blues as a facilitator of emotions, and blues as *antidote* to elements of a contemporary culture that many current blues fans experience as frustrating.

- Part II contains an exploration of the background for growing up in the 20th century. This section provides some historical insights as to why white baby boomers connect so powerfully with, and to, the blues.

- In Part III, we deepen the look at the life-changing gifts and potential of blues music that we began to explore in Part I. We look at the role of blues as a modern ritual.

- In Part IV, we look at the more ethereal components of blues music. Those that blues fans experienced as otherworldly, spiritual, or that provided a sense of restorative escape. Here findings from the previous parts of the book come together as we conclude what the relevance of blues music is to blues boomers. We then use these discoveries to explore the role of blues music to younger, future fans.

Chapter 2:

Who Are Blues Fans Today?

The typical blues fan today is white (well over 90%), and older (eight out of ten are between 45 and 70 years old). Based on my research, other surveys, and blues-related social media sites, whose administrators have given me access to their demographics, a preponderance of blues fans are men. Modern blues fans are generally better educated, have higher rates of home ownership, and are better situated financially than national averages. In addition to being white and generally middle-class, a typical blues fan today lives in the suburbs or in rural areas. He/she will likely have at least a two- to four-year college degree or a degree in a practical field.

I fit many of the descriptors of the typical 21st century blues fan myself: I am middle-aged, live in the suburbs, I fit the middle-class model and am well-educated. Each of us is obviously very different and has different preferences and idiosyncrasies. But with regard to demographic makeup, it was astonishing to see how largely uniform the blues base is today. There was very little ethnic diversity*. This concerned me, but confirmed what I had observed at blues festivals and blues concerts in the United States and Europe. I moved on as a researcher, simply documenting what I found.

It has been an eye-opening journey for me to suspend judgment about what blues music *is*, and instead focus on what blues music *does*. I found that if I thought less about whether I agreed or disagreed with the statements of

---

* There are likely pockets of more ethnically diverse blues fans today, who may not feel inclined to respond to surveys, or hang out in online forums about the blues, but who are still fans of blues artists.

blues fans, and instead simply listened to what they said, a new richness was added to my experience of the music. There were many treasured moments for me because they often were able to explain and describe their relationship with blues music in ways I could not have put into words myself. There were also plenty of blues stories that took me by surprise and added contrast or helped me gain new perspectives. As each interviewee tome me his or her blues stories, they linked to a virtual, vibrant tapestry that is the fabric of blues music today.

One might say that this book contains a representation of the collective "voice" of blues boomers. Historically, the role of blues music has changed, as the ethnic, cultural, social, and historical elements shaping blues fans also have changed. Therefore today's blues fans speak with a voice that is unique to their backgrounds and their experiences—just as contemporary blues music speaks a modern-day musical "language."

Blues Boomers Sing the Blues

Blues fans observed that our culture can be difficult to decipher and that media and popular culture offer entertainment but little substance. Author and clinical psychologist Mary Pipher observes:

> *We 'know' celebrities but they don't know us. The new community is not a reciprocal neighborhood like earlier ones. David Letterman won't be helping out if our car battery dies on a winter morning. Donald Trump won't bring groceries over if Dad loses his job. Jane Fonda won't babysit in a pinch. Dan Rather won't coach a local basketball team. Tom Hanks won't scoop the snow off your driveway when you have the flu. These vicarious relationships create a new kind of loneliness – the loneliness of people whose relationships are with personae instead of persons[2-1].*

Blues boomers often expressed a sense of fatigue with the way the world is today. They felt a loss of community where they live, were tired of much of our political and corporate processes, and expressed that they, in many ways, were fed up with the world they see. They worried about the rapid growth of technology and our lack of ability to deal with the onslaught of constant information streaming at us from all sides. Blues boomers expressed their distaste for a culture that showcases an abundance of superficiality, phoniness, and diversions. They stated that our media culture glamorizes; it makes the ordinary seem useless and bland. They felt much of it contributes to a shortage of emotional and interpersonal depth in our society. At the same time, these were elements that they stated they typically find in the blues or in the blues community: the blues offers a counter-cultural antidote to separation and superficiality.

Here are a few descriptive examples of typical statements from the study of blues fans indicating fatigue with the world we live in:

Well the only thing I guess I would say to that is June and Ward Cleaver lied to us. . . . I think we were, I can only speak for myself, I was raised to have certain expectations of what life in America was supposed to be and it was definitely not as hard as—not that I have it hard—but I've had to work a lot harder for the things that I was told should just happen.

Or:

I think it's almost a mob mentality type of thing that can occur within humanity where we almost lose sight of our individuality—of who we are. When we . . . start saying 'well, I'm part of this group; I should be like this. I should be like this group, or that group, or just a bunch of people and sometimes that can bring us false hopes and false ideas of what reality is. And then, when it hits you, it's not like that! That can lead people to even more confusion, and media doesn't help that very much. . . . And religion keeps splitting all the time, constantly splitting us into more and more factions. The spirit is supposed to be one, yet look what [is] going on in society. It's doing the opposite. It's just splitting, and splitting, and splitting. No wonder people are confused.

Or:

So I grew up in a Southern Baptist church, and you know, these are the right prayers, the right sermons and the right lifestyle. . . . I somehow believed that if you followed all the rules, and you did all these things that this religion . . . would protect you right? You wouldn't get heartbreak. Things would work out for you. I believed that for a long time.

A majority of blues boomers felt that a sense of emotional disconnectedness, a chase of elusive goals, and time constraints, were factors contributing to our modern daze:

I think we're definitely lonelier and more disconnected from each other in many ways—part of that has to do with the fact that people often live very far away from their family of origin—where they grew up—and so they don't have that instant familiarity. Plus the fact that we have our families, they're smaller. So we have fewer siblings to rely on, and be around, and aunts and uncles, and that kind of stuff so, and we're busier. We fill our time with things to do . . . being busy. . . . I think that's where some of the emotional disconnect for a lot of people is. I know it has been for me on occasion. I've lived places where I didn't know anybody and that is very hard. Made life miserable! If you're only motivated by money, if that's all you're interested in, then you're probably not going to be a . . . happy person because there's never enough. If you're happy when you're in a community, and you feel valued, and you can value others, then you're probably going to be happy—even if you're not making as much money.

Some mentioned that they felt that neither the media nor our politicians were trustworthy. Many expressed that they felt connected to the blues and disgusted by, and disconnected from, much of the rest of the world:

I don't believe anything I hear or see on TV news. I just want the news. Where's Walter Cronkite when you need him? The political correctness gets on my nerves. You can't say anything without being doomed for life. I don't like the news, because they tell you what they think about the news. I don't want to hear what [they] think, just tell me what happened. Like the presidential speech, and then you have an hour of people telling you what he said. I just heard him! Why are you telling me what he meant he said? . . .

With blues it's honest. It has feeling. I feel like I can touch it. I've seen guitar players—just see them get lost for a minute—just amazing. You're floored. . . . Why can't we all get along? . . . I feel sorry for people who are just being born. I'm totally disgusted with the government, both sides and in the middle.

A few Blues Boomers stated that although the times we live in are challenging to them, they are not really more challenging than previous times; that each era had its challenges to overcome. Yet, a deeper conversation typically unearthed some kind of insight about the specific challenges that face us in the modern world:

Marie: Do you think living in modern times is uniquely challenging to people?

Blues fan: You mean people—people?

Marie : Yeah I'm not even relating this necessarily to the blues. Do you think we live in uniquely challenging times?

Blues fan: [Sighs deeply] That was a long sigh. I don't know. I don't know that it's any more challenging than what anyone else has gone through. You know the generation before us.

Marie: So how might it be different?

Blues fan: Yeah that's what I was gonna say. Yeah it's certainly different, because you got this wonderful tool known as the internet which allows you to be in contact with everybody and nobody, because you really are. You're sitting in front of the screen but you're still alone. . . . It gives you the disguise of personal contact and relationships, but it's really not. That can be challenging—I mean I do it. I spend an awful lot of time on the internet, because that's what I do, but you have to be able to transfer that stuff, because you can be anything you want to be on the internet. . . . People do not learn how to relate on a one-to-one basis, or coexist actually. There's a

*great anonymity in posting shit on people's pages telling them they suck.
You're never gonna see them. I think we're losing a little bit of the human
context. . . .*

Professor of Social Studies of Science Technology, Sherry Turkle, finds
that a significant part of the difficulties with recent developments in
technology is the notion that we can edit our lives to appear perfect online.
We choose the photos we want to show—possibly edited in Photoshop to
be "just so." We edit our postings to be only those we want to broadcast to
others[2-2]. She writes:

> *Technology is seductive when what it offers meets our human vulnerabilities.
> And as it turns out, we are very vulnerable indeed. We are lonely but fearful
> of intimacy. Digital connections and the sociable robot may offer the illusion
> of companionship without the demands of friendship. Our networked life
> allows us to hide from each other, even as we are tethered to each other. We'd
> rather text than talk.* [2-3]

The notion that we are somehow uncomfortable with authentic
connection if we cannot edit our reality to appear flawless is probably an
undercurrent in many parts of our society. To counter this trend, blues
boomers broadly expressed that they valued relationships and connections
that felt somehow "real," and they appreciated honesty, genuineness and
straightforwardness. Many stated that they found these hard-to-find qualities
in the blues and in the blues community. There was in fact a constant stream
of comments about this topic of technology alienating us from each other.
Here are some examples:

> *People spend too much time on-line. They don't get out and socialize and talk
> to other people. . . . Email has taken the place of conversation.*

> *Our expectations, of what we believe others 'should' give us, has become
> almost impossible to fulfill. I think our brains are overloaded with pleasure*

endorphins from the immediate and constant interactions with others, even if we're miles apart, and we don't all negotiate being truly isolated very well today. I believe this is why the genre of blues is becoming more mainstream, more people are connected with those feelings of isolation and loneliness than ever before in man's time.

I feel the world or the country has become more callous, cruel people as well. Time has passed me by, I belong in the past. People are too busy and tired from working/stress to want to go out and be with people. On my radio show my saying is, 'Go get the CURE!!! Go see LIVE music!!!'

Our new attachment to each other means that perhaps we detach from ourselves somewhat and ignore the world happening at our feet and instead focus on being 'connected'. I feel we are more influenced by outside factors than ever before.

People text, tweet, or call and are hesitant to interact personally

Everybody is in their accommodation "interacting" online but not really interacting with other humans in any real way at all.

I have been a cop for 18 years. I see this! All the lonely people, where do they all come from...

A few comments lauded the internet because it had opened up possibilities for connection that they otherwise would not have had. Like anything, the value of the internet as a tool depends on the awareness of those who use it:

The friends I've discovered on the internet have enhanced my daily life simply with their own words/experiences.

I feel more connected, and have made and met more true blue friends through the internet, and have learned of music I perhaps never would have known about, and festivals/venues/events that I'd otherwise never known about. I now have a HUGE blues family, which wouldn't be possible without the internet! I love each and every one of them, too! Not superficially, but deeply, as I would family!

I believe the digital age has restricted some from their ability to socialize...I'm torn in this belief, because I feel that texting and social networks are becoming the NEW form of communication...For those on the periphery, I believe it enables them to stay in the shadows even more...I, however, am a social creature, so it actually enables me to network with more people than prior.

Chapter 3:

What is the Role of Blues Today?

A Brief Initial Summary

Unearthing the underlying mood of blues boomers with regard to their understanding of our modern reality gave some clues as to why blues music—and the qualities within the blues community—speaks to modern fans. Research professor Brené Brown echoes some of the collective voice of these fan statements when she finds that since 9/11, our culture has moved increasingly toward disconnection and fear. Each time our culture moves in this direction, we get the feeling that there is never going to be enough, so we must fight others in order to survive. Thusly we move away from connectedness and authentic relations. She states that if we feel that we have to fight every day to survive, and others are seen as competing with us or as a threat, we continually get some of our deepest fears confirmed. When we, on the other hand, are able to step out of this mindset of scarcity, and connect authentically with others, we find some of our deepest needs met. And blues music clearly provides this cultural antidote of authentic connection in many ways.

Summed up in just four words, the role of blues music today (beyond musical enjoyment) is that it can provide access to: *Fun, Authenticity, Connection and Escape.* These words headline the four main themes that surfaced throughout the research (Fig 1.):

1. Blues is fun: it includes musical appreciation in an entertaining, playful and relaxed context;

2. Blues enables authentic connection to one's own feelings;
3. Blues facilitates authentic connection to others, connection to community, as well as appreciation for emotionally connected "ancestors;"
4. Blues provides escape: authentic connection/connectedness to an experiential realm beyond the everyday.

Role of Blues Music Today

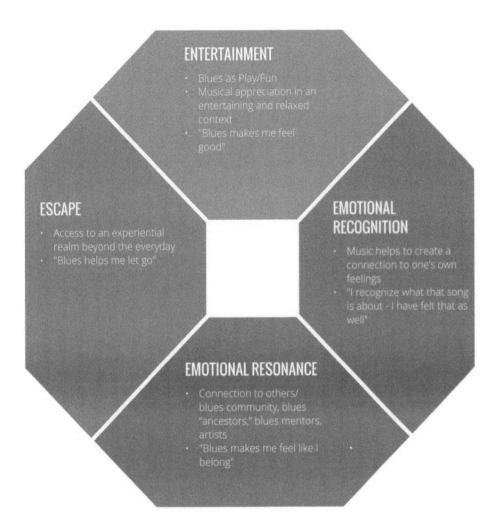

Figure 1: Four Main Relevancies of Blues for Modern Fans.

Chapter 4:

Blues as Play

Blues as Entertainment

We let our hair down when we go to blues concerts. We feel good when we put on a blues album at home or when we listen in the car. The blues is—and has always been—entertainment. Historically, blues offered a way for blues musicians to escape a crippling, back- and soul-breaking workload and to make a bit of cash playing music for people—whatever they wanted to hear. For original blues audiences, going to a dance or out to just listen to music, offered opportunities to have a little fun on a Saturday evening after a full week of work and no play. The music provided rhythms to dance to, and a chance to just be together and let all concerns and worries go for a brief moment in time. In *The Blues Fell This Morning*, Paul Oliver describes black dance halls, or "jukes," in the immediate aftermath of WWI, packed to the gills with dancing couples who "shimmied" and advanced their "shakes." Oliver writes: "The blues pianist or guitarist may not have called the gathering, but he was the most important member of the throng, demanding his liquor and his women, 'whipping' his guitar 'to a plank' and his piano to a 'jello'" [4-1]. The blues still serves this function of entertainment in the 21st Century with the performers at its center. In fact, entertainment, play, and fun are central, motivating factors for fans today. At the same time, contemporary blues fans rarely talked about blues *solely* as entertainment and fun, even as those aspects attract them and keep them "hooked."

Alligator record label president, Bruce Iglauer states in his preface to *Blues Philosophy for Everyone*: "Since the blues emerged from Southern juke joints and Northern bars into the mainstream of American and world music, it has become more of a form of entertainment and less of a form of a shared community folk music"[4-2]. Iglauer states that modern audiences still can "glory in the delight of simply being alive, as the creators of the blues intended"[4-3]. This ability of blues music to provide distraction, a relief from everyday woes, and escape into a shared universe of *joie de vivre* and play-time is well established. There is however, paradoxically, also a tendency to devalue the role of the blues as entertainment. Jay Sieleman, the former CEO and President of the Blues Foundation, illustrated this predicament. When we talked about his discovery of the blues, he said:

> *I came to it as 'music is entertainment.' Music is fun! And this is the most fun music there is. And I used to be sort of apologetic about that or embarrassed or whatever the right word would be. But the more I've read, the more I've found that "Geez, that's what the original purpose of the music is in the first place."*

Is there an implicit sense that being entertained by blues music is more superficial when it is enjoyed by a white middle-class audience? John Ruskey,* the first curator for the Delta Blues Museum in Clarksdale, Mississippi, states:

> *I think a person who . . . looks at the blues as pure entertainment, and nothing else . . . doesn't understand where it comes from, and doesn't really understand what it's talking about 'cause if you really have the blues, then you're not lying about what you're seeing, you're not glossing it over and saying that it's all harmony. Blues is about accepting reality. I'd say it's just*

---

* Mr. Ruskey was the curator at the Delta Blues Museum between 1992 and 1998. He is also the co-founder of the Delta Blues Education Fund. The Museum's website states: "Ninety-five percent of the DBE Program's apprentices are Black, and most have Native American heritage. Most come from impoverished families, and are between the ages of nine and 15. Many of the best apprentices are considered 'at risk' children in the local school systems. The Delta Community served by the DBEP is sixty-five percent African-American, and predominately rural/agricultural based." (www.bluesed.org)

a suburban mentality about looking at the blues just as entertainment, pure entertainment. [4-4]

For Ruskey, "entertainment" for the suburban crowd implies that it is inauthentic and "glosses over" the harsh reality of the origin of blues. Certainly, considering his work with disadvantaged children, and contact with the economic and social hardships of destitute families, it is easy to understand where he is coming from: comparatively economically and socially privileged middle-aged suburbanites dancing to the blues in park-like blues festivals clearly share a very different reality than that of blues originators. The degree of suffering and the longing for finding relief in the music then and now are obviously very different and not comparable. Nonetheless, an important part of the life-sustaining elements of blues music have always been about letting go, being free in dance and movement, and having fun. Oliver's description of early blues people shimmying and shaking in Saturday night abandon is telling—entertainment and enjoyment are at the very roots of the blues. It was then, and it is now. There are still elements of reckless abandon mixed in with cathartic elements of blues that does a body—any body—and soul good. This is imbedded in the offering of blues music.

Blues fans today go to blues concerts to have a good time, but this does not mean that the experience is one-dimensional. We will explore the various levels of blues experiences in the chapters that follow. But blues as musical entertainment remains a *primary* function of blues. It is what makes couples feel a shared bond when they together attend blues festivals, concerts and blues cruises; it is what makes people feel the need to dance and move around to the music without feeling judged; it is about just having a great time with other people; it is about listening to lyrics that make you laugh—or cry or both—within a short amount of time; it is about "getting into" the groove and feeling transported. That is all part of the entertainment, where and when all these elements combine.

Play time, having fun, being entertained, and finding time to just recharge our batteries are not necessarily areas of our lives we are taught have importance. Yet, according to the research of Dr. Stuart Brown, founder of the National Institute for Play, the importance of restorative elements in our lives is clear, and blues is a perfect vehicle for it. Ruskey demonstrates a common belief that entertainment is, per definition, superficial in white, middle-aged, middle-class, suburban circles. This can certainly be the case, as is often painfully obvious in many demographic groups, when it comes to contemporary, mainstream pop-culture. But interestingly, blues boomers were very clear on this topic. They expressed the exact opposite: they feel that their engagement with blues music offers them a chance to *get away from* what they see as a superficial, mainstream pop culture. They experience blues as an antidote to hollow shine and glamour. Blues is an art form that manages to have a multilayered significance—*even* when it is entertaining. Amiri Baraka (Leroi Jones) acknowledges both the entertainment aspect of the blues and its other layers in his book, Blues People:

> *Classic blues is called 'classic' because it was the music that seemed to contain all the diverse and conflicting* elements of Negro music, plus the smoother emotional appeal of the 'performance.' It was the first Negro music that appeared as entertainment, though it still contained the harsh, uncompromising reality of the earlier blues forms. It was, in effect, the perfect balance between the two worlds.[4-5]*

Again, the circumstances of suffering for the people about whom Amiri Baraka is talking are completely different and cannot be compared. The point about blues being used for entertainment all the way back to its inception however is repeated and important. Many blues boomers grew up with a work ethic that ridiculed play time and saw simple enjoyment as time wasted. Many of us glorify our busy schedules and filled calendars. Brené Brown

---

* These "diverse and conflicting" elements are still found in the blues when performers sing about feeling low. We will explore the ability of the blues to hold this tension between conflicting emotions and realities later.

observes in an online course, how our culture encourages us to see "exhaustion as status symbol and productivity as expression of self-worth." This is precisely one of the ten roadblocks that she states gets in the way of what she calls "wholehearted living"[4-6]. Our need for speed—our need to constantly be engaged leaves us feeling disconnected, overwhelmed, and lonely.

Stuart Brown explains that play is as crucial for us as oxygen. His studies have found that occasional play time is foundational to our wellbeing, to our ability to think innovatively, to unlock our inherent creativity, to problem solve, and to find a safe setting in which children and adults alike can learn how to pick up on social cues[4-7]. According to S. Brown, play is "preconscious and preverbal" [4-8]. What play does to us, or how it makes us feel, is an intangible quality. Thus it was often difficult for fans to put into words what they felt were the enjoyable benefits of listening to blues music. Many said that they were hooked on the blues, but that they could not really express why:

> *Yes, blues facilitates emotions in me. How, I mean it's kind of a question I'm trying to figure out myself, it's just a feel-good emotion…. It's just like a good cup of coffee; I can't explain why coffee makes me feel good in the morning.*

Others resonated some of S. Brown's conclusions of the benefits of restorative, inspiring elements in our lives, when talking about their experiences with the blues, such as the below statement:

> *If you have the blues and you're kinda down, if you're playing the blues— you're playing music that directly channels to your soul and that you turn into a conduit and through the expression of your soul, you can become happy. It takes your focus away from your problems and allows you understanding and clarity. It allows you a good feeling. It opens up doors for inspiration.*

S. Brown illustrates what it feels like when some of these important precognitive or preverbal elements of play show up in our lives. The meaning of these terms will be important throughout this book, and I therefore add a brief description of how I use these terms.

Precognitive, nonverbal, or *preverbal:* These terms are used interchangeably to describe a preconscious "language" that is facilitated in the blues (or between people) through music, rhythm, "groove," or musical expression. Such language expresses a feeling—or mental state—that can be observed as "doing something," yet cannot be fully captured verbally, conceptually or analytically. Therefore, when the term(s) are used, it is to describe something that has a "sensed" quality that is difficult to put into words.

To sum up S. Brown's definition of play, below I have paraphrased his descriptions of the seven beneficial properties of play,* adding my own comments *in italics* to indicate examples of how the blues provides these various elements. I have quoted fans in **bold italics** when a representative comment from blues boomers in this study illustrated the point well. According to Stuart Brown, the seven elements of play—here described as they manifest in the blues—are:

1. Apparently purposeless (done for its own sake): Not done for food or money—it is not done for any practical value. *Obviously, blues fans are typically not being paid or compensated for being fans or going to concerts.*

2. Voluntary: Not obligatory or done out of duty. *Being a blues fan is obviously an entirely voluntary endeavor.*

3. Inherent attraction: It is a source of psychological arousal and a cure for boredom. ***"I would say the blues provides a sense of relief that, gee, this is music that we so enjoy. It allows us to escape to our happy place, if you will. It's a form of escapism as well— I'll be the first to admit that definite form of escapism.""* It's**

---

* Dr. Brown's definitions of the seven aspects of play can be found in his book: Play: How it Shapes the Brain, Opens the Imagination, and Invigorates the Soul: (Brown S., 2009, pp. 17-18).

all about dance! You are missing the boat if you disregard the dance aspect—as this survey seems to do. The benefits of the BLUES are largely LOST if you aren't moving your feet."

4. Freedom from time: When fully engaged in play we lose a sense of time. *"That's my escape when I go to a concert like that. . . . It just brings me back to a place that I want to be so I'm in that moment and I'm enjoying it and I don't think about nothing else but what's going on at that time."* 95% of survey takers agreed that they often forget time and place, and stated that they "go with" the pulse of the music. *"I get caught up in a great tune or concert and nothing else matters."*

5. Diminished consciousness of self: We are fully in the moment and stop worrying about whether we look good or smart; we are in the flow.* *"The moment is what's important, right. You're here. Just enjoy it. Don't worry. Let go of it all . . . I love to dance . . . I want to let myself go in the music and I can feel it. . . . There is a lot of just going out and expressing yourself with the music and letting yourself go—and letting yourself feel all of those things, and it doesn't matter whether or not you look cool or not, and it doesn't matter whether or not you're the best dancer there—or you're the hottest chick there . . . . The only thing that matters is that you're out there with the music and you're letting it flow." "Even if I'm completely happy and stress-free walking into a concert or festival, I get even happier and just let go!"*

6. Improvisational potential: When we are willing to include seemingly irrelevant elements into our experience allowing new potentiality to emerge—and thus we allow new thoughts, behaviors, ways of being,

---

* Dr. Brown here, with the concept of "flow," refers to the work of the esteemed psychologist, professor, and writer, Mihaly Csikszentmihalyi, who discovered that people find a sense of genuine happiness in a pursuit of activities in which they are totally absorbed and forget time and place.

strategies, and movements to emerge. *"I just love a good jam. I really do. What it is about it is hard to say; it just pulls you in. And it's like 'holy cow what is this?' You just get released and all of a sudden, like I said, they'll bring it back in nice and tight—back to the one—and it's like 'I don't know what that was but it worked for me!'"* 94% agreed that it is important to them that the blues is improvisational and spontaneous. *"I love that the same songs come out a little different each time I hear them. I love to hear how the musicians create magic in the moment."*

7. Continuation desire: The pleasure of the experience drives our desire to do it. We want the activity to continue—and when it does, we will seek new ways to make it happen again. *"[The blues community] just seems like this very large, warm community that has a big enough stage to accept everybody and be friendly with everybody. It's one of the things—it's the drug that keeps bringing you back."*

The entertaining, fun, and attractive elements of blues as play function as an invigorating experience that brings blues fans joy and inspiration to go back to everyday duties and obligations. The effects of this play time require, however, that we embrace it and go with the experience. Thus someone with an overly critical mindset who continually seeks to analyze and critique the experience might miss out on some of its playful elements. Some blues fans stated that it was distracting to them if blues musicians used the stage as a platform for their personal and political views. Political commentary activates the analytical faculties, and with such an interpretive lens applied, an inner judgment is activated, possibly rendering the playful elements inaccessible for the participant. It is difficult to get lost in the moment, when one is busy analyzing it for what might be its flaws, or why it is not practiced by, or for, a group who rightfully can claim ownership of it, or while being annoyed with a political or religious viewpoint, particularly if it clashes with one's own.

This mindset of critique might also reveal itself when we set ourselves apart as those who "know better;" those who can "see through the obvious." It is often activated when we spend intellectual energy on discerning which styles of blues are "the real deal," and which are not. Or when we seek to speak for those whom we deem are too disenfranchised, too weak, or too unaware of their own misfortune to speak for themselves. Philosophy professor, Linda Alcoff, writes in an article in *Cultural Critique* that the "practice of speaking for others is often born of a desire for mastery, to privilege oneself as the one who can champion a just cause and thus achieve glory and praise"[4-9]. Please do not misunderstand. I am certainly not suggesting that having personal opinions about blues music, or anything else, is meaningless, or that championing causes and helping those who need a hand is not a worthwhile effort. I am simply indicating that judging whether a certain style of blues fulfills certain diagnostic criteria, or a certain population group is "allowed" to engage with the blues, gets in the way of our experience. And it makes sense; the analytical critique will likely shut down some, if not most, of such spontaneous enjoyment. The blues is not primarily an intellectual construct, and when we treat it as such, we often miss some of the power of its potential.

S. Brown mentions that if we enter into play "self-critical, competitive, and preoccupied …, we are unlikely to experience the benefits of play"[4-10]. In the study, blues fans talked about how the playful aspects they enjoyed in blues were more beneficial and fun some days than others, and it was often dependent on how relaxed they felt:

It kind of makes a difference, who you're with too. I went to see a local band. It was a rather small thing, but my boss had taken me there and I didn't feel as comfortable doing any of that [moving around, hollering] because my boss was there, right? So I didn't feel like I could really let myself go.

Chapter 5:

Those Darn Emotions

If We can't Describe it, Does it Mean it Doesn't Exist?

To work scientifically with emotions is uncomfortable.*
Sigmund Freud

Baby boomer boys typically grew up learning that expressing certain emotions is for sissies. They were taught that boys don't cry, whine, or complain, and that it is in their best interest to button up, shut up, keep the lid on, and stay emotionally unaffected when life throws them a curve ball. It is in many ways still silently accepted to develop a drug or alcohol dependency or engage in destructive—or self-destructive—behavior in order to deal with pent-up, repressed, or suppressed emotions. It is certainly often easier in the short term to skim the surface rather than openly talk about what is hidden under the frozen surface of muddy, emotionally complex waters. As adults, they are used to hearing cultural icons like Arnold Schwarzenegger talking about "girly men" and Donald Trump venting about "losers." Beaming down from the silver screen, Clint Eastwood points his Smith & Wesson at those who are portrayed as threats and tells them that going against his stone-faced determination will only make his day.

From Civilization and Its Discontents (1930). The sentence is usually translated: „It is not easy to deal scientifically with feelings." However, Freud's original sentence reads: „Es ist nicht bequem, Gefühle wissenschaftlich zu bearbeiten," and one can argue that his choice of the word "bequem" in this context could indicate discomfort, in addition to difficulty, with how to deal with emotions.

James Bond takes his martini cocktails shaken but never stirred, and stoic and heroic "real men" ride stone-faced and emotionally unavailable into the sunset after saving the day. In such pervasive cultural myths, women stereotypes watch the apparent show of alpha-male invincibility, with breasts heaving and eyes gleaming with poorly contained lust and endless admiration. This is the image of masculinity that many boomer boys were taught to admire and emulate. Dysfunction, loneliness, feelings of inadequacy, narcissism, abuse, sexism, and desperation often follow in its wake.

Seen on this backdrop, it certainly makes sense that the blues is attractive to this group of men. Blues and blues rock offer a matter-of-fact method of expressing and connecting to emotions combined with vigorous and expressive axe-wielding, harmonica-blowing, drum-pounding, or bass thumping displays of swashbuckling independence, (sexual) power, courage, and confidence. Many blues musician, role models express feelings while *retaining* a robust masculine integrity and identity. Women obviously find ways to connect to blues and express themselves within the format as well. But due to the fact that many more men than women are devoted blues fans, it is clear that blues offers something to men that, generally speaking, is not as intoxicating to, or needed, by women.

Every interviewee, whether male or female, talked about blues as being emotional music. Blues fans often struggled to describe exactly what blues means to them. *Yet they observed that it certainly affected them.* I want to use a metaphor to describe this occurrence. Quantum Entanglement is an observable phenomenon within quantum particle physics. When two particles have interacted with one another at some point in time, they somehow continue to respond simultaneously, rotating counter to one another if just one of them is being manipulated, *even if, theoretically speaking, they are across the universe with a distance of many light years between them.* Albert Einstein observed this fact and was perplexed by it. He called it "spooky actions at a distance." He couldn't explain it, and quantum scientists are still not sure why it occurs. We can observe it and describe it, but not explain it.

We often relegate that which we can observe, yet not explain, to be unimportant or "spooky." Yet, just because something cannot be explained does not mean that it is not happening or that it is invalid. This is the case with many of the experiences that fans described with regard to blues music. We will look into the most ineffable blues experiences in Part IV. Here and now, we will look at the emotional elements of blues, which blues boomers identified as central to their experience of the music, yet they often found difficult to define or describe, since these elements are neither rational nor logical. And it made perfect sense that we blues fans have a hard time describing what we observe in blues music; what is felt is not easy to put into words. Again, we must look to the observable effects of blues music; what blues music *does to us* in order to describe it by its actions, not its being.

The blues musician emotes expressively through music; the audience receives and interprets the music through feelings. This reciprocal relationship happens to varying degrees in all kinds of music. English psychiatrist and author, Anthony Storr, refers in his book "Music and the Mind", to British mathematician G.H. Hardy's "Mathematician's Apology," in which Hardy states that music and mathematics are often likened, yet, he states, music can "be used to stimulate mass emotion, while mathematics cannot." Music is not simply logically constructed patterns. Storr continues that music can "penetrate the core of our physical being. It can make us weep, or give us intense pleasure. Music, like being in love, can temporarily transform our whole existence"[5-1]. Blues boomers expressed similar sentiments in various ways, and they felt that blues music in particular was powerful in its potential for such emotional penetration.

Definition of Terms

In order to establish an understandable and describable foundation for our interpretation of the prevalent emotional, preverbal, and diffuse relevancies of today's blues music, here follows a list of terms that will be foundational as we move forward.

Front and center in this glossary is the definition of the concept of "connection." It became clear that, in the context of modern blues fans and their love of music, this term has four distinct expressions. Connection when referred to here is neither physical (as in making physical contact) nor theoretical/intellectual. Connection in the blues is an *emotional* connection. It was beneficial to an understanding of what blues fans expressed to separate the concept into four sub-categories which often proved to be interrelated. For instance, the blues can often be experienced simultaneously in two or more of the below versions of connection. This overlap is inevitable, and thus these sub-categories act only as leaky containers for the sake of description. **The four kinds of connection are fundamental to the description of the blues experience, and will be more fully examined later. Here is just a brief overview:**

1. ***Connection to self.*** Music acts as a personal "mood enhancer." It facilitates a sense of emotional *identification*. The blues, through this connection, helps us recognize and accept our feelings, rather than ignore or repress them. We experience ***emotional recognition***: "I know what the musician is singing/playing about from myself and I become more aware of my feelings through the musical experience." The fans often expressed that such recognition legitimizes their feelings. The listener connects, consciously or unconsciously, with emotions that, previously, may have been unclear, difficult to describe, or unwanted. Blues fans also express that it is possible to experience a state of moving *through* the emotions helped by musical involvement (catharsis)*.

2. ***Connection to others***: Connection to others is a feeling of kinship. It necessitates *first recognizing one's own feelings* in response to the music, and then connecting back to the musician(s), and possibly with other audience members or fellow listeners. It fosters a sense of

---

* See definition of catharsis below.

universality—we are all made from the same emotional cloth. Here we experience **emotional resonance.** Resonance includes a sense of mutually shared emotions. "I understand you better because I recognize that emotion, and thus now share in the experience of it with you—I resonate with the music, the musician, and possibly also my fellow audience members who experience this along with me." The fans often felt moved by such experiences, and mentioned that their own suffering was put in perspective by listening to, or understanding viscerally, the emotions shared by the musicians. It is a fount of compassion.*

3. **Connection to emotionally authentic ancestors:** A historical connection to emotionally transparent bluesmen and women—often back to African American masters—who led the way by sharing authentically all kinds of emotions including the experience of *walking through pain* rather than ignoring it.

4. **Connection to a higher power or an altered state:** A state of light hypnotic trance or lightly altered state of consciousness, in which a connection to "spirit," or simply an experiential state slightly beyond everyday awareness, takes place.

Catharsis: According to the Merriam Webster Dictionary, the root of this word comes from Greek *katharsis,* from *kathairein* to cleanse, purge. It has three meanings that were all expressed by blues fans:

> *"a) Purification or purgation of the emotions (as pity and fear) primarily through art; b) a purification or purgation that brings about spiritual renewal or release from tension; c) elimination of an [emotional problem] by bringing it to consciousness and affording it expression."*

Blues boomers described catharsis in their life with blues music as an experience of somehow moving *through* the emotion—and having a physical

---

* The origin of the word "compassion" is from Latin. It means to "suffer with" or "suffer along with."

manifestation or sense of the emotion as it passes through one's body. It can take many forms: crying or feeling tearful, a chill up the spine, hairs standing on end, shouting out, moving one's body in response to a feeling, a sense of being cleansed, feeling relieved, feeling tension release, etc.

Collective: Cults typically have one leader and everyone else follows along. These followers are part of the machinery: replaceable, and only valued if they function predictably and obediently in order to drive the tyrannical mission and agenda forward. There is no appreciation for individual thought, critical thinking, or dissent.

When the word "collective" is used in the context of the blues it has a very different meaning: it is a shared experience that depends on individual autonomy. The experiences resonate with others in a shared "field" of experience, but they depend on individual recognition of emotion, individual immersion, and individual freedom of thought, feeling and action. Coercion, force, or obligation are all counter to the experience in this kind of collective encounter where individual differences add virtual color and texture to the shared experience or engagement.

Authenticity: Finally, we will need to define the term "authenticity". Successful emotional connection does not happen if it is sent or received disingenuously. Authenticity however was a concept that many fans struggled to describe or interpret.

- Blues fans broadly defined the concept of authenticity in two ways that were therefore labeled accordingly:
  1. **Universally Authentic Blues (UAB)**: An emotional honesty that is a prerequisite for meaningful connection. Blues fans seek to connect authentically to a musical expression that is perceived as direct, honest, transparent, and "real." Authentic here means "without pretense." To point out and clarify when this kind of universal authenticity is being described I will often clarify by using the descriptor UAB.

2. **Context-Specific Authentic Blues (CAB):** The interpretation of what is considered "authentic blues" here depends on the contextual parameters applied to define it. Authenticity here, in other words, is about the context in which it appears: how the music is representative of, and therefore *traceable to,* a cultural, social, ethnical, or historical *framework.* When referred to I will use the descriptor CAB. We will dig into this all-important aspect of the blues later.

Now that we have begun to define a common language, let's dive into the emotional universe of the blues.

Chapter 6:

Emotions in the Blues – Why it Matters

Feelings shared in blues music are often universal in scope. They are shared across ethnic, cultural, national, political, religious, and social boundaries. Fans relate to emotions shared by musicians. More than nine out of ten blues fans found that one of the gifts in the blues is its capacity to remind us that we are all human, even when we encounter our limits, fail, or fall short. They connect to an emotional rawness in blues music; blues helps them release their own emotions and their involvement with the blues gives them new perspectives of their own feelings as well as those of others.

Blues fans were not concerned with whether musicians were black, white, gray, red, or purple. When it comes to Universally Authentic Blues (UAB), the experience of emotional recognition and/or resonance is not dependent on the era, ethnicity, cultural, or social context in which the music is performed. Emotions speak through the musician—and the blues fan recognizes the emotions within—loneliness, despair, heartache, joy, lust, feeling rebellious, feeling defeated, etc., and resonates. Clinical psychologist and blues lover Mark Winborn explores a Jungian analysis of the blues:

> *Internalization (i.e., introjection) occurs in the listener based on modeling by the blues singer. Observing or listening to the bluesman wrestle with and survive his emotional life, his pains or trials, gives the listener courage to face his own inner pain by connecting with what is universal in each of us through interaction with another.*[6-1]

Winborn's findings about internalization of such emotional recognition and resonance, as well as the potential for catharsis through the music (and historical identification with themes expressed by the musician), were echoed with conclusive strength when blues boomers talked about the role of blues music to them. The legitimization of emotions that happen through identification with what is expressed in the music furthers a sense of acceptance. Connected through the blues, we are not alone with an—at times—confusing inner universe of complex emotions.

Emotional Recognition and Resonance in Our Lives

It is one of the most loving things we can do—to truly listen deeply to another person, particularly if he/she is emotionally charged or upset. It does not in any way mean that we agree with what this person is expressing, or that we condone a certain behavior or belief. It simply means that we express willingness to walk in the other person's shoes for a bit, to express that we can understand how they feel. It is about just being there and observing from a place of compassion. Acknowledging the other person's feelings and validating that it is understandable to feel that way under the circumstances, creates a base of trust and makes others feel safe.

We live in a culture however, in which certain emotional responses or reactions are often made suspect. It is not a given that we will be understood if we express our feelings openly and it is therefore often not safe to do so. We are taught to hide how we feel from an early age. Author Don Miguel Ruiz, who bases his writings on ancient wisdom as shared by the Toltec, calls this *Domestication*. It is the notion of trying to live up to our parents' and other role models' perceived expectations at any cost for fear of falling short—of not being "good enough"[6-2]. This is, I believe, an accurate assertion and therefore it often does not feel safe to share how we feel, because it can backfire. But consistently tailoring our responses to externally applied parameters that are not necessarily representative of our own values, morals, or ethics as we attempt to "fit in" or "do what is expected of us" can leave us conflicted and feeling disengaged or disconnected. As a result, we often hide our honest feelings whether it is appropriate or not. We want others to think of us as strong, good, brave, well-behaved, self-contained, cool, "acceptable members of the tribe," etc.

Personally I learned to play it safe, to apply emotional suits of armor, and be stoic – and as a result I can easily fall into behavior that is nothing short of passive-aggressive. It takes awareness and constant work to identify it. And if things go well, and all the stars align just right, I can mindfully choose another response than just clamming up, applying the stigmata marks, and slamming the door as I walk out. My family hates it when I do it. And they feel emotionally stuck, too, when faced with such mind games that do nothing but encourage a wild goose chase through wrongly perceived assumptions about how we mutually feel about a certain situation. In my case, this hard-to-avoid behavior often hides what I don't want to show: I feel vulnerable and I have no clue how to deal with something at that moment, so I pretend to be strong or project certainty. Emotions are often difficult to express straight-forwardly, because it was not modeled for many of us how to do so, or we instead have internalized how to use insincere, sarcastic, or angry expressions of emotions, when we finally do let them out. Of course this is one of the wonders inherent in the potential of blues music—it can facilitate honest and direct expression.

"I am Never Alone in the Blues"

This statement was often made by Blues Boomers. They felt a sense of familiarity when they interacted with blues music. Many felt a sense of commonality or "belonging" with the music, the musicians, and also often with fellow blues fans, and they perceived this familial feel as a gift in their lives.

Growing up, blues boomers were typically not needed to secure the survival of the family. In previous generations, every family member performed a function: helping with the harvest and livestock, apprenticing in the family business, cooking, or helping rear younger siblings. This kind of responsibility toward family or community members gradually became less prevalent in the lives of suburban baby boomer children. This freedom, on one hand, allowed them to get an education and connect to a sense of independence. Yet on the other hand, there were ramifications of this liberation that took away the young child's or teenager's sense of being needed, and therefore being implicitly valued or important. Our sense of self-worth instead had to come from more diffuse or indirect achievements, such as grades, diplomas, money-making potential, status symbols, achievements, associations with "important" people, and titles. This trend continues for young people growing up today, and these kinds of desired achievements are emotionally one or two steps removed from a sense of belonging to a group; they are instead based on achievements that further self-promotion and/or self-aggrandizement, such as: "I nailed the test," "I got that big promotion," "I married the most beautiful/handsome/wealthy spouse," "I won," or "I sealed the deal."

Contrast this achievement-based reality with a time when everyone had to chip in to get the grain in the barn before the rain came, or grandma was ill and food had to be brought to her through the snow. Young people, as well as everyone else, had an important part to play in the survival of self and others. And there was an innate satisfaction of accomplishment that came from being an integral, and needed, part of the team. Nobody really needed to praise young people for their deeds. They received an implicit sense of belonging and of having made a difference by participating. They were important; they had tangible responsibilities.

Nobody wants to see a return to the times when children were put to work and denied an education. But at the same time, it is important to point out what was lost on the altar of self-sufficiency and having to find our sense of belonging and self-worth almost solely in the sum-total of our individual accomplishments. We are encouraged from many cultural sources to pretend to be lone vigilantes: to go it alone hoping for recognition. We do not have a family or a village that pulls us through if we fail. And it is an immense personal pressure to have to succeed or fail solely on our own terms. This is another reason for why we tend to sweep our anger, fear, desperation, grief, jealousy, etc. under the rug where these kinds of "unwanted" emotions fester and become unrecognizable as they become mixed, aged, and fermented into an unrecognizable hodgepodge of hidden emotional charges. We don't want to show "weakness" or project "failure." And if we choose to confess our doubt, sadness, or fear to someone, we are likely met with comments such as: "just think positive thoughts," or, "look on the bright side." Our vulnerability makes others uncomfortable and they don't know what else to say or do.

Fans expressed that listening to, or playing, the blues often helped them identify, express, and accept certain difficult, contradictory, or complex emotional states as a part of their life experience. And that it felt like such a relief to not have to go there alone. The blues was like a friend that kept them company through it all.

The Relationship Between Thoughts, Feelings, and Actions

Being emotionally congested affects our ability to think and act clearly. Emotions play a part even in rational decision-making—and, in fact, in most other cognitive processes. The emotions we consistently ignore influence our actions subconsciously. Understanding the importance of the "Emotional Life of Our Brain" is a recent discovery. In the book of the same name, neuroscientist Richard Davidson writes that prior to the 1970s, research psychologists thought that emotions were "little more than annoying flotsam that got in the way of the brain's more august functions, namely, cognition, reason, judgment, and planning."[6-3] They preferred to focus on the supposedly more dignified and impressive areas that were used for logical reasoning. Until recent decades, learning about our emotional responses was regarded as an exercise in futility; they were seen as relevant only in order to help patients deal with psychological *dysfunction*. Davidson's research shows that emotions are, in fact, pervasive in all kinds of perfectly healthy brain functions. Emotions do not *interfere* with rational and cognitive behavior and decision making; they are instead an intrinsic part of them. Davidson continues:

> *There is no clear, distinct dividing line between emotion and other mental processes; they blur into each other. As a result, virtually all brain regions play a role in or are affected by emotion, even down to the visual and auditory cortices.*[6-4]

Emotions help us understand ourselves, each other, and everything with which we engage. They are central to our learning process, and they filter and interpret what we encounter. But even if research has identified emotional awareness as important to overall well-being, most of us still experience a significant "lag" in learning how to relate constructively to our emotions and how to make sense of, and integrate, them in our daily lives. Our domesticated conditioning becomes like an inner voice that tells us what we "should" have done, what we "should" feel, and how we "ought to" behave. We withdraw from emotional closeness, and this withdrawal is often simply because we find it difficult to describe the emotional complexities we carry within. Since we cannot adequately explain it, we simply deny, minimize or repress it. If, however, we can find safe networks of other people to share our feelings with authentically, we can gradually free ourselves from the "shame web"[6-5]. In blues music, the artists often humorously, transparently, and non-judgmentally express all kinds of emotions, and just having this modeled feels like a relief.

Of course, part of the predicament facing many in Western culture today is that we live in what transpersonal researcher, psychologist, and author Dr. Charles T. Tart, in his book "States of Consciousness," calls a *consensus reality:* it is implicitly expected of us, if we want to fit into social constructs, that we follow expectations of how to behave and appear.[6-6] If a silent, grin-it-and-bear-it, stoic approach has been modeled to us instead of emotional authenticity and transparency, we are often stuck when it comes to expressing ourselves appropriately. Instead of giving voice to our feelings, we hide them.

But in the blues, we can step slightly out of this "consensus reality" and live a little on the wild side. Many fans stated that they felt that blues music contained an element of rebellion—in blues we can visit openly with of all kinds of emotional states.

Thoughts, emotions, and actions are three interrelated layers of our personal realities. Emotions are the bridge that links thoughts and actions. Thoughts about our world are based on previous experiences and beliefs. Emotions are based on what we have internalized, been taught, and our emotional style. Davidson refers to "emotional style" as a combination of genetically inherited, relatively fixed traits (nature) and the non-fixed ones that we can alter using various "mental activity ranging from meditation to cognitive-behavior therapy" (nurture).[6-7] We either "take action" or stagnate in inaction; in a very real sense, action (or inaction) is the outward manifestation of the dialogue between our thoughts and emotions. Yet often, we bypass the emotional layer and go straight from thoughts to action. When we do so, we mostly act from a mindset of "should," "ought to" and "need to" (the messages of our domestication). Doing so can lead to our being perceived as insincere and inauthentic by others. We are stiff, awkward, and formal. Or we might appear cold, calculating, and uncaring. However, if we bypass the "thought" layer, and communicate directly from emotional experience to action, we run the risk of becoming gut-level reactive, instinctual, and possibly imprudent. We fail to involve the higher levels of cognition, and react in ways that might ultimately harm ourselves and others. Emotional balance in our lives thus depends on an open, aware (relatively unrepressed), and reciprocal dialogue between thoughts and emotions carried into action (see Figure 2).

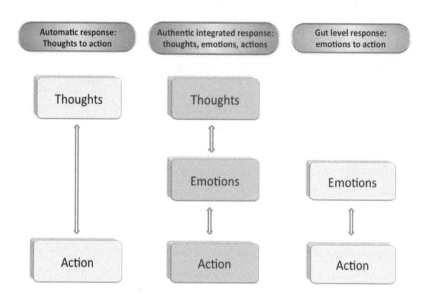

Figure 2: Three Kinds of Responses: Automatic, Integrated, or Reactive

When we, whether as a learnt behavior or by choice, consistently ignore, deny, or repress our thoughts or feelings, we eventually become hijacked by them. This hidden material then oozes out in the form of stress, anxiety, rage, abuse, depression, worries, etc. We feel shameful about why we are the way we are, and, in the worst-case scenario, do something irreversible out of desperation. However, most of us simply deny, ignore, repress, and don't talk about it and suffer in silence. A new book researching the history of addiction, "Chasing the Scream – The First and Last Days of the War on Drugs," by Investigative Journalist, Johann Hari, finds that precisely a sense of isolation and a lack of meaningful connections, in which one feels safe enough to express oneself authentically, that is one of the primary causes of addiction.[6-8]

Baby Boomer Blues

As a group of mainly white, middle-aged baby boomers, typical, modern blues fans are clearly neither marginalized nor economically disadvantaged. But statistics indicate that people in this demographic are not immune to emotional pain; in fact, evidence points to the contrary. In 2014, seven out of ten suicides were committed by white, middle-aged males.[6-9] One recent study from The National Institutes of Health concluded: "Whites aged 40-64 years have recently emerged as a new high-risk group for suicide."[6-10] The phenomena of lethal overdoses from both legal and illegal drugs have increased every year since 1970 and have never been higher. A bulletin from the Centers for Disease Control reads, "Rates have increased nearly fivefold since 1990 ..., [and] age-adjusted rates of drug overdose death for whites have exceeded those among African Americans since 2003. For both sexes, the highest rates were in the 45-54 year old age group."[11] The same bulletin states that from 1987 to 2007, there was a tenfold increase in the medicinal use of strong prescription painkillers known as opioid analgesics (e.g., Vicodin, Oxycontin, Dilaudid), and that in 2007, resulting deaths from these prescription drugs outnumbered those from cocaine and heroin combined.[6-12] By 2008, death by poisoning (of which 89% were due to drug poisoning) was more prevalent than death from car accidents.[6-13] The latest numbers show that *one and a half time as many* people in the US die from drug overdoses than car accidents, and the percentage of deaths from opioid medication continues its meteoric rise.[6-14] Today, 8% of white baby boomers admit to current use of prescription opioids. This is the highest percentage of any population group followed by non-Hispanic blacks at 6.5%.[6-15] From 2002 to 2012, the percentage of people between the ages of 50-64 admitting to illicit drug use has doubled.[6-16] Alcoholic beverage sales increased from $90 billion annually in 1990 to $162 billion in 2010. Measurable, serious psychological distress is now proportionally *the highest* among people aged 45-64, along with those who struggle financially.[6-17]

While white, middle-aged people use pain medication in record numbers, and white men are among those most likely to end their lives by suicide, paradoxically white middle-aged men simultaneously also hold most positions of power in North America.[6-18] A recent article in Fortune Magazine stated that "of all the Fortune 500 CEOs, only 23—or just over 4%—are minorities, a classification that includes African Americans, Asians, and Latin Americans."[6-19] A study from 2010 shows the average age of incoming CEO's at S&P 500 companies as being 52.9 years of age.[6-20] The median age in the US Congress is 60.[6-21]

While being white and middle-aged are traits of the most powerful group in the United States, many people in this group also suffer from significant, diffuse, or acute emotional pain. They feel anxious, depressed, and powerless, and therefore turn to prescription drugs, illicit drugs, alcohol, and suicide in record numbers. While many people in this group do not suffer in traditional economic or social terms, they are not *immune* to suffering. We explored previously that emotional pain often comes from repressing emotions that are considered undesirable. But no matter how much we dull difficult emotions with prescription medicine, street drugs, or alcohol, no matter how many luxury items we purchase, no matter how desperately we pull at our lone vigilante bootstraps, the "difficult" feelings do not go away by ignoring them. They might morph, seem to lessen by our inattention to them, and thus become unrecognizable, but research is clear that they continue to wreak havoc on our lives no matter how much we deny them or seek to repress them. And our senses of isolation and loneliness grow the more we seek to convince ourselves and others that we are doing just great. Brené Brown writes that "one of the greatest barriers to connection is the cultural importance we place on 'going it alone.' Somehow we've come to equate success with not needing anyone."[6-22]

Emotional Recognition and Resonance in the Blues

Since we are culturally conditioned to hide or divert many of our unwanted emotions, it can be a huge relief to encounter people who treat emotions matter-of-factly—who don't pretend. To varying degrees, blues boomers expressed relief when they sensed emotional recognition, or "labeling," in their encounter with blues music that made them aware of their own feelings, whether they previously were able to identify them or not. Here are a few examples:

> *You can have happy blues, but usually to me when I get happy—it's when I listen to the blues and I find out that somebody's doing just as bad if not worse than I am (laughs). So I know I'm not alone. You know? You can relate to it absolutely. You can relate to somebody else's troubles or somebody else's problems. I think it's an emotional form and that emotion translates into music as an expression, as an outlet, or as a release.*

Or:

> *Reflections that are more about ourselves if you really listen . . . experiences other people have had. In AA, they have speaker meetings, and every once in a while somebody tells your story—and the blues is like that. Every once in a while I go, 'That's me. That's what happened to me.' I feel that it's just like sometimes somebody has gotten into my head and they've made a song out of it, and I like that.*

The blues has served this function since its inception. Professor of Afro-American studies, Julius Lester, states that "the roots of the blues . . . are social. The rural bluesmen were intent on telling their listeners what they already knew but could not articulate."[6-23] A blues fan astutely made a parallel observation:

The blues continues to speak to my own pain and my own joys when I have those experiences; and sometimes when I have a hard time expressing my own emotional state, I can express it easier by either listening to a song or repeating some lyrics to somebody.

There were many variations over this same theme:

To me the blues is music from the soul that says everything, whether it has words or not. It says everything with feeling. I can't put it in any other words. I love the blues guitar but it's—even with the guitar, it's speaking to me. It makes me feel. And sometimes some of the sassier ones say things that I would not be able to say myself.

Many fans were also clear that blues helped them feel connected to others. This is emotional resonance—when they not only recognized their own emotions, but also felt a part of the shared emotional experience. As an example:

The genuineness of blues: the openness and how it relates to life and the soul and the spirit too. I mean people need to know that they're all connected and that there's not just this one person, not just this one group, but, hey, look, we are all in this together. All of us.

When blues musicians share their feelings of grief, loneliness, heartache, as well as their joys, celebrations, humor, etc., members of the audience benefit in subtle yet powerful ways from this sharing. They recognize emotions expressed in the music from their own experience and resonate with others in new ways. Fans often expressed that blues breaks down boundaries between people and create a common bond as exemplified in this statement:

When you're at a blues festival, you might see people that might be intimidating to you in some other setting, whether it's the way they're dressed, or their hair, or maybe a tee shirt they have on, or something like that. But

*when you see that same person and you know that they are part of . . . the
blues and you can see that they are enjoying it just as much as you, there's a
bond there that wouldn't normally exist, or at least a fence is broken down.*

Fans also voiced that resonance is not *dependent* on a live setting:

*That's just so much more real. I can't even explain it! I would listen to the
original, whoever that was, and go 'Now this is the part where I can hear that
emotion.' So it was kinda just the joy of learning of the music, really. It was
the joy of learning who these artists were and learning about their lives. That
was another thing that came as an outgrowth of buying people's CDs—I
started to read whatever biographies I could find online. In some cases I bought
books or checked them out from the library, but I just tried to learn about the
artists themselves.*

Fans often exhibited this curiosity to learn about the artists, their stories,
and how those stories emerge in the emotions within the music. Blues allows
a cycle of inspiration that includes individual as well as a common "field" of
shared experience:

The Cycle of Inspiration

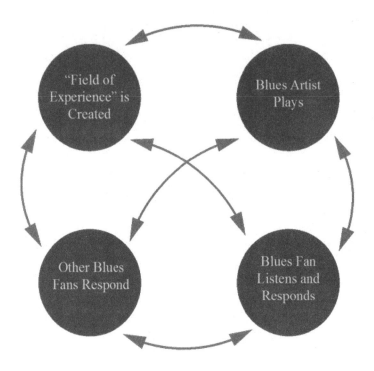

Figure 3: Emotional Recognition, Resonance, and Mutual Inspiration

A few blues fans mentioned that they were extremely fed up with political correctness and having to be careful with what and how things are carefully calculated and convolutedly edited before it can be expressed. And most blues fans felt that there is a level of insincerity in popular culture—and sometimes also in their own professional and private lives—that turns them off. They loved that the blues feels immediate and not pre-meditated.

Chapter 7:

Tellin' it Like it Is

"Tellin' it like it is" is a way of releasing or expressing all kinds of emotions. Fans stated overwhelmingly that they form the most powerful connections to the music and the musicians—or their fellow audience members—when musical expressions felt transparent and real versus pretentious and contrived. This was a consistent predictor of whether the music felt restorative or not: that it felt "real" even if the topic of the blues song was a sad one. The honesty of expression was key. This is one of the gifts of the African American tradition that (re-)emerged in white culture through the blues: the ability to express emotions more authentically, transparently, and matter-of-factly. In her book about "Black Life and Culture in the United States," Rhoda Goldstein quotes Julius M. Waigughu: "The African peoples have strived, against terrible odds, to communicate and exchange their joys and sorrows and achievements throughout their history. It takes an unusual people to survive and be creative under similar circumstances."[7-1] Neurological research that proves Mr. Waigughu's point that it is possible to achieve increased emotional resilience, when you have an ability to share all kinds of feelings in aware ways, emerged several decades later. In our brains, clusters of neurons receive signals from various spots on the surface of the body (skin) in the somatosensory cortex. Likewise the insula, a buried piece of the cerebral cortex, communicates with internal organs of the body in a reciprocal manner. The somatosensory cortex is also involved in perceiving internal sensations, such as when we feel aroused or angry. This internal communication between these centers in the brain and our bodies is connected to our level of self-awareness. It is found that high insula activity is connected to being more self-aware and better able to accurately identify and describe emotional states. The opposite is also the case, so lower activity in the insula signifies that a person is more disconnected from their emotions.[7-2]

Emotionally transparent musical expressions that are prevalent in blues music might thus directly help us become more aware with regard to our emotions in general. It is clear that the blues helps us identify and acknowledge emotions. David Rock, who works on development of a new science of leadership, synthesized the term "NeuroLeadership" as the discipline of the practical application of neuroscience to modern management and leadership theory.[7-3] His research indicates that the practice of "labeling"—meaning actually saying out loud, or internally recognizing, a felt emotion—facilitates a diminished stress response. He states that simply defining "the emotional experience in a word or two without going into the story of it . . . automatically dampens the stress response" to it.[7-4] The blues tradition has always included this element of emotional transparency. Whether singing about time in prison, lost love, hopelessness, lust, or hope of getting to a better place, artists were typically well-versed in the art of speaking their truth, thus labeling their emotions. In "African American Communication: Exploring Identity and Culture," Michael Hecht and Ronald Jackson echo the definition of itutu (mystic coolness/grounded awareness) when they state:

> *Although African American culture stresses a positive and emotional outlook on life, this is juxtaposed with a strong grounding in reality. African American culture places a high value on 'tellin' it like it is'. Again, this realism is reflected in the lyrics of blues and gospel music as well as rap and hip-hop music, all of which portray the difficulty of life and advise a cool, steady, and persistent toughness needed to overcome this difficulty.* [7-5]

In 1967, Lee Rainwater wrote:

When . . . Negroes use the expression, 'Tell it like it is,' they signal their intention to strip away pretense, to describe a situation or its participants as they really are, rather than in a polite or euphemistic way. 'Telling it like it is' can be used as a harsh, aggressive device, or it can be a healthy attempt to face reality rather than retreat into fantasy. [7-6]

"Telling it like it is" is the blues term for exactly what David Rock calls labeling of the emotion. It is a matter-of-fact way of just stating the emotion without sinking into deeper analysis of why the emotion exists. It is about simply and unceremoniously naming it. In cultures that place an emphasis on politeness and emotional restraint, repression of feelings is done to fit into social conventions. And as we have seen, it carries a price. According to Rock, suppression does not lessen the level of stress or arousal in the limbic system, the main seat of such emotional experiences. In addition to maintaining the level of stress or agitation, suppression causes *additional* stress by decreasing our ability to remember things. A study by Steven Most, Marvin Chun, and David Widders confirms this relationship between higher stress and distractibility. It shows that people who are more prone to stress, worry, and pessimism suffer from higher degrees of *emotion-induced blindness* than people who are less prone to stress. In studies, testers displayed difficulty performing simple tasks if they were shown an emotionally distressing image immediately prior to doing the task. The more prone to stress and worry testers were, the less able they were to willfully counteract the distracting effects of the distressing images.[7-7]

The more we suppress our emotions, the higher the degrees of diffuse, but ever-present, stress and anxiety we experience, and the more distractible we will be. Furthermore, when we suppress our emotions, others intuitively seem to "know" that which we ignore, as they sense we are not being authentic.[7-8] Such shadow sides of suppression were, and are, commonplace in European-American culture, which interdisciplinary scholar Jerome Braun, in his book about the nature and psychology of civil society, calls a "neurotic culture." Braun writes that repression at the root of such cultural neuroses is rarely entirely successful, and thus often comes out in "twisted ways." He states that our culture models a tendency to sublimate our repressed emotions into a supposed "cure-all for all personal unhappiness," which can be found in a focus on "achievement." The result is the creation of what he labels "successful neurotics." [7-9] When successful channeling of emotions into "achievement" is not possible, stress, anxiety, and worry follow, along with other more sinister forms of existential angst. And even if all achievements have been gained (successful marriage, job, retirement, investments, etc.), a sense of emptiness and lack of fulfillment is often still present. Here Braun echoes similar findings mentioned previously to those from Brené Brown's research in the realm of the social sciences.

Lee Rainwater's thoughts about the concept of "tellin' it like it is", that "it can be used as a harsh, aggressive device, or it can be a healthy attempt to face reality," is, I believe, acutely perceived. The first is a prescription for immediate (aggressive) release and long-term stress production, the second can include a healthy way of stress release. If we look around in popular culture, we see the "harsh, aggressive" aspects of the practice used in political campaign speeches and when talking heads debate publically on TV. This version of telling it like it is supports a cultural creed that favors those who shout the loudest. It can be used as a battering ram in the "winner-takes-all" mindset, which is not conducive to authentic emotional sharing. It offers a quick relief that is not unlike that of scratching a mosquito bite. It feels good for a second, but long-term it only makes the effects of the bite worse. For many of us though, this version of talking tough is a more culturally accepted mode of expression than sharing an emotionally complex but authentic underlying sense of uncertainty or vulnerability.

Will the Real Winner Please Stand Up?

In a 1995 interview with Canadian blues and roots record man and broadcaster, Holger Petersen, ethnomusicologist folklorist and author Alan Lomax said:

We're now facing that in this new very hard-boiled rational, big-time-bottom-line society that's emerging here amidst prosperity, a man's not much better than his qualifications, you know? If you haven't got them, you don't eat, and neither does your family. So we'll begin to sing and feel the blues, you know?
7-10

The 2006 comedy-drama, low-budget film, *Little Miss Sunshine*, rose to unexpected popularity, grossing in excess of $100 million worldwide. It was nominated for four Academy Awards, and won two. Michael Arndt, who wrote the screenplay, talks about his inspiration:

One of the things that was an impetus to write the script is [that] I remember reading this interview with Arnold Schwarzenegger where he was talking to a group of high school students—high school students—and he said, 'If there's one thing in this world that I hate it's losers. I despise them.' And I thought there is just something so wrong with that attitude . . . . There is something so demeaning and insulting about referring about anyone as a loser. I wanted to attack that idea that in life you're either going up or you're going down, you know, it's all about status and impressing other people... It's this winner take all society where one person is going to get the million dollars and everyone else is a loser, and I just despise that mentality. . . . And to a degree a child's beauty pageant is the epitome of the ultimate, meaningless competition that people put themselves through. 7-11

The movie examines the human cost of a society, where a struggle to achieve individual success (as exemplified most glaringly by the "meaningless competition" of very young girls required to appear flawless in front of judges) creates loneliness and despair in an attempt to excel, impress, and be the winner that, per definition, makes everyone else losers. Unhappiness and feelings of alienation happen because competition for individual success pits people against each other in an endless pursuit of the winning slot. *Little Miss Sunshine* depicts a society in which fame and appearance trump competence, and where superficial gloss and looking like a "winner" is the normative standard by which all are measured. In this world of posturing and glamour, there is no compassion or authentic connection between people. There is no room for failure, pain, vulnerability, or self-doubt. Rather than talking about the problems, they are dealt with by ignoring them. Each character tries to cope by using the prescription for success in suburbia: go it alone and craft your own happiness on your own terms by using the harsh, aggressive prescription for competition at any cost. The results? A suicide attempt (the uncle), a vow of silence and impenetrable isolation (the teenage son), silence around a heroine drug addiction (the grandfather), stress and chain-smoking (the mom), and desperate self-aggrandizement and eventual failure (the dad). As family members one by one fall apart emotionally, the VW bus that carries them on their odyssey also gradually breaks down. In fact, moving the bus forward can only happen when they all get out and push: a symbol of how togetherness and teamwork, rather than a mindset of "I win, you lose," is foundational to belonging rather than simply conforming. They find new appreciation for each other as they learn to connect without judging themselves and others. At the same time, they stop depending on externally applied rules for "success."

Brené Brown writes:

Perfection is not self-improvement. Perfectionism is, at its core, about trying to earn approval and acceptance. Most perfectionists were raised being praised for achievement and performance (grades, manners, rule-following, people-pleasing, appearance, sports). Somewhere along the way, we adopt this dangerous and debilitating belief system: I am what I accomplish and how well I accomplish it. Please. Perform. Perfect. [7-12]

I don't know about you, but I probably have elements of all of the characters in *Little Miss Sunshine* inside. I identify this interior landscape as my "success-focused neuroses." When I think that achievements, events, things, or success in and of itself will make me happy, I get disappointed. Even if I get what I was hoping for, it leads me to immediately go hunting for another achievement. I have a sense of emptiness inside that constantly looks around to be filled. And, conversely, when I stand in the audience at a blues concert and resonate, or sit around the dinner table in deep conversation with friends or family, I know that this sense of belonging and heart-to-heart connection ultimately feels more satisfying to me than any additional diploma or achievement. I still go for the diploma though: it is not an either/or proposition. I personally am the happiest when there is a balance between my sense of achievements and an inner joy of contributing and belonging. Likewise, I am the happiest when I succeed at striking a balance between acknowledging my emotions and using them to inform and empower, rather than let them dictate, my choices. It is not easy and I often fall short. Fans frequently expressed that being authentic is somehow easier when they are within the blues community. Here they find some respite as the music invites them into fellowship. They focus on ways of connecting, rather than competing, with others.

Historically, blues artists often stood squarely in personal, and public, unashamed acknowledgment of their emotions. Some performers got stuck in the emotions, expressed them harshly and aggressively, and burned out— or they may have made them into quite the "story," as Rock might say. He writes: "Your ability to regulate your emotions instead of *being at the mercy of them* is central to being effective in a chaotic world" [emphasis added]. [7-13] Some bluesmen and women, in impossibly harsh and unforgiving circumstances, may have lingered in the "storytelling" part of the emotions, becoming increasingly pulled into a sense of despair and victimization over their situation. There are numerous examples of bluesmen and women who lived self-destructive lives.* Living entirely at the mercy of one's emotions, whether in or out of the blues, is probably just as destructive and dysfunctional as emotional repression.

---

* I am referring to Robert Johnson, Charley Patton, Son House and many others. It seems likely that the myth of the "27 club" (artists like Jimi Hendrix, Janis Joplin, and Brian Jones, who all died at that age from self-destructive behavior) speaks archetypally to this mythological layer of self-destruction and "lingering in the story of the emotions," or living "at the mercy of the emotions." These artists are commonly beloved as martyrs to a life of being uncompromisingly in the realm of emotions.

Chapter 8:

Universally Authentic Blues

Looking For Honest Expression

As mentioned previously, two main definitions of authentic blues crystallized from the data. Much blues music would clearly belong in both categories simultaneously:

1. Blues that is deemed authentic by its historical context or "group membership" and what I thus labeled: Context-specific Authentic Blues (CAB). Some blues boomers found it difficult to use the word "authenticity" in relation to contemporary, white, or middle-class black blues performers, since the blues originated with a different ethnic or social group in a different era. Authenticity here is based on contextual factors such as geographical location, race, time period, social and cultural backgrounds, influences, and even musical equipment availability. Authenticity here means that the artists play it congruently in relationship with their contextual factors.

2. Authentic blues as it pertains to honest expression and thusly played from the heart to be received by the heart: Universally Authentic Blues. UAB is communicated through a blues form, but is never based on imitation alone. The musicians' immersion in the moment allows the synthesis of cultural, social, musical, and emotional experiences to be communicated with integrity. Authentic blues is dependent on good musicianship, as defined by the musician's ability to connect emotionally within, to effortlessly allow personal

involvement to merge with the musical format, and to transmit this through musical expression to others. *What constitutes such felt authenticity is entirely subjective.* In UAB, the meaning of "authenticity in the blues," exists in the context of emotional honesty and universality of emotions. It is not defined by *who* plays it, but instead by *how* it is played by the musician (and by how it is interpreted by the listener).

It makes sense to define the word authenticity carefully at this time of the evolving blues saga to avoid endless discussions about what is "real" or "authentic" blues. I find that often these discussions are, at least partially, based on unclear consensus regarding definitions of these terms. We will explore UAB in this chapter, and delve into parts of the context-dependent elements of blues (CAB) in Chapter 17.

Almost all blues fans agreed that the blues seems vibrantly alive, authentic, and more "real" than other genres. The two most commonly chosen "bottom line" statements about the blues (out of 21 possible) were that blues feels less commercial and more organic and real. The interviews deepened and furthered this finding. Most of the interviewees also emphasized that it was important to them that the performers were emotionally transparent and/or honest in their delivery. In the vast majority of cases, when fans talked about authenticity in blues, they were referring to UAB:

Marie: But how do you gauge, how do you figure out that this is authentic?

By the way it makes me feel. If I listen to a song and it grabs me a certain way, or . . . I get a certain sensation from it, or it brings me to a whole new place, I know . . . that's truly authentic. That's what I like listening to versus there's some songs that I like, but they just don't do that for me. I don't know . . . that's tough to answer. It really is.

Or:

The authenticity . . . it's not just that I can relate to it. I think it's also that . . . the everyman can relate to it. That every…just the common person can relate to this emotion or this . . . you know, 'Call my job. I had too much weekend.' Who hasn't had that experience?

Or:

*Blues affected me on a deeper level. On an inside level, you know, more than just your average what you hear on the radio, but blues is something more. It touched something in my heart and that's what made the difference. It was what lit up the blues over everything else—realizing that was the truth. That it was genuine. That's what I need to do. Now **that's** me.*

UAB is not a simple concept. In order to communicate emotions authentically, a musical language is used that has less to do with technique and more to do with a certain kind of musicianship. It is based on acute listening skills allowing musicians to engage reciprocally with the immediacy of the ever-changing creation process. As an example, Mick Fleetwood— who replaced Aynsley Dunbar in John Mayall's band in 1967—has claimed that he felt that Dunbar lost the gig with Mayall "because he was too proficient." Fleetwood continues that it was Peter Green who championed the switch to a less technical drummer by approaching Mayall stating that Fleetwood's "simple, straight-ahead" drumming would benefit the musical expression they wanted to achieve.[8-1] Similarly in Walter's band, I have witnessed technically brilliant drummers get passed over at auditions for more intuitive drummers. If a drummer, for instance, wanted to agree in advance of starting the song, which—out of a handful of possible styles of shuffle—Walter wanted him or her to play, it was an immediate, yet possibly unconscious, warning sign to Walter. If the drummer couldn't feel his or her way into the music, it might not be a good fit. Likewise, musicians who want to write charts of the music locking it into fixed, pre-determined forms—or who play the same solo the same way every night—eventually also find themselves gradually moving on to other bands, where the focus is less on intuition and intense listening, and more on technical prowess, composition, or exact reproduction of existing material. There are plenty of musical styles, and plenty of bands, where this kind of approach is desired and appreciated. Obviously, it has to be mentioned conversely, that there are plenty of technically adept musicians who can play the blues well, and Walter, and many other blues bands, employ some very technically skilled musicians. But they need to *also* be able to enter into a realm of spontaneous exploration, acute listening, and immersion into a fluid process of spontaneous improvisation based on "feel."

In UAB, musicians speak a poignant musical language that is difficult to explain. Many blues musicians talk about the difficulty in getting the notes to "speak." Playing them is not enough. Singing the lyrics is not adequate. There is another quality needed that has to be internalized for the musical expression to come alive. Guitarist, Michael Bloomfield said:

> *The first blues I remember was a T-Bone Walker song called "Glamour Girl". That was just a whole other thing. I was playing the same notes that they were playing, but when I would take my solos they weren't the same. What I was playing was like fast bullshit – it wasn't right at all. Those cats were using the same notes, and it was all right. I just couldn't figure out the difference.* [8-2]

Here Bloomfield addresses the fact that playing the blues authentically is not just about mastering a musical form or technical ability, but rather about an immersion into deeper layers of authentic sharing. UAB is a spontaneous—and complex—musical language. In order to experience UAB, conventions and the social rules of engagement are often put aside. We can observe in their stead a certain anarchistic element of rebellion; emotional honesty does not adhere to conventions, and is typically born out of a deep need to communicate without filters. More than 90% of blues fans stated they connected to a certain rebelliousness in the blues. Playing the blues honestly requires the performer to dig deep in the interior universe of emotions. It is the antithesis to "keeping up appearances" and "falling in line."

John Mayall

Let's take a brief look at John Mayall to describe how we may talk about authenticity in blues, beyond African American blues originators. First let us look at him as an artist in the realm of context specificity (CAB): Mayall is authentic to the synthesis of postwar Britain and to what must have been a deeply-felt desire to escape or transcend the brown, drab, postwar, stiff-upper-lip environment. His blues contains a search for lively expression, vivaciousness, excitement, and relevance of immediacy, for which he found the tools in the African American blues tradition. His music is a synthesis of a deep knowledge, study, and respect for African American blues tradition and a personally developed musical expression. He has his own singing style; he does not have an African American voice, but his voice works within the format, powerfully and unapologetically. The context of escape from postwar Britain and search for new potentialities thus merged seamlessly in Mayall's blues through personal immersion in tradition, unique synthesis of influences, personally felt elements and a signature sound.

Within the format of UAB, our brief analysis of his music might look like this: his song writing is at times painfully honest and transparent (for instance "Memories" from 1971, which chronicles loneliness and desperation in the wake of his parents' divorce, teenage angst, etc.). Mayall is a versatile and talented musician in his own right, but one must not overlook his brilliance in creating a "blues academy" of sorts for up-and-coming blues musicians—especially guitarists (Eric Clapton, Peter Green, Mick Taylor, Walter Trout, Coco Montoya, etc.). Here he teaches the improvisational elements of the blues and pushes and conditions his (technically masterful) players to also tap into the moment and let go of perceived expectations: to be spontaneous, find their authentic "voice," be themselves, and be real. Mayall epitomizes that, for him, spontaneous elements of the performance are paramount. Often Mayall will change the key of a song on stage without warning and play what he feels like playing exactly at that moment—set lists be damned! Mayall exemplifies that UAB is about authentic expression in the moment. Mayall's blues depends on how he and his musicians feel, and how he and the band interact with each other and the audience at any given moment. His recording style is also based almost entirely on improvisation, and he often will not do second takes in the studio. He chooses to surround himself with first-rate musicians, so these spontaneous first-takes become auditory pleasing experiences, precisely for this reason: to go with the immediacy of the music and let it bloom in the moment. Mayall's blues is an ever-changing and personally direct statement of a musical commitment.

Healing Connections in Universally Authentic Blues

A study from the psychological and cognitive sciences concludes that humans are skilled in recognizing "negative emotions" (anger, disgust, fear, and sadness) across cultural barriers. In other words, whether we live in a small African village or in a Western metropolis, we can recognize expressions of emotional distress across cultural differences. That study also found that happy, jubilant, celebratory, and playful human sounds are, at the same time, not as easily universally recognized and identified cross-culturally. [8-3] It follows that we can thus more easily pick up on and recognize the sounds of human sadness, distress, grief, fear, anger, and frustration no matter our social and cultural conditioning. When we share the sounds of our painful experiences, we share a universal preverbal common "language."

On an archetypal level, the blues speaks a universal language that simply allows us to feel that we are not alone when we move through difficult experiences in our lives. Many blues fans commented on how they found solace by resonating with this discovery:

Growing up in school as a kid, you know, I used to get bullied. I was the little guy. I had to learn self-defense and all that stuff. But yeah, I was bullied and made fun of as a kid, and, you know, I felt kind of like a loner. Didn't always fit in with everybody else, what have you. I can relate to a lot of things in blues music like being stuck here, being stuck there, being told to do this and to do that. Knowing you can't go here, you can't go there. So yeah, I say I can definitely relate to a lot even though the African Americans in the eras of slavery and share cropping obviously had to deal with far worse. The things they had to endure were insane, which we have not eliminated in this world yet in any shape or form. This is another thing that makes the blues even so much more relevant today, when you just look at the world. . . . Good blues is timeless. I mean it will always be good no matter when. I mean ten years from now you could turn that song on, and it will still evoke that emotion, and will be just as good as it is today or was 20 years ago.

Bruce Iglauer said in his interview with me:

The blues looked oppression in the face, and provided emotional healing to its victims. The magic of the blues is that the healing force of the music is so strong that it speaks to those who didn't grow up in the culture that created it. I've traveled around the world with blues musicians and seen them wield this healing power on audiences that couldn't understand the meaning of the words, but could still feel the emotions of the blues. So, intense oppression was the forge that created this hugely resilient music.

Iglauer later spoke about his own experience of emotional resonance and recognition which obviously is foundational in UAB:

I certainly could feel the 'tension and release' in some songs. As a teenager, I had a lot of personal angst, and blues helped me deal with it. So the notion of suffering did connect with me intellectually and emotionally.

Growing up in a 1950s, upper-class, Jewish neighborhood in Chicago, Michael Bloomfield didn't have economic worries or social oppression to deal with. However, navigating an emotionally abusive environment was a fact of life: he was often ridiculed, especially by his father. Being shamed for not being a jock, for being chubby, and for not wanting to follow in dad's footsteps as a businessman all contributed to give him a sense that he didn't belong. He found he was recognized and treated compassionately in a more emotionally forgiving world, namely the world of African Americans. His childhood friend Fred Glaser said:

> *Michael's father would be embarrassed to introduce him. 'Sit over there, Michael, and don't tell anybody you're my son. I'll take care of your check later. Just sign your check. Go sit over there and don't bother me.' It hurt, but we would go and sit where he told us. The black guys would be nice to us. . . . It was just another example of the way we would go around white people and be treated well by black people. It was another way of connecting with blacks and breaking away from whites.*

Implicit in this world of African Americans was the approach and music of emotional honesty. Glaser continues:

> *The key to what it was really all about was breaking away from these rigid, conservative white people. . . . That's what the music is. The music is the outpouring of that feeling; it's a visceral creation, you know, a creation of that feeling. We just wanted to be among these nice [black] people and have some fun and not be screamed at, because we liked music and art.* [8-4]

Likewise, blues boomers often report relief in sharing emotional experiences through the musical and social outlets around the blues scene, in which they find authentic emotional resonance with others—musicians and fellow audience members alike. They refer to the blues milieu as a place where they feel that they do not have to hide who they are. It was very common to just feel a sense of being "at home," being safe, and feel accepted in the blues milieu. As an example:

> *I don't feel I have to put on any airs. . . . No, I'm totally myself when I go to a blues show. Very comfortable! Very at ease! I don't have to worry about what anybody thinks. I don't feel like I have to put on anything. It's just very spontaneous. You're just there! (Laughs)*

Blues singer Janiva Magness stated:

That's how printed [the blues] is on my psyche. It made me feel like I was connected and like . . . somebody else feels like shit. Somebody else knows this broken thing in me. Somebody else gets it. Somebody else gets what it's like to try to come through that and come out the other side. Somebody gets my rage.

Magness points to the fact that the blues meets us where we are. If we need to identify with someone who is experiencing pain like we are, then the blues allows it. It frees by allowing us to navigate the pain together. Stuart Brown writes: "Music, dance, and painting, . . . bring people together to 'sing with one voice.' Art is part of a deep, preverbal communication that binds people together. It is literally a communion."[8-5] This preverbal communion is easily accessible in blues music. A few blues boomers, described this sense of identification as life-saving in scope:

I suffer from depression and PTSD and I know that there are times when I am so down. And I just can't do it anymore—and I can put on some good music and it brings me out of that. It's more than a therapist. It's more than the medication. It will actually activate my brain cells to do what I can't do without it. . . . There's times when there's this sass in me [that] comes out and I can identify with a nasty old lady and sing some blues, and that feels really good too, you know? It's just something that I don't think I could do without if that makes any sense. I know I wouldn't be here.

J.B. Hutto, a Chicago bluesman, stated in an interview with Bruce Cook:

Blues is my bag. Singing the blues—let me put it this way—you get the chance to tell the public what you're thinkin' and what you're doin'. See, you catch the heart of the public with the music. . . . A lot of people have [similar] kind of problem[s]. You get with a band that's good and you got a good voice, then you can handle it. [8-6]

Many fans talked about their participation in blues concerts as somehow transformative:

> *I think the blues explains it how it is. . . . It doesn't sugarcoat life. It takes the negative and can even turn it into a positive. . . . Even though it's called the blues and people talk and sing about some bad things sometimes, I can't ever remember coming away from a blues concert feeling bad. It's always really good even though what I might be hearing is people's despair or troubles—it's not sung about in those fashions.*

Brené Brown's research indicates that the act of sharing is healing. She implores: "Practice courage and reach out! We have to own our story and share it with someone whom we can count on to respond with compassion." [8-7] The blues provides a place where differences of economic and social standing, political persuasion, and other dividers, to a large degree, fall away and a sense of connectedness and communion is possible. Author and music journalist, Art Tipaldi said:

> *There's a real special community. . . . It's the shared, soulful, honest experience. We went on the cruise two weeks ago and Ruthie Foster was doing a one-hour Sunday gospel session. When you walk out of there with those 300 people who were at that, you have all shared the most magical soulful moment and you just look in each other's eyes differently.*

Part II

Blues Boomers:
Wired for the Blues

Chapter 9:

My Blues Story

I know about wanting to go it alone. I grew up an only child and learned early on to be self-sufficient. The world seemed filled with competitors. It was difficult for me to decipher other people, both in my home and outside of it. Going it alone became a way of life for me and remains my default emotional setting. When Walter became seriously and very visibly ill in 2013 after a decade of increasingly frequent health crises, I found myself at the end of a long phase of being emotionally paralyzed. The wall of uncertainty facing us had me trapped. For years, I had chosen to deny the reality of his disease (he had Hepatitis C) both privately and publically. He wanted to continue playing music for people as long as possible, and I knew playing music was going to give him encouragement and strength. So I hid most of what was really going on. I hid it from myself, from Walter, and from the world. Was I repressing that which I didn't want to face? Was I living in denial? Maybe – it was a coping mechanism for sure, and it was also founded in a litany of practical concerns. I believe that is the case for most of us. Living in emotional congruence is a nice ideal, yet how much we want (or are able) to be emotionally transparent with ourselves and others varies depending on our situation.

The lid blew off my silent secrecy in March of 2014, when doctors told us that the love of my life had 90 days left to live if he did not get a liver transplant. Two of our three sons were still in middle and high school. Medical bills were piling up on my desk where performance and recording contracts used to lie. My salaried work as Walter's manager obviously depends on him being able to work. A family friend, Kirby Bryant, started a fundraiser to help us survive financially. Seeing the fundraiser go "live" activated in me a sense of being worthless and weak. Admitting that we needed help felt like the ultimate defeat. Much to my surprise, we were not met with judgment or condemnation, but rather deep caring and support.

I started blogging for the supporters of the fundraiser as a way to thank the many contributors for their love, support, and prayers. I continued writing as a way to update the community that formed around us. My pain, my anguish, and my frustration, as well as my Sisyphean work to help Walter survive, became shared experiences. I increasingly just wrote how I felt. It was raw and unpolished. I shared from a place of deep sadness, desperation, and fear, and I sent it out for people to read via social media. The community, in turn, responded with comments, love, desperately needed financial support, and prayers. I felt their embrace. They stood by us and showed such compassion. I read in the many comments from perfect strangers that they understood what I was going through. It made me feel accepted even if my emotions were a mess, and our life situation was far from perfect. The inner peace of that realization was immense. The sense of commonality I felt with others was especially powerful because there was no pretense. Their responses became a daily source of revitalization for me. I received notes and comments from this community that my sharing somehow also helped some of them deal with things that were going on in their lives. Comments came from readers in India, the Middle East, Europe, Australia, New Zealand, South, and North America. The common humanity linked us across time and place, and the connection was life-sustaining for me. Maybe for the first time in my life, I did not fight this fight with my inner emotional demons in the dark secrecy of my own doubt. And it gave me strength.

Previously, I assumed that there would be many problems with revealing painful and raw emotions publicly, and especially when asking for help. I had only shared the victories of my life and self-righteous political commentary on my Facebook page. I felt I had a reputation to protect. I had always edited my life to appear smooth, happy, and secure. I strove to appear self-sufficient and project an image that I was in control of my life. However, through this experience, my stoic façade cracked and became a virtual bloody mess. As I chronicled our struggle, I opened my heart. The honest sharing became my lifeline. Oscillating between vulnerability, desperation, and occasional bursts of strength, I found that being authentic was like the trust-builder game in which you fall backwards and others catch you. Every time I wrote an update, I jumped backwards into this embrace of perfect strangers, and each time, my confidence in human beings grew. I felt surrounded with kindness, generosity, understanding, and support.

This community gave me strength to continue my trek through the medical nightmare we were in. It didn't make my pain go away. But I felt our fight was not just mine, not just Walter's, not just our kids', but shared and therefore somehow less difficult to bear. It strengthened a desire in me to also give back in some way to the community that believed in us. I felt connected to others in a way I had not felt before. One day it dawned on me that this is precisely one of the miracles of the blues: the ability to authentically share life's joys and sorrows, to feel part of a community, and to be connected to others without pretense. I had become a "blues writer," and my stage was the written page. My writing was my music. I sent my emotions out to the online community, who, much like an audience at a blues festival, responded with "shouts" of recognition and support, sending energy back. They inspired me to keep up my spirits, to keep fighting for Walter, and to keep writing. It became a communal circular breathing of love and support. Walter and I had the blues. And we were not alone even if we were feeling down. In fact, this was the most connected with other people I had ever felt.

I began to appreciate with new understanding what Walter had been talking about for years—how his audience inspires him, how it holds him, and somehow co-creates the music with him as inspiration flows back and forth. How, on such special nights, magic is created in the moment not just by Walter and the band singing and playing, but by their becoming a part of a spontaneous manifestation of connection in a mutually felt, musical exchange of authentic human emotion, where all individually contribute to create a shared field of experience that feels somehow greater than the sum of its parts. Indirectly and unwittingly, I experienced a part of the miracle, the mystery, and the majesty of the blues in my moments of writing from my heart. The blues—and telling it like it is—became my lifeline.

That mysterious lifeline that I felt in those moments offered yet another vantage point from which to view the relevance of blues music. My research showed that other blues fans experienced connectedness through the emotional transparency of blues as well. Our default tendency to deny, minimize, or repress our doubt, fear, and vulnerability is a part of what makes us admire and respect the originators of the blues: people who were socially, economically, and culturally oppressed, but who often led the way into a more emotionally transparent universe. Blues helps us know how we feel. Blues helps us find acceptance with the "blue notes" and the imperfections in our own lives. **Blues helps us acknowledge it so we don't choke on our own stoicism.**

Walter has told me about burly, bearded bikers who hug each other while tears stream down their faces as they listen to a blues tune that evokes a particular memory or emotions they might not have wished to acknowledge or digest. And suddenly, in the safe container of a blues concert, they can let it go. I have watched members of the audience come into blues concerts with bitter wrinkles on their faces, only to leave laughing and carefree—visibly transformed. I have heard stories of suicides averted and hope rekindled due to a particular blues song, or through an individual's interaction with members of the blues community. I have experienced moments at blues concerts in which time and place seemed to merge, and audience and musicians were like one organism. In such moments, separation caused by social distinctions, political persuasion, ethnicity, or culture ceased to separate.

In the following chapters, we will point our lens of observation back to the 1940s, '50s, and '60s. It is central to understanding the role of blues music for its fans today to first explore often-ignored elements of the postwar environment in which baby boomers grew up. We will focus on emotional residue in the wake of certain historical events and circumstances rather than the events per se. It is a virtual ride back in time to discover the fertile field that existed for the blues to cross over from the black community where it originated into white culture. To explore this topic, we will start by taking a brief look at the musicians who synthesized African American blues tradition with white culture as examples of people who were able to appreciate, connect to and integrate cultural trends that were floating around in the times they were in.

White Blues – Black Blues

White musicians who discovered the blues often felt that they could not really live up to black blues masters. Instead, they mixed musical traditions into new expressions and thus contributed to continuing manifestations of the blues format. Among these first musicians in the United Kingdom in the 1950s were Alexis Korner, Chris Barber, Cyril Davies, Lonnie Donegan, and Long John Baldry. Later in the 60s, John Mayall, Eric Burdon, Bill Wyman, Charlie Watts, Eric Clapton, Peter Green, and many others. Belonging to the first wave of postwar, white musicians in the US, who tapped into black blues tradition, studied it, and wished to play it as a recognizable genre themselves (beyond other genre descriptors such as "folk") were John Hammond, Jr., Paul Butterfield, Mike Bloomfield, Charlie Musselwhite, and Elvin Bishop.* These white musicians were instrumental in bringing awareness of blues music to white audiences, and in doing so, they contributed to the process which allowed blues music to transcend previous times' racial boundaries. Or, depending on your view, they stole a musical style that was not their own and removed it from its cultural cradle. It is indisputable though, that white musicians playing the blues clearly made the

---

* In the US, there had of course been many white performers who had been influenced by blues, R&B, boogie-woogie, and jazz prior to the 1960s. Rock 'n' roll was hugely influential—also abroad for British musicians—and was clearly a powerful manifestation of African American music transitioning into white culture. Jazz, particularly traditional jazz and New Orleans styles also made early inroads into white culture.

genre reach further and wider into white culture. By the time blues emerged as a defined "genre" in the 1960s, the ground was tilled, fertilized, and readied by at least a decade of musical emergences from black musical tradition that were mixed with white sensibilities. Some of these musical manifestations were known as skiffle in the UK and as rock 'n' roll, folk, or hillbilly in the US – or they were squeezed in under the label of country music. Eric Burdon describes that in the late 50s, musicians all over the UK rallied around "the blues flag," but that they were not yet aware of it as a collective discovery. Each group of musicians in various areas of the UK seemed to discover it independently, and be surprised to find other groups of musicians in other towns who were experimenting with similar musical amalgamations. It thus literally sprouted in various areas of the UK spontaneously, particularly in Newcastle, Liverpool, London, and by extension, the red light district in Hamburg where British bands—mainly out of Liverpool—went to entertain the public.[9-1]

I have always wondered why white audiences discovered and embraced certain styles of music more quickly or easily, and certainly more broadly, when it was performed by white performers. I couldn't find good answers for this phenomenon until I came across a recent study by J. Kilev Hamlin et al., called "Not Like Me = Bad: Infants Prefer Those Who Harm Dissimilar Others" that might *begin* to explain why people embrace a certain style of music when it is played by people that look and sound like themselves. The study found that infants between the ages of 9 and 14 months showed a preference for puppets that displayed helpful behaviors and disliked puppets that were destructive. However, when a helpful puppet was from a different race and/or with an unfamiliar language, the infants overwhelmingly preferred a puppet displaying similar or familiar racial and linguistic traits as the infant, *even when this puppet displayed harmful behaviors.* The tendency intensified and was more pronounced in the older group of infants.[9-2] These findings *might* help explain why having white jazz, rock 'n' roll, and blues performers performing *their* versions of African American-inspired music helped garner the attention of the white population—the music seemed easier to relate to when performed by musicians who were similar in outward appearance. Thanks to this default, innate "setting," we humans are, at least partially, wired to ignore, or even exclude, others who sound or look different from us. In addition to this inborn gravitation toward, and familiarity with, similar others, there were plenty of other circumstances that made the white baby boomer generation ripe and receptive for the matter of fact expression of blues music.

Chapter 10:

Postwar "Suburban Mindset" in the United States

As the cataclysmic events at Nagasaki and Hiroshima heralded the onset of the nuclear age, they symbolized more than the end to World War II. Paradoxically, even as the Allied forces had won the war, there was a latent sense of unease and fear. These diffuse fears in the population were kept hidden by the celebratory euphoria apparent around the end of Nazism. But the mushroom cloud etched an indelible image onto human consciousness—it was clear that humanity now rested perilously on the edge of possible self-annihilation. This knowledge was mitigated in the US by a conviction that as long as the "good guys" had these god-like destructive capabilities, it was all right. And almost immediately, this notion was shattered in 1949, when the Soviet Union also achieved these powers. It became clear that human survival now rested on a precarious and paradoxical balance of power dependent on restraint, and ultimately, and probably more significantly, on a desire among nuclear-holding powers to self-preserve. In a strange way, the possibility of mutually assured destruction brought an uncomfortable—or reassuring, depending on our vantage point—notion that we are all in this together no matter how much we disagree. The rules of engagement were re-written in this new reality, yet in many ways, we often (still) fight to maintain old prewar views and moral codes because they somehow seem to promise a cloak of perceived security and order in a paradoxical and perplexing world.

The postwar populace often struggled to contain the implications of such an all-encompassing change of reality. They just wanted to move on into a functional everyday reality where they could concentrate on everyday matters.

The sweeping perspective of watershed change was relegated to the basement of their psyches. And often, postwar survivors wished to throw away the key to this awareness, enter into the kitchen, put a pot on the stove, and concentrate on the business of finally being able to feed, clothe, and house their own families. A focus on the family, and on that which one could be in charge of personally, gave an illusion of much-desired security. Having a safe home in which one could close the door to the outside world became ever more important.

Professor of history and social sciences, Kenneth T. Jackson, writes of the post-World War II zeitgeist that "for more than five years, military necessity had taken priority over consumer goods, and by 1945 almost everyone had a long list of unfilled material wants."[10-1] Since WWII followed closely in the wake of the Great Depression, Americans had experienced a period of 16 years in which scarcity of food, jobs, and housing plagued the population. Jackson states that in 1947, six million families were living with relatives and half a million were living in Quonset huts or other impermanent homes.[10-2] Before WWII, various political attempts to help the housing situation were tried. The Public Works Administration, under the leadership of Franklin D. Roosevelt, created programs that encouraged private enterprise and also extended a helping hand to local authorities through federal loans to improve circumstances with regard to housing. This approach was largely ineffective. The incentive to build housing for the poorest, even secured by federal loans, was not enticing for investors. In 1937, the United States Housing Authority (USHA) was created and these federally supported housing projects finally got underway. Roosevelt wrote to his chief housing official in 1938 that:

> *Today marks the beginning of a new era in the economic and social life of America. Today, we are launching an attack on the slums of this country which must go forward until every American family has a decent home.*[10-3]

During the war, much attention was diverted to creating temporary housing around manufacturing plants that supported the war effort. But the federally funded housing program remained in place and was ready to be launched after the war. The notion of each family having its own home came to symbolize the American postwar "Dream" in which the underlying awareness of nuclear threats and complex international affairs could be dulled by a mirage of self-reliance and creature-comforts. Before the 1920s, the more well-to-do often lived outside cities. They did not live in farm communities that were often poor, but rather in grand style in idyllic green Gardens of Eden. According to Harvard professor John R.Stilgoe, these suburban settings, small communities, or estates dotted the countryside outside of the chaos and squalor of the inner cities. Political and business power players typically had their residences in these green countryside estates.[10-4] These idyllic communities outside the polluted air of the inner cities were largely the idealized models that later were sought after, emulated, and mass-produced in the creation of suburbia.

Other than supporting the housing program, the government also sought to give incentives to encourage marriage and childbearing. During the war, the United States government supported married couples by sending a check to wives of soldiers who were at war. For each child born, this check was increased. Soldiers were encouraged to marry and have children before they headed out to war, as their wives and children would be taken care of financially in their absence.[10-5] After the war, housing was desperately needed for the returning soldiers and their new families. And in this postwar environment, the focus was often on family values as measured by the number of children. The ability to feed them was seen as a measure of material success, forming an ideal environment for further population growth and a symbol of national strength and freedom. Studies show that deprivation over a long period of time changes the mindset and priorities of those who are deprived. Research professor of sociology, Glen Elder, writes:

Lastly, it is clear that economic hardship experienced in the Depression made an enduring contribution to views on "things that matter" in life. The one common value across men and women is the centrality of the family and the importance of children in marriage.[10-6]

In the early 1960s, an influential leader in the women's movement, Betty Friedan wrote in her book, *The Feminine Mystique*, that because of the sense of confusion, separation, and vulnerability in the wake of WWII, both men and women sought the "comforting reality of home and children."[10-7] This family-centric climate, combined with an unprecedented building boom wherein builders had federal mortgage assurances, and an overarching American postwar mindset of having lived victoriously through hell on earth, created an almost inexhaustible urge in the population for peace and quiet, privacy, and the ability for the individual to shape his or her own destiny. The success of the nation in war and peace became synonymous with high levels of home-ownership, an abundance of consumer goods, and a plentitude of new children to form future armies of consumers. Every American family living comfortably, each in their own home, became not only the measuring stick for personal as well as national success, but also a symbol of a victorious nation. Franklin D. Roosevelt stated this vision in 1933: "A nation of homeowners, of people who own a real share in their land, is *unconquerable.*"[10-8] These words were obviously uttered long before the reality of possible nuclear annihilation cast its shadow opervasive power over the national awareness. The notion, however, that individual homeownership and autonomy combined created invincible national strength, lingered. Again, the uncomfortable reality of a changed world-view was collectively repressed to the national subconscious only to surface in a single-minded focus of ridding the US of future potential enemies. It also surfaced within the country's borders masked as witchhunts toward "sneaking" domestic socialists, ethnic minorities, drug addicts*, and those

---

* Johann Hari's recent book, *Chasing the Scream*, is about the politics of addiction in the pre- and postwar environment in the USA—including the racial over- and undertones of this endeavor. I highly recommend it. Another excellent book about the postwar focus on individual autonomy over social welfare and how this mindset took hold with religious over- and undertones is Kevin M. Kruse's book *One Nation Under God*.

who otherwise looked or acted "suspiciously" (read: those who appeared somehow different than the white, all-American, conformist mainstream).

In the postwar years, as the Cold War mindset added to tension, keeping up the appearance of being victorious and strong was thus (subconsciously) important on many levels for the individual and national self-image.

Repression, Fear, and Identity in the 1950s

In the late 1940s and early '50s, Alfred Kinsey, and later, in the mid-to late 1950s, Masters and Johnson, lifted some of the taboos around human sexuality through their study findings and reports, which were publicized widely. But for many in suburbia, the new sexual liberation only meant a new to-do list of expectations. In addition to newly installed suburbanites feeling pressure to appear as symbols of a victorious nation (successful, independent, and brood-producing), couples now also felt they had to be uninhibited and playful in the bedroom. As taboos were broken down, and new sensual experiences were entering the parental bedrooms in Suburbia, a new secret sense of sexual inadequacy was also born, as the *King James Version of the Bible* competed for space with Masters and Johnson's latest book about the female orgasm on the bed stand. And no matter if the big O was now becoming a part of popular vernacular, sexual and emotional repression did not just disappear overnight.

For many, life in postwar suburbia included bouts of intense private anxiety masked by public bravado. The undercurrent of anxiety, as mentioned before, stemmed from a range of causes, including fear of nuclear holocaust and a sense of feeling inadequate, alienated, or not up-to-par with the demands of a fast-changing world. Other issues stemmed from the gender role-reversal—or role-shift—that happened in the wake of the war. Women had been encouraged to work outside of the home to help the war effort, but after the war ended, they were expected to once again stay at home, iron shirts, and vacuum floors with starched aprons, perfect hair, and after the kids were put to bed, to be hot to trot in the boudoir.

African Americans returned from the battlefields to a racially-biased, segregated America. White and black soldiers had a shared purpose during the war, and now, once again, blacks were told that their peacetime contributions to society were less important and/or not appreciated.

In the 1950s, movies, television, and media in general often portrayed the era as carefree and idyllic, with a few iconic exceptions, such as the movie "Rebel Without a Cause." Relative material wealth after the war came to symbolize an idealized and happy public image that was often just a façade. On the home front, as (mainly white) suburban neighborhoods flourished, many women heard a "problem without a name" murmuring in the corners of well-appointed living rooms. Betty Friedan captured the sense of emptiness that was pervasive among dutiful white housewives of the postwar era. In spite of "luxuries that women in other times and lands never dreamed of," Friedan found suburban women suffered from a hunger "that no food can fill." According to Friedan, the notion that this problem could be solved by "more money, a bigger house, a second car, [a move] to a better suburb" only made the emotional congestion and feelings of inadequacy worse.[10-9] It did, however, fuel the rapid economic growth of the era, as the war machine production transitioned to peacetime consumer goods. Friedan was among the first to shine a light on the fact that American commerce thrives as long as people are kept in a perpetual state of "underused, nameless-yearning, energy-to-get-rid-of state of being."[10-10] Friedan speculated that this did not happen as a result of a conspiratorial plot hatched by corporate America, but rather as a "byproduct of our general confusion lately of means with ends; just something that happened . . . when the business of producing and selling [10-11]

One might draw a parallel to the words of President George W. Bush in the immediate wake of the terrorist act on September 11th, 2001, when he encouraged Americans to continue their "participation and confidence in the American economy. . . . We will come together to take active steps that strengthen America's economy."[10-12] The purpose was to inspire resilience by not letting disaster deter people from living their lives. But to connect this resilience with materialistic consumption, indicates that the notion of tying patriotism to consumerism has followed us into the 21st century.

Postwar books like J.D. Salinger's *The Catcher in the Rye* encapsulated the zeitgeist of the postwar generation's dilemma. The protagonist, Holden Caulfield, sees through the hypocrisy or "phoniness" of the adults, but at the same time idolizes a fictitious childhood state that probably never existed— a Neverland. Holden identifies the inauthentic behavior of others, yet is unable to avoid it himself. This theme of "phoniness" in J.D. Salinger's book circles around the anxiety inherent in a repressed and inauthentic existence— and the inability to escape it—as no role models are available to show the way. The book is set against a backdrop of alienation, anxiety, and confusion. Holden seeks connection with others, and at the same time fears the unpredictability of such intimacy; he is stuck in a perpetual no-man's-land on a blind search for meaningful connections in a desert of human superficiality. The theme resonated with the baby boomer generation, and *The Catcher in the Rye* became and remained a best seller for adolescents, some of whom found that they, too, lacked good role models for what it meant to grow up in the shadow of the war. Repression, denial, and avoidance often created a "phony" environment leaving youngsters longing for something they could truly believe in, relate to, and find authentic and "real."

The following section on Post-Traumatic Stress Disorder is included to illustrate *one* example of the emotional costs of attempting to put aside that which is not easy to deal with. Members of the Silent Generation* were often silent because of perceived expectations to keep up appearances, suck it up, and make it all work: to make daily life in the suburban utopia look good and hide anything that did not fit the image of a picture-perfect family.

---

* Those born roughly between 1925 and 1945 – typically the parent generation of the baby boomers.

The Cost of Pretending

In the postwar rush to portray strength and security, it was difficult to accept that answers to complex problems, such as global, local, and personal effects of war, were not always found in simple and easy-to-effect "bang-zoom—you are going to the moon" type solutions. The invisible wounds in the wake of any war affect many more people indirectly than those who were originally in the line of fire. The war comes back, even if it is won, with the damaged nervous system of returning servicemen, wounded veterans, economic aftershock, and fear of future repercussions.

Post-Traumatic Stress Disorder (PTSD) is one such insidious and wide-ranging consequence of war. The diagnosis of PTSD did not exist prior to 1980. The National Institutes of Health made the following statement in 2010: "Much of the general public and many mental health professionals doubted whether PTSD was a true disorder. Soldiers with symptoms of PTSD often faced rejection by their military peers and were *feared* by society in general" [Emphasis added].[10-13] In WWII, the medical profession and the army were aware of the condition. It was not called PTSD, but that does not mean that it was not medically, albeit secretly, well-established as a neurotic reaction to traumatic experiences. Quiet and ashamed avoidance was the preferred method of dealing with PTSD on all levels. Because of the stigma attached to suffering from these kinds of "nervous disorders," it was not something a soldier would admit to without the risk of being labeled a "coward" or "yellow," and there was a great deal of confusion as to the legitimacy of the terms "Combat" or "Battle Fatigue." Acknowledged or not, the disorder went home with returning servicemen of all ranks, but acknowledging such "weakness" was diametrically opposed to the expected public image of a strong soldier who was greeted around the world as a war hero. It was practically unpatriotic to admit the reality of feeling an inner hell in the afterglow of a seriously successful victory of war. Nonetheless, numbers from the Veterans Administration Hospitals from 1942 to 1948 show a drastic increase in cases of "neuropsychiatric disorders."

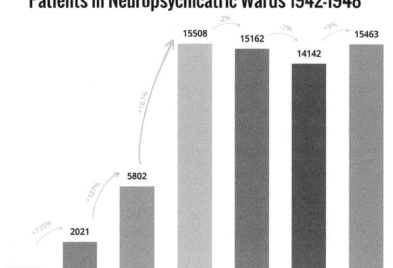

Patients in Neuropsychicatric Wards 1942-1948

Figure 4: Patients in VA Neuropsychiatric Wards[10-14]

The effects of PTSD often show up many months or years after the original trauma occurred. Furthermore, these numbers only indicate hospitalized cases. The majority of PTSD symptoms were dealt with in private, in shame, and behind closed doors, with only the wife and children as terrified witnesses. It is safe to say that the war, in many ways, came home to the American dream home, where it was allowed to fester, manifest, and create what a study conducted by the Anxiety and Depression Association of America later labeled a "secondary traumatization" for the family members.[10-15] A study from 2002 concludes that:

> *When a member of the armed forces is killed in combat, family members receive condolences from "a grateful nation." When that combat veteran survives to struggle with PTSD symptoms for decades, we still need to extend a*

compassionate hand to that family to help them overcome the isolation in which they all too often find themselves.[10-16]

Such help was rarely, if ever, offered to post WWII veterans and their families. The hidden humiliation of not living up to the All-American ideals dug trenches of shame and feelings of impending doom in the psyches of many postwar families. It was, in fact, a living nightmare.

Since Spielberg's 1998 film *Saving Private Ryan* started showing the "other legacy" of WWII, several books have surfaced chronicling the life of the Baby Boomer generation growing up with a "combatant dad who truly never left the battleground." [10-17] Likewise, the recent movie *Railway Man* is based on a true story about Eric Lomax, who was tortured as a POW by the Japanese in WWII. Following the release of the movie, his family described in a newspaper article his unwillingness to talk about what happened to him during the war—his total emotional absence, and how the torture he received in the war, lingered in his mind for decades, in effect torturing his family by its silent and repressed presence.[10-18] Lomax was a British soldier, but his experience was no doubt also typical for American soldiers returning home. In her book *The Hidden Legacy of WWII*, American author Carol Schultz Vento chronicles the horrors of a homecoming father from WWII who cannot connect emotionally, who drinks, and has nightmares: he is in effect unable to escape his inner demons.

After WWII, with no official diagnosis available, and in the face of a taboo against discussing the negative human effects of war, much psychic residue and reactive fallout was swept under the proverbial rug. And simultaneously, socially accepted behavior was portrayed by TV shows such as "Leave it to Beaver," in which idyllic and exceedingly well-dressed everyday lives were orderly and safe. It was a world in which "Ozzie and Harriet" gracefully agreed that "Father Knows Best," and if everybody just did the morally right thing, nothing really awful could ever happen. This mindset of refusing to deal with, or name, problems was also prevalent in dealing with all kinds of domestic abuse, alcoholism, divorce, and other personal problems that arrived on the threshold of the suburban home. Just because things looked great on the surface, and material goods were accessible and plentiful, the emotional wellbeing of the postwar generation was not as easily maintained as the perfectly manicured lawns and new paint job on the Plymouth in the driveway. Behind closed doors, in the private eco-system of the picket-fenced suburban lot, things were rarely as easy as American Pie, yet it was paramount to make it seem so. One lacked a language to describe inner desert landscapes that grew evermore desolate as outward appearances were continually kept artificially "greened."

Later, we will get to the liberation of elements of the postwar psyche that became possible when blues and blues-inspired music entered into the equation. But first, we will explore a bit further around the postwar generation: baby boomers, and the exhilarating but challenging times in which they were raised.

The Multigenerational Family Becomes Nuclear

The multigenerational family did not typically make the transition from the city to the wide, picket-fenced, sidewalk-lined streets of suburbia. Whereas families had coexisted and co-parented before, the suburban ideal did not typically involve cohabiting with grandma and grandpa. While about a quarter of all families had multigenerational living arrangements in 1940, the number of such arrangements steadily declined in the postwar years. Pew Research states that immediately prior to WWII, about 25% of the population lived in "extended households." By 1980 only 12% did. Pew attributes one of the key reasons for this change to the "rapid growth in the nuclear-family-centered suburbs."[10-19]

Simultaneously, the closeness of living together diminished. Grandma, grandpa, aunts, and uncles were no longer needed to help in the household. Washing machines and gas-powered lawn mowers were part of the arsenal of modern conveniences that allowed greater self-reliance and independence within the nuclear family. In an article in the "Family Coordinator" published in 1971, Jack Balswick and Charles Peck state that "as society becomes increasingly mechanized and depersonalized, the family remains one of the few social groups where . . . the primary relationship* has still managed to survive."[10-20] Marital relationships in this new "depersonalized" society relied on more abstract elements (such as affection) to survive, while they previously had been bound by the functionality of working relationships. Such new demands on the relationship, the authors argue, increase the risk of divorce. Furthermore, Balswick and Peck find that "inexpressiveness is a culturally produced character trait which is characteristic of many males.... It is suggested that in growing up, boys are taught that expressiveness is inconsistent with masculinity,"[10-21]. They conclude that the new trends that were then arriving with the hippie movement "along with the blurring of sexual distinction in fashion may very well be the shattering of the strong, silent male as a glorified type."[10-22] And they speak to the generational change in emotional expectations between the Silent Generation and Boomers: "Youth in general are critical of inexpressiveness and [seek] candid honesty in interpersonal relations."[10-23]

Baby boomer boys often gravitated toward a more expressive male role model rather than their Silent Generation dads, who frequently didn't speak up but did what was expected of them while on emotional lock-down. But if the silent and strong male role model was not always fulfilling for boomer men growing up in the shadow of the war, where were they to look? Many felt conflicted about how to express their masculinity: old stereotypes modeled by their parents' generation felt stiff and awkward, but they were still reluctant to leave it behind. The hippie movement offered an alternative, which brought with it male role models that were less about machismo, and more about peace, love and understanding – and certainly sex, drugs and rock 'n' roll. But this new model proved effectively unsustainable or difficult to live by once marriage, job, and children entered into the equation.

---

* Primary relationship in sociology is referred to as being "based on ties of affection and personal loyalty [that] involve many different aspects of people's lives, and endure over long periods of time. They involve a great deal of interaction that focuses on people's feelings and welfare more than accomplishing specific tasks or goals." (Crossman)

As families depended less upon each other for collaborative efforts in the home, and various needs were "filled" by consumer goods, another convenience further eroded connectedness and meaningful exchanges between family members. In the 1950s, TV dinners and pre-packaged food items were not only acceptable, but commercially encouraged. Families stepped away from the dining room table, and dinner conversation became a thing of the past; eating in front of the TV was the new ideal. This phenomenon really took off after 1954 when Swanson ran a successful advertising campaign promoting the plastic tray with peel-back foil wrapping.[10-24] The trend was to strive for an increasingly convenient and self-sufficient existence and status symbols of the era were thus expressions of this trend. Each family ideally lived in their own home and, if they were part of the new, relatively privileged middle class, took care of their own lawn, with their own entertainment center (radio and TV) and mode of transportation (the family car), all neatly arranged to appear flawless. Perceived security and comfort was supposed to equal "happy," and many felt that if they weren't, there must be something wrong with them.

In the book, *Suburban Nation*, Andres Duany, Elizabeth Plater-Zyberk and Jeff Speck find that the suburban model of building was based on a "rational model that could be easily understood through systems analysis and flow charts." They find that "historical precedent and human experience" were no longer considered; rather, town planning became a matter of logistics in an excited rush to replace the old with new, technologically-planned sprawl.[10-25] Suburbia was organized around functionality. Housing tracts were pods of residences, as opposed to the mixed-use construction of previous times (shops, schools, hospitals, taverns, work, and homes mixed together) which had allowed more "experiential richness."[10-26] In addition to these pods of residences, suburbs consisted of isolated strip-malls, office and business "parks," and civic institutions like schools, town halls, and roadways that connected the various disjointed components. Convenience and isolation became keywords that described this modern construct of American postwar suburbia, rather than an intimacy of experience and an emphasis on human connection.[10-27]

In this increasingly prosperous, but often desolate, landscape of the 1950s, a new form of music captured the youth. This music offered a language to speak to emotional turmoil that allowed spontaneity and freedom of expression. We will explore the explosion that was American rock 'n' roll shortly, but first let us jump across the pond to the UK.

Chapter 11:

The Background Story of the "British Invasion"

Drab and Brown – The UK Postwar Reality

Before the 1960s, it was easier for African American performers to get their careers off the ground in Europe, and in Britain particularly. Some Britons were fascinated with music that came from a different place than mainstream American offerings. These Britons explored another side of the American reality through music that was forged in the ashes of slavery, the ongoing blaze of sharecropping, and industrial, impoverished cityscapes. They explored what was on the dark flipside of the shiny silver dollar—the ongoing oppression of an entire race of people. Britain became pivotal in the dissemination of American blues abroad, and also in the reintroduction of this music to American shores.

As Britons gathered in the streets for joyful and euphoric celebration at the end of World War II, sorrow and sadness was latent under the surface. During the course of the war, 264,000 British servicemen and 90,000 civilians had been killed.[11-1] The Great Depression had been sandwiched between two world wars. In both—and especially in the second—the destruction had extended to British soil. Through extensive bombing during WWII, Britons had suffered their share of the German air offensive. Rebuilding was a gargantuan task, and the financial toll was by some described as a millstone around the UK's neck. Britain was broke. In 1946, they had to borrow money from the US with interest. The loan was not paid off until 2006. The people of Britain did not experience the relatively immediate switch from wartime economy to consumerism, as was the case for Americans. Additionally, the UK received a great deal (26%) of the money from The Marshall Plan – or the European Recovery Program—that was extended by the US interest free to war-torn European economies after the war. A paper from the National Bureau of Economic Research (NBER) indicates that The Marshall Plan, among other things, enabled them to build "successful mixed economies" (economies that contain a mix of private and public ownership).[11-2] But rebuilding daily life was a slow and painful process. Rationing continued in the UK for almost a decade. Beginning in 1946, bread was rationed for two years, even though it hadn't been during the war. Potatoes were rationed in 1947 – 48. Even into the early 1950s, people lined up to get basic food items due to shortages: sugar, butter, cheese, margarine, cooking fat, meat, bacon and tea were all rationed. Finally, in 1954, rationing ended in the UK.[11-3]

Historians Janet and John Shepherd write that the many years of deprivation before, during, and after the war turned the desires of people toward family values and having children. "Traditional family values dominated: 'male breadwinners,' full-time 'stay at home' married housewives, and 2.4 children were the safe and traditional ideals that many strived to accomplish in order to offer a perceived kind of security and order to their families."[11-4] This is obviously very similar to the mood in the US immediately following the war. In 1945, the Welfare State was created in the UK. It consisted of the National Health Service, family allowances, as well as child allowances. It was made possible by a fund that everyone paid into, and from which those in need could receive aid. Children were seen as a shared investment in the future requiring sacrifice and discipline:

> *The post-war era placed a high importance on child welfare. Children were the future; it was 'to them the new welfare state was devoted'. The critical importance of the family as the 'indispensable framework' for a child's development was also recognized.* [11-5]

A shared sense of striving for a better world for all was a stated objective. Shirley Williams quotes British economist and social reformer William

Beveridge as saying: "The object of government in peace and in war is not the glory of rulers or of races, but the happiness of the common man."[11-6] The creation of the Welfare State, mixed with business-friendly policies that furthered private enterprise, was born out of a desire to help everyday people achieve happiness and be content. One might note that this sense of social responsibility was also present in the US in the policies of the New Deal enacted in the time before the war, yet as mentioned previously, this mindset of social responsibility faded rather quickly after the war in celebration of individualism and patriotic conformism. In the UK, this socially progressive awareness was mixed with a desire to further traditional values: a mix of conservative personal ideals and progressive social policies.

The British populace was under immense pressure. Growing up in postwar UK was anxiety-producing: Shepherd and Shepherd state: "At all levels, schooling was full of rules and strict discipline. . . . Pupils were often 'made an example of to deter others.'"[11-7] Children were to be raised with high morals, preferably in an upstanding household with their mother at the stove. Test scores and measurable success were crucial to demonstrate how investments in children's education could pay off. To be deserving of recognition, one had to work hard, and achieve measurable and quantifiable markers.[11-8] This individual success was thus also a gift to the greater society that believed in and invested in the young. Pressure to perform was ubiquitous.

The general mood of the British population was affected by a sense of "profound resentment and anxiety at Britain's loss of imperial status."[11-9] The British gradually lost their self-image as a major global political and financial power-player. In December, 1962, Dean Acheson, who helped design the Marshall Plan as Secretary of State in Harry Truman's White House, was invited to give a keynote speech at West Point. His speech included his thoughts about Britain having a hard time finding its self-identity after the war:

Great Britain has lost an empire and has not yet found a role. The attempt to play a separate power role—that is, a role apart from Europe, a role based on a 'special relationship' with the United States, a role based on being head of a 'commonwealth' which has no political structure, or unity, or strength and enjoys a fragile and precarious economic relationship by means of the sterling area and preferences in the British market—this role is about played out. Great Britain, attempting to be a broker between the United States and Russia, has seemed to conduct policy as weak as its military power. [11-10]

The need to preserve personal images of identity and integrity intensified as the expression of national identity became increasingly perplexing. Alistair Davies and Alan Sinfield comment in their study of postwar Britain that:

Many of the leading British and American commentators on postwar British culture have echoed his (Acheson's) sentiments. For them, the politics and culture of postwar Britain have been defined by evasive inwardness and nostalgia (Hewison 1977, 1981, 1986), cultural retardation (Wiener 1981), middle-class conformism (Nehring 1993), anti-technological romanticism (Veldman 1994) and insularity (Piette 1995). [11-11]

Britain was searching for a meaningful national identity after the war, and finding a synthesis between tradition and modernity was not a simple task, especially since new influences, particularly from the US, had been flooding British shores. This new influence was paradoxical: it was fresh and new, and yet this newness sat in the shadow of an awareness that the US was also the country to which Britain owed an immense monetary debt. During the war, there was an influx of Allied Forces from the United States and Canada on British shores. As much as these friendly forces were there to help, it was a barrage of foreign culture nonetheless. From 1942 to 1945, almost 3 million Americans disembarked in the UK (a country consisting of around 45 million people at the time). A perceived "cultural imperialism" was felt in the wake of their presence. They partied in clubs and pubs alike, dated English girls, and lived comparatively lavishly on army bases dotting the English countryside. According to Paul Ward's study of *Britishness Since 1870*, as the end of the war neared in 1945, a slight majority of British people (58%) felt favorable toward Americans. The following year, this approval rating dropped to around 20%. Americans quickly became viewed as self-obsessed, spoiled, and insincere:

> *American 'boastfulness', 'immaturity', 'materialism and commercial preoccupation' and 'morals' were cited as reasons for dislike. One man told Mass-Observation that the USA was not prepared to supply Europe with food yet was 'prepared to flood the world with their atrocious films, full of slop, bad manners, inaccurate history and the general marvelousness of the American people'.[11-12]*

The strong influence from the vibrant, demonstrative, free spending, and youthful Americans annoyed Britons. Perhaps a sense of crumbling self-identity played a part: a sense of underlying resentment of having been, in the very recent past, a confident, powerful, self-contained, and proud country. After WWI, Britain stood strong. It had expanded its ability to control trade and foreign policy. By 1922, the British Empire held control over 458 million people—one fifth of the world's population at the time.[11-13] In the course of a few decades following the war, the United Kingdom transitioned from being "the empire on which the sun never sets" as a measure of its size and scope, to being an empire crumbling at the seams, the empire on which the sun had set. Therefore, as the United States was increasingly successful at establishing its economic and military superiority after the war, the memory of American GIs and their youthful, national self-assurance became unpleasant and distasteful to many Britons.

The older British generations especially were not enthusiastic about the American "youth" culture that was propagated through Hollywood movies and jazz music. Immediately following the war, Harold Wilson, as President of the Board of the Trade, expressed fear that Hollywood movies corrupted morals and were not representative of a true British way of life:

Speaking as an ordinary cinema-goer, I should like to see more films which genuinely show our way of life. I am tired of the sadistic gangster ... films [made by] diseased minds which occupy so much of our screen time. I should also like the screen writers to go up to the North of England, Scotland and Wales and the rest of the country and to all the parts of London which are not so frequently portrayed in our films.[11-14]

Wilson was trying to stem the tide of cultural influences that were flooding his country. It was an uphill battle that he lost!

The Americans' brash confidence, however, was often intoxicating to British youth. British youngsters were brought up in the sunset times of a crumbling empire's conventions. Their emotionally reserved elders were careful not to overstate anything. But the young generation emerging from the shadow of the war was hungry for new, vital, and exciting modes of expression. A mid-1960s study from the University of Birmingham about the popular press's representation of youth subcultures in postwar Britain suggests that:

Youth was, in both papers [the Daily Express and the Daily Mirror] and perhaps in the whole press of the period, a powerful but concealed metaphor for social change: the compressed image of a society which had crucially changed, in terms of basic life-styles and values—changed, in ways calculated to upset the official political framework, but in ways not yet calculable in traditional political terms.[11-15]

A tangible tension between "the old ways" and the new was ever-present under the surface in the postwar years in Great Britain.

For many, particularly among younger generations, America stood as a giant: a representation of modern conveniences, boldness, innovation, exciting new forms of music, Hollywood glamour, and military and material might. It truly appeared to be the land of freedom and endless opportunities while the millstone hung heavy around the necks of all in the UK. In the more tradition-bound and war-beaten United Kingdom, there was a sense of Americans as loud-mouthed, brash, and arrogant teenagers crashing the adult dinner party. These Britons took pride in the traditions that were part of their way of life, in spite of—and for some because of—the fact that it included limited emotional expression: "stiff upper lip, and that sort of thing." In the United Kingdom, the make-up of the empire had been based on a pedigree-dependent, class-based system. Now, the proponents of the new welfare state encouraged a broader part of the population to reach for success. Some young Britons were intrigued with a different way of doing things; they looked to America with a mix of intrigue and envy. The bounty of the American way of life offered what seemed like intoxicating possibilities.

In the decades after the war, the US became increasingly a consumerist paradise: the place where a ritual of the "pursuit of happiness" was enacted again and again, accompanied by the sound of the cash register, and where one could buy anything the heart (or mind) desired. David Wright and Robert Snow describe how consumerist rituals are advertised and marketed to promise a kind of perpetual nirvana, where all needs were to be continually and effortlessly filled.[11-16] These rituals of consumption exemplified salvation from scarcity to some starved Britons, while it contributed to what made America appalling to others. For some British teenagers during and immediately after the war, the appeal of America was materialistic. It promised endless release from scarcity. To other youngsters, it (secretly or not) was the way Americans carried themselves with a sense of confidence that wasn't class-or pedigree-dependent. And for some it may have been a combination of things as expressed in American movies, music, and cultural icons. Others saw America as a country with gross racial inequality, double standards, and a superficial materialistic focus. Yet, no matter how Britons viewed Americans, they were unable to ignore them!

After WWI, recordings of American jazz reached a few record collectors and select music lovers on British shores. In the 1940s and particularly after WWII, there was an active group of musicians in the hip traditional jazz circuit in the UK. Artists like Humphrey Lyttelton, Mick Mulligan, George Melly, Kenny Ball, and The Saints Jazz Band reached a wider group of enthusiasts. However, this music did not reach the mainstream: a confluence of unique circumstances was required for this music to reach the masses. For the Britons, who found jazz and blues early, African American music came to embody and represent some of what made America complex, alive, provocative, paradoxical, and intriguing. Such was the case with Chris Barber, who became one of the pioneers who brought American blues and gospel artists to the United Kingdom and his brand of traditional jazz and blues to both the US and mainstream audiences in the UK. He, along with chief harbingers Cyril Davis and Alexis Korner, thus contributed to a continuing, cultural, cross-fertilization after the war—through music. I met Barber in London at the Classic Rock Awards show in November of 2013 and had an opportunity to interview him over the phone later.

A British Musical Trailblazer: Chris Barber

During WWII, Barber was a violin-playing teenager who wanted to study mathematics. His father was an economist and statistician and his mother a headmistress. Both parents had big hearts and were actively involved with causes devoted to helping better conditions in countries "where there was barbarity and things."[11-17] He was headed toward academic pursuits when American jazz and blues intersected his path. Barber had a transformative experience when he first heard African American music. The connection was solidified through a book he found on a trash heap on an American air field at RAF Bassingbourn near Cambridge. It was a book co-written by Mezz Mezzrow, an American musician who in the 1920s left his comfortable, well-to-do, Jewish, upper-middleclass life to learn jazz by immersion in the black musical community—an unthinkable act at the time. Through being exposed to African American musical styles during the war, and then reading about it in the book, Barber received an initiation into what he described to me as his "musical priesthood." I asked him what it was about this music that stood out for him, and this was his response:

> *Well, I mean it was kind of life-altering music in a way. I had heard of it,*
> *and I knew of the traditions but not much about the music. . . . The difference*

is black America, white America and everything like that. The members of my family were political people and we had all kinds of books. We'd set out the position – and recognized the trouble with the whole system and how it is in America, how it was in America I can say now, and had been of course in Europe several years before: the racism business....

So the whole idea to me was of the music being – having to do with this culture –their folk music. When I first heard more about it was during the war, about '43 or '44. I heard some on the radio and I liked it and I'd even written in to American Forces Network to get a record played on the program for the jazz thing* and what happened was that when my – I was at school – my school had evacuated itself from London to a farm, which belonged to one of the teachers in a town called Royston, which is about 35 miles north of London in the direction of Cambridge. Four miles away was an airfield called Bassingbourn, which became the headquarters of the 8th Air Force. So the flying fortresses, B17s, were mostly based there. . . . We used to cycle. We would stay at my house in the morning before breakfast to go and watch the B17s landing from night bombing raids in Germany, which meant us lying on the ground in the ditch beside the road that went beside the airfield and the planes used to just clear the barbed wire to get on the ground, so it was quite loud.

An interesting thing about Americans was their music. Particularly how the American Forces Network was, how different than British broadcasting it was. American music seemed so alive and real. So we were wandering about at the airfield, and we noticed that on the way, back of one of the big buildings, there was kind of a heap of rubbish. America had quite obviously reached a point in civilization where everybody buys things they're never going to want, and throws them away. Like in England we only started doing that recently. I mean junk things. Stupid idea, and so a whole lot of things got thrown away that were in perfect condition. And there was a pile of books – of pocket books. I looked through them. I saw one of them was a book called "Really

---

* The American Forces Network broadcast a program, called "the Jubilee Show," in which only African American artists were featured.

the Blues" by Mezz Mezzrow. He was a white jazz saxophone player of
Russian descent. But he came from Chicago and he played with black bands
and so on in the late 20s. He did a lot of things with black groups in the 30s.
The main thing is that he wrote a book, which was about jazz, blues, the
philosophy, and what it meant to the life of black people in America. The
whole thing was beautifully described. It was co-written by a Pulitzer Prize
winning journalist whose name I've forgotten.† But it was, it was actually well
written. I think he did the writing. Mezzo talked to him about it. And so
having read that book, it was like some people read the Bible for the first time
and become almost a priest. They can't help it. Well, I read that book and I
became a priest.* [11-18]

Barber and Mezzrow ultimately shared an experience with musical art
forms that were foreign to the culture in which they were brought up, and
that allowed a musical expression that was new, exciting, life-affirming—and
transformative. Chris Barber became a practicing "priest" in jazz and blues.
Inspired greatly by Mezz Mezzrow, Barber changed course and decided to
pursue what was then termed "race music" full time. As described by
Mezzrow, it united the social justice element of Barber's upbringing—the
concern for the downtrodden—with expression that seemed so "alive and
real." I asked Barber to describe the living situation at the time, and what it
was about the music that played so powerfully to the British psyche,
particularly in the postwar period. *"It was brown and drab,"* he answered.

*Bear in mind, we had rationing, rationing, rationing! You had to give in
coupons to be able to buy things. There was so little stuff to buy. Food and
certain kinds of other things were restricted. The government couldn't let
manufacturers make stuff and sell it when the people were not willing to buy,*

---

* *Really the Blues* was published first in 1946, so Barber's walk about the airfield must have
been after the war ended.

† Bernard Wolfe co-wrote the book with Mezz Mezzrow. On the back of the book it reads:
"*Really the Blues* was published first in 1946 and was a rousing wake-up call to alienated young
whites to explore black culture and the world of jazz, the first music America could call its
own.... Above all, Mezz championed the abandon available to those willing to lose their
blues."

because they had to export it to get enough money to pay back the loans we got from the USA to help during the war. The Americans had made these kind of cheap but effective ships called Liberty Ships to ship stuff across the Atlantic during the war and of course they got sunk by submarines quite often. But those ships—they were making them and selling them to us. So we had to pay money back. We had to get out of debt. It was a terrible crisis. There was nothing going on. You just couldn't go abroad for holidays. I remember in '48 my mother had some friends in Paris and my sister-in-law went to Paris for a week, and she was only allowed to take £2 out of the country in English money. But that's the thing: England was very poor then, and we made ourselves poor trying to win the war and in fact help to defeat the Nazis, which was quite important. And there you go (Laughs). . . . It was a drab—a very drab country indeed. And the popular music was mostly dance orchestras! Doris Day—that sort of thing. They danced to dance orchestras, which were playing largely what you heard in Hollywood musical films of the 30s and otherwise just foxtrots and quicksteps, you see. [11-19]

I asked Barber if he felt that there was a resonance in the British population going through such prolonged hard times after the war—a resonance with the African American plight, slavery, share-cropping, etc. Following is our exchange:

Well I don't know about that. They didn't realize it was black music. We didn't go out saying 'listen to black music or else'—we just played what we liked. We talked about it. We didn't say it wasn't. They mainly heard it, liked it, and felt it. Felt what it was: the freedom and the expressive nature and the real feeling behind it. That was a great success. So from about 1953 or so people were going to jazz clubs. Now of course jazz clubs had a great advantage in Britain because you—if young people are gonna go somewhere to hear music, it has to be done in a place where they're allowed to go. In the USA where they sell drink, you can't go without a proof of being 21 years old. Couldn't then, you can't now.

Marie: So in England . . . if you had a separate room with no bar you could bring people down to 16 years old.

Chris: Exactly. That's right.

Marie: And so that gave an opportunity for a younger crowd to hear this music.

Chris: Exactly so.

Marie: So now they would hear it. They were coming out of this drab, brown, sort of indebted, feeling "down," kind of everyday life-experience, and then they hear this music that is so different than the sort of manufactured Hollywood gloss.

Chris: They liked it. Of course!

Marie: So they liked it because of why? Can you put some words on what it was?

Chris: They didn't know why. Most of them didn't know why.

Marie: No, but you know why.

Chris: I knew why. Sure. I played it.

Marie: So can you tell me in your words, what it was that caught them? What was it that caught you? What was it that was so different about this?

Chris: It was music played with feeling; with expression of human emotions.

Marie: Yes.

Chris: And singing songs that also expressed playing good, straightforward human emotions, and not kind of all dressed up in fancy language.

Connecting to oneself and others through the emotional immediacy of African American music changed Barber's life, and through his jazz, skiffle, and blues bands, scores of (particularly young) people in the United Kingdom and Europe got to hear this African American-influenced art as interpreted through his music.

Being a white trombone player, a self-professed "Cambridge Man," helped Barber open doors for this music to get played in places where it otherwise wouldn't have had a chance to go. Barber saw music as his priesthood, but it was not about preaching. It was simply about providing music for people that allowed them to have a good time and experience joy and "good straightforward human emotion." And the slant of his band toward the "bluesier" side, and "the black side," is something that set his band apart. Inspired by Mezzrow, Barber knew that there was something in this African American approach – something that could enrapture others like it had him, and like it had Mezzrow before him. And for many of the early British pioneers of blues and jazz, like Barber, it was the African American musical tradition that captivated and really bowled them over. This music "did something."

Chapter 12:

Musical Bridge-Builders

Blues Infusion into White American Culture

Mezz Mezzrow was from Chicago and born into a family that was white, Jewish, and "respectable as Sunday morning, loaded with doctors, lawyers, dentists and pharmacists."[12-1] Mezzrow had *his* conversion moment, in which he let go of his pedigree and immersed himself in the universe of African American music, after he had been on an adventure in 1915 to Missouri with a friend. They had been "riding the rails" and were soot-and-dust-covered and "dark-complexioned to begin with." He was called the n-word and refused service at a lunch counter. In Mezzrow's awareness, the experience combined with a memory of his rabbi telling a friend that "King Solomon and the Queen of Sheba were all colored, and maybe the whole world once was colored."[12-2] At this moment, he decided that he "belonged on the other side of the track. . . sticking close to Negroes."[12-3] He felt a kinship with black people, an immediacy and connection that were absent in white, upper-class society. Mezzrow married an African American woman.

A few decades later, and on another continent, Barber's first wife was also black. Both of these marriages occurred at a time when interracial marriages were rare. In America they were also illegal. Both Mezzrow and Barber came from well-established middle-class or upper-middle-class white backgrounds. Both swore off the expectations and pursuits of their families to engage in different and, at the time, controversial professional careers. They both felt that African American music offered them an alternative way of being: a portal to an alternate language that was immediately relevant. Mezzrow felt that intense *joie de vivre* was a part of this kind of musical training, which at times included a risky immersion in life lived uncompromisingly. Here, in the 1940s, after many years of struggle, Mezzrow talks about communicating in a language that allowed his life-experience and musical expression to join and form a powerful and life-affirming, nonverbal expression.

> *Those twenty years of striving and failing had all gone down into my fingertips, so that now, all of a sudden, I could tickle the clarinet keys and squeeze out the only language in the whole wide world that would let me speak my piece. And you know what my piece was? A very simple story: Life is good; it's great to be alive!"* 12-4

Now let us jump to the mid-1960s. Like Mezzrow, Michael Bloomfield left his white, upper-class milieu when he discovered and immersed himself in African American music. Bloomfield was born into a wealthy family. He was also Jewish— like Mezzrow—from Chicago and he became an influential white blues guitar player in the 1960s. He helped capture the imagination of many American white youths when he played his firebrand of electric blues guitar in bands with both white and black members. He championed the feeling of African American blues guitar. Fred Glaser, who was a friend of Bloomfield's since childhood, said in an interview:

> *The key to what it was really all about was breaking away from these rigid, conservative white people and being attracted to these liberal, non-judgmental, kindly black people. That's what the music is. The music is the outpouring of that feeling; it's a visceral creation – you know, a creation that feeling. We just wanted to be among these nice people.* 12-5

Bloomfield considered himself an apprentice among black musicians like Muddy Waters. He felt reverent in their presence:

A lot of these cats were old enough to be my father. And I had that sort of feeling – they were like dads, y'know. Like a father relationship. And I had to be polite. They were the older masters of this thing. It was like being with old classical musicians. They were the classics of the blues. I was very, very polite. [12-6]

Bloomfield compared the support he received from his musical mentors with his father's angry reaction, frustrated at having a son who did not live up to what was expected of him. And as we have seen previously, it was paramount in 1950s America to conform to expectations and not appear to be "different." Being different was often equated with being un-American and bore a heavy price of shame for Silent Generation parents.

My father used to break the guitars. He called them 'fruit boxes,'* and he'd just take'em and break'em up. He wanted me to be everything that I wasn't. He wanted me to be a jock, he wanted me to be a good student, he wanted me to be this and that. He just didn't understand. [12-7]

In blues music Bloomfield felt free to be who he was, and the African American musicians supported him. They were kind and gave him clear and honest feedback when they mentored him. Among blues musicians, he was encouraged to pour his heart into the creation of that "visceral feeling." He also felt connected to the history of his ancestors. He felt that blues music also connected him to traditional Jewish music on the wingtips of musical immersion:

There were sections [of Chicago] where there were old Jewish people, Talmudic Jews, Hasidic Jews. They'd be chanting in these old synagogues, and you'd think you were in Israel 2000 years ago. The music sounded like blues, the wailing of it. [12-8]

---

* A likely reference to what his father saw as a less than manly occupation by a "silent and strong" traditional male type.

Bloomfield found that he could take some of the musical traditions he found himself attracted to, of which that of the African American was by far his favorite, and let them merge in him to form his own honest expression. He wasn't African American—Bloomfield begrudgingly acknowledged that. But in order to play authentically, he found it possible to go into his emotions and experiences and not simply imitate his heroes. Instead he found that when he acknowledged his many musical and personal influences, he could articulate something that was true to *his* authentic expression:

> *The hillbilly area was another music scene. You'd hear mountain songs, right out of the Kentucky Mountains, cats singing 'em, women singing 'em while they was working.... It was just amazing. I wanted to make sure I could play like Robert Johnson, play like Furry Lewis, and play all this stuff, too. And I still didn't know how it all fit in. But all of it came together – it sort of melded together and coalesced and came out in my playing. Still, in my heart of hearts, I would strive to sing like Ray Charles if I could, and play exactly like B.B. King. If I could play exactly like B.B., Junior, I'd be content. But I had to accept myself for what I was.[12-9]*

Bloomfield united black and white musical traditions in America in the 1960s. Barber connected traditions beginning in the 1950s UK, and Mezzrow was similarly a "bridge-builder" in America, mainly during the 1930s and '40s. All three were hungry to embrace music from African American culture that filled them with feeling and "honest human expression." In addition, Mezzrow and Bloomfield felt alienated from their own kin. In very real ways they were emotional refugees from a pretentious and cold white culture.

Chris Barber, along with others in the 1950s UK, was influential in bringing many American blues artists to the United Kingdom and broaden the awareness and popularity of their music beyond exclusive circles, where before and during the war the blues had been studied by wire-rimmed, glasses-wearing intellectuals, musicians, and artists in smoke-filled back rooms. In the late 1950s and early '60s, Barber worked and traveled (also to the US where he performed and sought out new talent) to build a considerable mainstream audience in the UK to whom he featured artists such as Muddy Waters, Sister Rosetta Tharpe, Big Bill Broonzy, Sonny Terry and Brownie McGhee. Some of these musical heroes were ones he initially heard during the war on AFN. Gradually, British bands embraced the art form and started playing their own versions of it, and it took on a life of its own.

Mezzrow, Barber, and Bloomfield are examples of musicians, who, each in their own way, helped African American musical art forms transcend racial barriers. They bridged cultures and indirectly also helped give black artists a more recognizable and relatable platform across social, cultural, and ethnic borders. There were other such bridge builders, the audiences—especially younger ones—who were receptive to another manifestation and amalgamation of African American and European American music brought by other bridge-building ambassadors. This music was known as rock 'n' roll.

Rock 'n' Roll in America

In 1946, pediatrician Benjamin Spock became a celebrated voice for new styles of childrearing. He encouraged a more flexible and "feeling" parenting style. Spock discouraged the practice of raising children in a manner that was based on military-style parenting intended to harden the individual. This led to a conflict for the baby boomers' Silent Generation parents, who found themselves in a virtual philosophical no man's land. Many felt inclined toward applying more traditional, regimented, and stern advice, like that of behavioral psychologist John Broadus Watson, who, in direct opposition to Dr. Spock warned against giving children too much affection. According to him, children should be treated logically and rationally, like small adults.

The government supported not only housing loans and investment in infrastructure, but also the education of American youth. In this safer and relatively prosperous environment, a new generation of 1950s teenagers felt contradictory emotions themselves, and often chose to climb over the picket fences of suburbia to leave the TV dinners untouched in the soft glow of the

Ferguson TV console. They were curious and had time and money to spend. They grew up with the ubiquitous fear of nuclear holocaust and a paradoxical worldview. They were told they were part of the best and strongest country in the world, and at the same time that they needed to be ever-vigilant, suspicious, and indeed fearful of those who were different. One might speculate that the speed with which America had developed in less than two hundred years from being a colony dependent on the British Crown to—after the Second World War—being the most powerful nation on earth, coupled with all the changes in the fields of economics, technology, social expectations, morality and family structures, had happened so fast that the personal as well as national mindset struggled immensely to catch up.

Wes Smith writes in his book about the Pied Pipers of Rock 'n' Roll that although the white segments of Silent Generation parents at this point generally appreciated African American musicians such as Count Basie and Duke Ellington, Rhythm & Blues, by contrast, was seen by many as: "ghetto music, loud and lewd. The performers sang black and sang proud."[12-10] When this music reached American youths in the 1950s, they were hungry to embrace it. Music became a refuge and symbol of liberation from boredom, convention, and emotional restraint. These teenagers were hungry for something new, something that felt authentic; something that could define their uniqueness and set them apart from the generation that preceded them. They were like a barrel of gunpowder waiting to go off. Probably nobody caught the underlying potential for capitalizing on this unexploded teenage potential better than Sam Phillips in Memphis and Alan Freed in Cleveland. In an article about the Cultural Revolution that birthed rock 'n' roll, Clifford Mayberry quotes Phillips, who on a hunch virtually invented Elvis:

> *[Teens at the time] had emotional starvation, and the most active, imaginative years of your life were going to waste because you didn't have a thing for just sheer enjoyment, or an ability to say 'hey this would help me make contact with this girl or boy.' Believing that the vehicle would come from blues music, Phillips reflected, 'Thank God that the statute of limitations didn't run on the blues and what came from it.'[12-11]*

For most whites prior to the mid-1960s, the blues was perceived simply as one of the expressions of African American R&B that was largely irrelevant to them. Ragtime and jazz had partially bridged musical appreciation across racial divides in earlier generations; these musical expressions had symbolically surveyed the area and put up an important but flimsy rope "bridge." A link that nonetheless prepared the way for the virtual four-lane suspension bridge of the century: rock 'n' roll! This musical art form combined the inherent rawness and repetitive simple chordal structure of the blues with a new youthful directness, as well as a more powerful "rocking and rolling" pulse that felt sexual. Rock 'n' roll musicians represented an embodied physical connectedness mixed with music that contained a hypnotic simplicity. In the emotionally repressed homes of suburbia, tension between old and new moral codes was omnipresent. The directness of "ghetto music" was therefore demonized and feared, especially by older generations, those who had put the lid tightly on their personal mason jars of homemade "jams." Robin Wood writes about repression and its symbolic emergence in another medium—that of horror movies:

> *One might say that the true subject of the horror genre is the struggle for recognition of all that our civilization represses or oppresses, its re-emergence dramatized, as in our nightmares, as an object of horror, a matter for terror, and the happy ending (when it exists) typically signifying the restoration of the repression.*

In horror movies, the return to the established repressed norm—the perceived order in the psychological universe—might be the happy ending. With regard to rock 'n' roll, there was no restoration of order. Once the lid blew off, it could not be put back on again. The Silent Generation couldn't unring Johnny B. Goode's rollicking bell. For the establishment, rock 'n' roll was equivalent to a monster being unleashed—a virtual King Kong of many decades' worth of repressed urges, unvoiced thoughts, and stifled boldness—that was released right into the midst of the young, white, teenage generation. And the result was earth-shattering.

On March 21ˢᵗ, 1952, Alan Freed, a Lithuanian-born Jew and radio deejay in Cleveland, put on an event he called "The Moondog Coronation Ball," which by some has since been called the "birth of rock 'n' roll" (this is the reason that the Rock 'n' Roll Hall of Fame today is located in Cleveland). In anticipation, Freed promoted the affair relentlessly on his radio show. More than twice the 10,000 people the arena could hold showed up. It was pandemonium. The hullabaloo surrounding this event was just a first hint at the energy waiting to be unleashed among the youth (that at this point was black as well as white) growing up with paradoxical tensions since the end of WWII. The white press was quick to label the crowd a "mob," and the black newspaper, the "Call and Post," which called Ray Charles a "blasphemer," called the concert's music: "garbage, trash, a shocking display of gutbucket blues and lowdown rhythms."[12-12] The concert was stopped— even before it really got going due to the police shutting down the venue— largely because of a massive and unruly crowd that had broken through the gates and crashed the party. The sound of rock 'n' roll activated fears of that which is alien and therefore threatening to conformity among people who longed for a homogenous, predictable, and conventional society. One could sum up the conflict like this: the Silent Generation wanted predictable peace and security, while the baby boomers sought to live on the edge, explore, and experience new sensations. Rock 'n' roll—as jazz had before it—was interpreted as subversive and dangerous. It was regarded as a drug of sorts that compromised and destroyed otherwise good, orderly, and law-abiding youngsters and turned them into frenzied sex machines, wild with chaotic screams while their bodies flailed in (what looked to the uninitiated like) demonic ecstasy.

Johann Hari writes about how these latent fears were also foundational to the war on drugs, particularly as it was conducted toward the African American community. This drug war was the brainchild of the first commissioner of the U.S. Treasury Department's Federal Bureau of Narcotics, Harry Anslinger. Hari mentions how black musicians were particularly in the crosshairs of the enforcers of the war on drugs:

Jazz was the opposite of everything Harry Anslinger believed in. It is improvised and relaxed, and free-form. It follows its own rhythm. Worst of all, it is a mongrel music made up of European, Caribbean, and African echoes, all mating on American shores. To Anslinger, this was musical anarchy, and evidence of a recurrence of the primitive impulses that lurk in black people, waiting to emerge. 'It sounded,' his internal memos said, 'like the jungles in the dead of night.' Another memo warned that 'unbelievably ancient indecent rites of the East Indies are resurrected' in this black man's music. The lives of the jazzmen, he said 'reek of filth.' [12-13]

The disdain for, and fear of, African American-inspired musical expressions such as jazz, blues, and certainly, rock 'n' roll was shared by most whites and upper class, or "nice church-going" blacks alike. If black oppression and white repression were like monsters partially unleashed through the power of rock 'n' roll, the music became the nightmare apparent, a virtual horror show for those who sought to attempt to screw the lid on ever tighter. The fears of older generations only added to the mystique of the music that reverberated throughout America as an unstoppable force in the 1950s, virtually ruling the airwaves. The gunpowder met both ignition source and oxygen to create a powerful societal explosion.

This more daring, direct, and sexually-charged style of music became the soundtrack to a time of massive change. The gyrating hips of Elvis Presley and the frenetic energy of bad boy Jerry Lee Lewis took black, bluesy, musical expression and merged it with a desire to blast away old conventions and silent repressions; it was a realm of new excitement and reckless attitude. A host of performers mutually shared inspiration back and forth in the black and white formation of rock 'n' roll: Little Richard, Chuck Berry, the Big Bopper, Buddy Holly, Ike Turner, Fats Domino, and many more.

In Britain, rock 'n' roll inspired new bands who had grown up with and appreciated the music of black blues artists. The foundation of the Rolling Stones, the Beatles, the Animals, the Who, and Led Zeppelin rests in this amalgamation of the spirit of embodied, emotional directness from black blues, and the new confidence, rebellion, and assertiveness of black and white rock 'n' roll. These British bands mixed their influences with humor, swashbuckling style, and a new kind of self-assurance. The inspiration to be direct and unashamedly oneself stemmed from their internalizing the expressive directness and emotional transparency and authenticity of African American musical tradition. The British bands took pride in showing exactly who they were—in their use of fashion, through their use of language, and most importantly by making the music their own. When British bands of the 1960s featured American black blues musicians on American TV shows, and talked about how blues had influenced their musical development, the mutual trans-Atlantic musical inspiration came full circle. White British musicians effectively brought attention for American blues musicians such as Howlin' Wolf and Muddy Waters to mainstream listeners in their own country. The trans-Atlantic musical bridge was thus crossed twice: first by men like Barber bringing black blues performers to Europe, and then later via white Britons who brought awareness of the blues with them back to an American baby boomer audience.

It took the import of American blues music translated and venerated by Britons, rock 'n' roll, a cultural evolution, the break-down of old rules, the Civil Rights Movement, and a sense of fatigue with the old rules of engagement (or lack thereof!) for the new musical doors of perception and expansion to open up wide. The 1950s and '60s were wild decades, each in their own way, of social and musical change, when blacks broadly were leaving the blues to continue their creation of musical styles, and whites were embracing and mixing styles in new ways.

Next, we will hear from a blues fan whose grandfather owned a plantation in the Deep South. In the 1960s she found herself in many situations involving music and race that she couldn't quite understand. The blues worked its way into her awareness and changed how she viewed African Americans, and how she, ultimately, found herself in a situation where much of what she had been told by her elders fell apart at the seams. Her story also speaks to the topic of why whites historically have been so (often secretly) fascinated with black culture, including becoming absolutely bowled over by the blues.

Chapter 13:

White Fascination with Black Culture

Changed by the Blues

JP was born and raised in Gulfport, Mississippi. She often visited her grandparents' plantation when she was growing up. She discovered the blues sound by accident as a very young person because of her proximity to its origins. This is not typical for the vast majority of the blues fans I interviewed or surveyed for this book. Most found the blues later via recorded music, radio, TV, or live concerts as teenagers or adults. Her experience however offers a glimpse into the white plantation family, and the confusion swirling around the rules of engagement during the breakdown of old racial prejudices and new inroads of integration. Her voice adds a perspective that reflects blues music's ability to reach beyond the color barrier into white awareness. JP speaks of her first encounter with the blues around 1960:

I was born in Mississippi, and my grandmother lived in the Delta. We took frequent trips up there growing up, and I think my first experience with the blues was when I was a little older. I think I was six. We stopped at a little station to get gas and I got out to stretch my legs. And there was this old black man across the street at a little bitty house—I mean it was a shack—and he was sitting outside on his porch—I guess playing guitar—and he had a big old hound. I remember the dog because I wanted to go pet it. But the music was so pretty, and it was so bluesy, and I just stood there. . . . I was just mesmerized.

Visiting her grandparents gave JP a glimpse into a world of "black workers" that was strange and foreign to her, and whose presence, and music, beckoned to her in ways that she could not talk to anyone about, since she was not allowed to have any contact with the workers. She never asked why. Her language still reflects the sense of absolute separation, the intrigue—and the almost magnetic pull she felt toward the black culture she observed on her grandpa's plantation:

Well, my grandpa had a plantation—my daddy's daddy—and of course he had black workers that worked the field. I remember this one little girl that used to help her mother. I remember her name. I have such a vivid memory. Her name was Izzy; her eyes were huge. I don't know if I'm the only one that had any connection with these people that were out there, but for some reason, she and I had a visual connection. To this day I still think about her because that's where I first heard all this music. I don't know where their music was coming from because we weren't allowed to go near their housing, but they played a bluesy kind of music. I guess it was by record player. I don't know. I remember walking the railroad tracks one day going that way and hearing that music, but I knew if I got caught back there I would get in trouble. . . . I'm thinking: 'Wow!' It was like, you know how the hair stands up on you? . . . That's the feeling that I got with this music. Where is this music? And who are these people? It was like, this is nothing I never heard before, and it just did something to me. It was like a lifting and I wanted to hear more of it. And I dared not go back and tell my Grandpa, or my daddy, that I was back there, 'cause I would've gotten spanked. . . . It was just like a whole new awakening. We went to church. We sang and stuff like that, but this was nothing like that. . . . It was raw.

JP felt attracted to this raw bluesy music and to the people who played it—it "did" something to her. She was forbidden by her culture, her family, and the rules of Southern plantation etiquette to talk to them. But the experience never left her. Ten years later, Joyce researched the blues for a high school project. She studied the history of sharecropping and slavery. She learned about her family's involvement in it. I asked her if she felt a sense of guilt specifically about her family's treatment of the black workers, and about the treatment of blacks in general at that time, in her milieu:

JP: You run in and out of situations. I think the first encounter I had with that guilt was at Catholic school. I was in 6ᵗʰ grade, and they allowed the first black girl to come to our school. And she was dissed by everybody. Nobody would have anything to do with her. Nobody would play with her on the playground, and I felt so bad for her that I took her under my wing. And I paid the consequences for it if that makes any sense. You know we went to a couple of outings, and they wouldn't allow her in because she was black, and so I sat out with her—out front. And I kinda lost a couple of friends over it, but I felt like this girl didn't deserve to be treated the way people were treating her. They should allow her to come to school. Then the next year, they let 15 more in. So it wasn't that big of a deal. I kinda felt bad for her, and I felt guilt—not guilty—but why are they doing this? Because she wants to come to us and she was a very nice girl . . . that one's the first one that comes to mind as far as introducing a black person to a white person's school: the reaction from other people. All she was trying to do was go to school. She was Catholic, she was allowed, but all those other years black people weren't allowed in our society. . . . She was actually the first one, but I don't know. A lot of different things happened along the way, but as I got older, it got easier because a lot of things had changed. Even as my daddy got older . . . he made friends with black people and stuff. But I was thinking earlier on, we weren't even allowed to talk to them or look at them. But as you got older the barriers started to break down, and it wasn't so bad. But when I was young, it was real bad.

Marie: Why do you think there was this implicit understanding that you could not talk, or befriend, or even really look at black people?

JP: It was just forbidden. You weren't allowed to sit with, talk to, be near— they weren't allowed to use the same white restroom you used. They weren't allowed on buses. They had to walk. . . . I remember our big treat with my grandma when she was alive. My daddy's momma would take us downtown to Woolworth—to the soda fountain—and treat us to a soda. Two of us, because we were from a big Italian family. She would take two of us a week and bring us downtown, and I remember the first time she saw a black person at the counter. She just had a fit, and said: 'don't look that way! Just sit straight and drink your soda, and we're leaving!' She was very upset they let a black person in, and I'm just sitting there thinking—me and my cousin Mary went with her that time—and we both kinda laughed about it, 'cause we didn't see anything wrong with it. This little kid was just drinking a soda, but my grandma was pissed. She really was.

Marie: And did you have a sense, what specifically it was she was uptight about? What was it about African American people that was taboo for her?

JP: Well, you know . . . that time I was . . . around six or seven at the time. That time, when we were growing up, you just didn't associate. The thing was, they were the ones that had the plantation, and I'm thinking: 'why is she being so uppity about there being a black person here drinking a soda, when they have them out working their fields?' . . . . You were just born into it, and you had to live with it. However, it gave me a whole new respect for blues people and . . . the culture back then: segregation, everything we grew up with back then. I'm thinking: 'why would these people be treated differently, when their music is just so great?' . . . There were a lot of questions that we . . . didn't talk about growing up, because you weren't allowed to, and you just . . . I don't know. When I got into high school—I wish I still had that paper—I did one of my term papers on the blues, and it was on display for two or three months. And I was really proud of that paper. . . It just kinda went from there. I just really got into it.

JP's fascination with the blues turned into a lifelong interest and love affair. Her story shows the difficulties for a white person growing up in the Deep South to break ranks with the dominant worldview of her family and her peers. Issues revolving around slavery, black workers, and black rights were clouded in taboos and opaque rules that weren't talked about. Again we can notice a theme of avoidance and lack of transparency in talking about that which was easily observable. Joyce's experience was unique among the people I interviewed because of her direct encounter with black culture from a Southern segregation-era point of view at an early age. The wounds of segregation are still raw today. What is not unique about her story is her fascination with African American culture.

Blues Creation Story

Nobody really knows how the blues was created. It consists of fragments of musical traditions such as: church music, Irish folk music, Appalachian tunes, Hawaiian guitar music, African American musical traditions, including a syncopated, as well as a repetitive, rhythmic pattern, and vocal timbre and delivery. The *composition* of blues may be influenced mainly by Western tonal structure: the format of 12 bars, rhythmic simplicity (versus very complex African drumming patterns[13-1]), as well as the classic tonic, subdominant, dominant, tonic structure (popularly described by musicians as 1-4-5)—all of which are recognizable European elements. However, the vocal delivery, blue notes, treatment of lyrics, repetitive drone-like elements, syncopation, and emphasis on the "here and now" and the personal are likely African-inspired elements. Ethnomusicologist Charles Keil quotes rural singer Mance Lipscomb as saying that "the form, the expression, and the content of the blues" predated WWI.[13-2] Keil finds it is impossible to find proof of a rural African American blues style, or form, before 1915. He is also clear that the music had its roots in the "oral traditions, work songs, ballads, field hollers, ring shouts" of the African American community."[13-3] But there is one thing we know with absolute certainty: the blues is a synthesis of epic proportions. It is music that was served right out of the American melting pot, originated, stirred and blended in the Southern states by African Americans.

The first blues *recording* was of W.C. Handy's song "Memphis Blues," an instrumental number by the all-black "Victor Military Band" in 1914. A few months later, it was recorded with lyrics by white vaudeville singer Morton Harvey. But going back further, we see that all the musical elements of the blues certainly existed previously in the black community. They were referred to as Plantation Songs: songs and rhythmical patterns that accompanied work and play. They were magnetic. It took someone from Europe—a cultural outsider—to bring Plantation Songs into the awareness of white society.

In 1895, toward the end of a three-year engagement in New York City as Director of the National Conservatory of Music, Czech composer Antonín Leopold Dvořák observed that there was no definable and distinct American musical art form. Americans sought to emulate European musical tradition in their conservatories, concert halls, and at recitals, but, he noted, a distinctive, American sound was absent. He found, however, that snippets of musical brilliance from the *African* American culture stood out to him: music that to him represented the "voice of the people" and an expression of "true feelings." Without naming or branding it, he encountered the sonic blueprint that later became blues music—an event of discovery that is normally ascribed to W.C. Handy, a decade later, in 1903 at the Tutwiler train station. In an 1895 article for Harper's New Monthly Magazine about "Music in America," Dvořák wrote:

> *The most potent as well as the most beautiful among [American songs], according to my estimation, are certain of the so-called plantation melodies and slave songs. . . . The point has been urged that many of these touching songs . . . have not been composed by the Negroes themselves, but are the work of white men, while others did not originate on the plantations, but were imported from Africa. It seems to me that this matters but little. One might as well condemn the Hungarian Rhapsody because Liszt could not speak Hungarian. The important thing is that the inspiration for such music should come from the right source, and that the music itself should be a true expression of the people's real feelings. . . . An American reporter once told me that the most valuable talent a journalist could possess was a 'nose for news.' Just so the musician must prick his ear for music. Nothing must be too low or too insignificant for the musician. When he walks he should listen to every whistling boy, every street singer or blind organ-grinder. I myself am often so fascinated by these people that I can scarcely tear myself away, for every now and then I catch a strain or hear the fragments of a recurring melodic theme that sound like the voice of the people . . . . Whether the original songs which must have inspired the composers came from Africa or originated on the plantations matters as little as whether Shakespeare invented his own plots or borrowed them from others. The thing to rejoice over is that such lovely songs exist and are sung at the present day. I, for one, am delighted by them.[134]*

Clearly, the discussion about how blues music was, or is, synthesized, is one that has been ongoing at least since Dvořák's article was written in 1895. But Dvořák, being a respected European composer, had a platform from which he was able to call attention to something that was otherwise easily overlooked in those times—the African American synthesis of various influences had a potency that was intoxicating. Honesty, "realness," beauty, accessibility, immediacy, and much more were qualities of this music. It seemed to come from the soul of humanity. This music, forged by African Americans in the horrifyingly extreme physical and emotional "heat" of Southern plantations, was transformative, also for outsiders that came in contact with it.

Sixty years later, in 1955, music critic and author Henry Pleasants, in his controversial book *The Agony of Modern Music*, asserted that worldwide musical leadership had passed from Europe to America. Not, he argued, because American music was more complex and serious; on the contrary, because it was less technical, more spontaneous, and ultimately relevant to the masses.[13-5] Although Pleasants bemoaned this development, he nonetheless shone a light on what was incontrovertible—America had moved from having no distinguishable musical style of its own to developing styles of music that had taken the world by storm. And these styles of music would not have been created had the blues not been there first. American music had found its voice from the African American music that Dvořák was among the first to name as the "sound of the people."

A Shame-filled Pastime: Minstrelsy

For many reasons, throughout the past few centuries, and often with upsetting, dangerous, and disrespectful consequences, whites have been fascinated with African American culture. Often ignorance, greed, and repressed urges have driven white fascination to abuse, exploit, and ridicule. It has obviously had appalling consequences. Historically, it is a fact that whites love to imitate blacks. Controversial historian Thaddeus Russell writes:

Whites imitating blacks is America's oldest pastime .... White entertainers imitating black songs and dances became a common sight on the streets of major cities .... By the 1840's, ... whites all over America were acting black. 13-6

A white person in blackface was (and is) an offensive practice, especially when it was done to ridicule and offend. There was another component of the practice that was likewise offensive, but less malevolent: many whites desperately wanted access to their emotions, but would or could not allow themselves to do it. Blackface allowed a vicarious access. In the documentary, "Ethnic Notions," UC Berkeley history professor Larry Levine says:

Hundreds of thousands – perhaps millions – over the years of white people in all parts of the country have gone to the theater and watched white men pretend they were blacks. I think in part what they were watching was more complicated than merely whites masking themselves. I think they were watching whites release themselves as blacks. Suddenly these whites who were just like them would dance and sing – show emotions openly and cry and laugh. I think there was something cathartic about that. So I think blacks have played this role in our society: they would be some sort of surrogate. 13-7

African American music and culture was caricatured and ridiculed in minstrelsy, and white entertainers capitalized on it. By the end of the Civil War, an element of malevolence, stemming from Southern whites' bitterness toward newly-freed slaves was further added to the practice.[13-8] In an anthology about the minstrel tradition, David N. Lyon observes that the minstrel show was a world of make-believe that was comforting to its audience because it "defined black culture in a manner which rendered [it] comic and innocuous." Further, it brought relief to white audiences to see actors portray black culture in a way that was carefully managed and orchestrated for specific effect. As such, it had "both conscious and unconscious levels of meaning."[13-9] Minstrel shows served a dual function of making black culture accessible through a vicarious thrill, and at the same time provided a setting that sought to justify the ridicule of blacks. What did whites access vicariously? And why did they feel the need to render an oppressed and impoverished segment of the population "innocuous"? It is one of the areas of our historical past that is very painful to contemplate.

In white culture, there was a need to rationalize why slavery, and later segregation, were natural, necessary, and "right." Historian Winthrop Jordan argues that slavery was justified by using economics to rationalize its necessity, but in reality it was also a practice that was propagated from a need to conquer, exploit, and humiliate that which appeared to be different from oneself. Jordan mentions the frequent comparisons between apes and blacks. Various studies showed similarities in facial structure or "proved" that male apes and black women would have sex if left to their own devices.[13-10] This was seen as evidence that blacks were more closely related to apes than to humans. Such "scientific" findings were then used to justify the inhumane treatment of blacks. Jordan writes:

It may serve as a reminder that the "mind" of any age arises from widely disparate levels of psychic activity and that "ideas" persist according to the measure of their deep-rootedness in psycho-social necessities.[13-11]

Perpetuating the bigoted image of blacks as "less than"—serving to ridicule, and implicitly confirm a sense of shared white superiority—was part of what the white population found comforting about the minstrel parodies. The comfort was obviously preposterous. At the root of the ridicule was a psycho-social need for ritual access to a collective absolution found in the confessional box seats of the minstrel theater. Eric Lott writes that the dividing line between black and white cultures in the 19th century was "property and sexuality."[13-12] In minstrelsy, there was both a suggestion of vicarious sexual experience and justification for further exploitation. Both were found on the altar of lampoon and ridicule. Lyon continues that "at the same time:

Whites wanted to possess the power they attributed to blacks, which was primitive sexuality, and also be free to carry on the sort of social relationship

with blacks which led to miscegenation and economic exploitation. A more
subliminal need was doubtless a need for some mode through which whites
might expiate any guilt they felt over all these associations. The extent to which
blackface constituted a mask permitted the white who hid behind it to
maneuver within the hierarchy of these functions." [13-13]

Whites often justified economic exploitation of black slaves by attributing a more "primitive sexuality" to them, which of course was also a part of white addiction to black culture: the continual loop of guilt, repression, and obsession. The mask provided vicarious access into a universe that was off limits to "good American citizens," [13-14] that which was repressed in the collective shadow of white culture. It was fascination with and for the forbidden fruits, while seeking to justify seeing black slaves as "less than human," that allowed white needs and wants to be projected. Again we can observe that psychic, mental, or sexual material that is consistently repressed and ignored doesn't go away. If it is not carefully and mindfully addressed, and brought into the light in ways that allow expression and thus transmutation into conscious existence where it can be *appropriately* addressed, it reappears in twisted ways using the now shameful residue of its shadow to manifest as its demonized gestalt. Here it manifests as a now uncontrollable force that seeks to belittle, vilify, and terrorize those who in any way awaken reminders of that inner desire, which was repressed, hidden, and denied in the first place. Obviously, denial and repression are themes surrounding this issue that go further back in time than WWII. The fascination with black culture is also closely tied to conflicts surrounding human sexuality. We will look at this next.

A Brief Outline of Sexual Repression and Slavery

Northern European and American whites have a long history of vilifying and ignoring emotions. Part of this process of denial is sexual repression. The view of humans having a sinful/sexual/emotional body, and on the other side, a spiritual/pure/rational mind runs deep in Western culture. As an example, we can explore the moral code of one of the leading writers on health and wellness in the late 1800s. John Harvey Kellogg was an esteemed physician, businessman and co-creator of the Kellogg's Cereal Company, as well as co-founder of the American Medical Missionary College. He promoted sexual abstinence in his personal life (even in his married life). His faith was Seventh Day Adventist, and he took his literal interpretation of his religion and merged it with his medical practice. As a result, he advocated practices such as applying carbolic acid to the clitoris of young women to prevent sexual arousal. He understood masturbation, or any sexual urges, as threatening to human health and civilized society. Kellogg suggested wiring the foreskin of young boys shut to effectively prevent an erection, as well as applying electrical current to the sexual organs at the time of arousal.[13-15] He deemed that these preventive measures would be efficient tools in ridding society of all ills stemming from sexual urges. He was also a proponent of circumcision of boys with no anesthetic, "especially . . . [to] be connected with the idea of punishment." [13-16] Further, he preached that having intercourse in marriage was simply "legalized prostitution."[13-17] Kellogg was just one of many respected medical practitioners of the time who interpreted the sexual drive as something to repress and inhibit *at all cost.*

One of the undercurrents of the Southern white establishment's strong sentiments regarding the abolition of slavery was neither political nor economical. Lee Rainwater states that "moralism permeated the subject of Negro sexual, marital, and family behavior in the polemics of slavery apologists and abolitionists."[13-18] Emancipation meant that white plantation owners lost their easy access to silently sanctioned sexual release through sexual abuse of their slaves. In studying the history of human sexuality in America, John D'Emilio and Estelle B. Freedman found that some Southern moralists espoused white husbands having unrestrained, yet discreet and hidden, sexual relations indiscriminately outside of the confines of white planter class marriage because it "protected the virtue of white women." Such phony, pseudo-moral standards were carefully maintained to provide a "safety valve" of sexual male release, protecting the hypocritical purity of a largely sexually-deprived, white marriage.[13-19] Historian Eric Lott agrees with this assessment and calls this double standard of white male hypocrisy central to what he calls the "libidinal economy" of slavery.[13-20]

As Africans were brought to America, their sexuality was often targeted for punishment and exploitation; as they were enslaved, mothers, fathers, and children were separated and family ties torn asunder. Men as well as women were sexually mistreated, and their fertility and sexuality was abused and commodified. American folklorist and ethnomusicologist, Alan Lomax writes:

> *When they get to be fourteen, fifteen years old, they breed them with whatever man they had in their stalls.... They took any man that weigh from 195 up and they put them in stables like they do stud horses, and jacks and bulls. They didn't have to work. They keep them for breeding and stuff.*[13-21]

Black women were of course the main target for sexual abuse. Their sexuality was extremely fascinating to Victorian era white men. Slave women, in spite of being held in captivity and treated like property, often conducted themselves with an inherent confidence about their bodies. Having been raised in an environment unlike that of puritan society women of European descent, they behaved differently than uptight, white, planter-class wives. Lomax continues that slave women themselves appreciated, and were appreciated by, their communities for their "capacity to bear and rear children" and that a baby born to an unmarried woman was desired proof of her fertility.[13-22] Professor of history at UCLA, Brenda E. Stevenson, agrees in part, but states that this was not universally so. Some black elders frowned upon girls having premarital sex. However, due to a tradition of matrifocality, the black community could often take in and raise children of unwed mothers.[13-23] The women were, in turn, expected to give back to the community in other ways, but there was often no judgment attached to sexual conduct. On the contrary, fertility was a valued component of black society.[13-24] Stevenson finds that black women often had a joyful and proud relationship with their bodies, which was in stark contrast to the prevailing white interpretation of sexuality as forbidden, hypocritical, or the root of all evil. She writes:

> *Slave women usually frowned on blatant female exhibition or promiscuity. This is not to say that they were ashamed of their sexuality. Nor were they shy about the promise of sexual pleasure or human procreation that they as women embodied.* [13-25]

White males observed that the Africans didn't have the same convoluted hang-ups with regard to their bodies and sexuality, and that was secretly and privately an explosive attractor. This observation was part of the rationale for treating black slaves as less than human: in a universe of strict moral codes, repression distorts and mauls human relationships. And African slaves were its innocent victims while whites wielded power to mask their feelings of shame.

It is important to mention that the planter class enjoyed obvious abusive material and sexual privileges that the vast majority of whites did not. Poor southern and northern whites post-Civil War did not (typically) have access to sexual release through rape, abuse, and exploitation. However, various degrees of sexual and emotional repression were also a factor in the lives of other groups of white society. For them, minstrelsy served partially as a cathartic ritual in an artificial and imagined universe, in which the black man and woman became unsuspecting conduits for white repression and guilt. In addition to these sexual overtones, and possibly just as damaging to blacks, minstrelsy also offered access to a more playful aspect of existence. Thaddeus Russell quotes the Northerner Frederick Law Olmsted, who toured the South for a year in the 1850s. For Olmsted, the different work ethic among the slaves stood out to him. Whites, steeped in the protestant work ethic, were encouraged to work from dawn to dusk. Perceived laziness carried "a heavy price of shame"[13-26] and hard work was a virtue. However, according to Russell, due to the lack of incentive inherent in being held as property, some blacks *understandably* felt no shame in under-performing.

It was, rather, a way of one-upping their owners. It had to be done creatively and carefully in order to avoid punishment. Some sought to get out of work with "sham sickness." On the Bowles plantation in Mississippi, Olmsted observed, for instance, that of the "159 sick days missed due to illness in one year, only 5 were Sundays, when there was the least work to do."[13-27] Since slaves were forced to labor, never benefited directly from their efforts, and rebellion or escape was not possible, avoiding work as much as possible was one of very few possible acts of indirect protest. Watching this behavior annoyed and intrigued whites. Again we can watch a double-bind fascination stemming from white intrigue with black culture that nonetheless is yet another example of whites abusing, misunderstanding and misrepresenting blacks.

After the Civil War and until the 1940s, it bears mention that there was also a huge population of white sharecroppers in America's South. They were likewise at the bottom of the economic and social ladder and just as tied down financially. According to an article by Charles C. Bolton from the Mississippi Historical Society, there were many poor whites, who shared the plight of sharecropping. "By 1900, 36 percent of all white farmers in Mississippi were either tenant farmers or sharecroppers. By comparison, 85 percent of all black farmers in 1900 did not own the land they farmed."[13-28] In Alabama, white sharecroppers outnumbered black sharecroppers in the 1860s and in the early 1900s. Due to the Black Migration north, the majority of sharecroppers in Alabama were white.[13-29] Professor of history, Dan T. Carter, quotes George Wallace, who later became the governor of Alabama, talking about an encounter with a white sharecropper in the early 1930's. The sharecropper expressed that America was the "strongest country in the world," and could "whup ever' country in the world. We could whup'em all put together or we could whup 'em one at a time," to which Wallace later reminisced:

The sharecropper's greatest pride—for himself and his country—was the ability to 'whup somebody,' said Wallace. He had 'fought to live, he fought to

eat, he fought to exist. . . . Southerners my age and a little younger, we were
fighters because we went through a period of time when we fought to exist. 13-30

White sharecroppers, although as economically squeezed and dependent as black sharecroppers, did not have to deal with the oppressive Jim Crow laws that effectively kept blacks in a vice of fear, intimidation, and segregation. The perceived strength of the country became an important confidence booster for poor whites—they felt that because of group membership in white America, they were a legitimate part of something great, even if they were struggling mightily to get by. And vilifying, attacking, and hurting those who were even further down the societal ladder, and those who were different, became an outlet for silently sanctioned—yet horrifyingly misdirected—repressed frustration, shame, and fear.

Blackface minstrelsy continued as a genre until the time of the Civil Rights Movement. In minstrelsy, whites gained access to a less restrictive, less morally convoluted way of being through the use of caricatured projections. But there was undoubtedly also, particularly for disenfranchised and economically exploited classes of whites, elements of wanting to "whup'em" in their demonic enjoyment of the send-up. Nonetheless, whether due to needs repression or poverty, all aspects of blackface minstrelsy were clearly hurtful, demeaning, and devastatingly misguided.

The following anecdote from Walter's life illustrates the tendencies of confusing the outward "reality" on display in the 1950s and the reality kept behind closed doors. We see here also, how the search for permission to feel and be real was often projected onto black performers, or, in this case, white performers in blackface.

Walter's Al Jolson Moment

Walter grew up in a household where mom and dad were trying to maintain the illusion of a happy marriage, as the reality of dysfunction continually crept through the cracks. Their divorce became final when Walter was seven years old. He grew up with a tension he did not understand. Each of his parents struggled through a lonely internal battle that they couldn't find words to express. Instead, jealous rages and silent accusations were served up as side dishes to their TV dinners while the family watched Ozzie and Harriet portray the sought-after image of family perfection. Walter loved music, all kinds of music, but it was particularly his dad's record collection of jazz and blues that spoke to him. He was enthralled with performers who could express what he didn't have words for, music that matter-of-factly expressed some of the emotions that were like wordless screams inside of him. The music allowed him to make momentary sense of the conflicting messages all around him. He could find himself in the music. He could sit back and be enveloped by a universe of sound that didn't judge. On very special occasions, Walter and his mother wept together when they listened to a particularly sentimental song, and here he found an emotional bond that momentarily allowed release of that vulnerability which was otherwise kept quiet, turned to blame, or ever-present, angry accusations. Walter was also exposed to whites in blackface. And he loved it. He would listen to "Mammy" with his mother and they cried together. The difficulty in navigating the environment of mixed messages due to repressed emotions vis-à-vis race and public displays of emotions in the late 1950s can be illustrated by the following incident.

Walter's mother and father are hosting a dinner party. The house is squeaky clean and all the finest silverware is on display. Suddenly, an ominous odor fills the dining room as little five-year-old Walter emerges from the kitchen with soot all over his face and his mother's white, now soot-stained, gloves on his hands. He puts his hands out and starts singing "Mammy," wishing to impress the guests with what he considered to be an emotionally-charged tribute to Al Jolson. Walter fully expected to ravish the guests with his emotive efforts, and was hoping to elicit tears, hugs, and closeness. Upon the first few notes escaping his vocal chords, his mother notices him, and gasps in horror. The bond Walter felt with his mother when they had listened and cried together before, was suddenly broken by her utter embarrassment at the messy-looking child and the intense smell from the smoke of Walter burning wine corks on the electric stove. He was severely scolded. His confusion about the mixed messages he received became internalized. He didn't understand it, but he knew he was drawn to music that allowed him to feel. And this music was most often the music of black performers, or in this case, it was a white performer imitating blacks.

1950's Hipsters and Minstrelsy

In 1957, Norman Mailer published the essay *The White Negro*. It reads like a protracted primal scream. He explains that humans in post-WWII reality were thrust into an accelerated historical rhythm, where the rules of sublimation that worked in previous times were now inefficient, leading many to experience an over-stressed nervous system. Mailer paints a picture of the postwar reality played out on a backdrop of the potential for human extinction: the threat of nuclear war and holocaust. This reality was, according to Mailer, akin to the black man's reality of constant danger in which "he subsisted for his Saturday night kicks, of the body and in his music he gave voice to his rage and the infinite variations of joy, lust, languor, growl, cramp, pinch scream and despair of his orgasm."[13-31]

Mailer divides his contemporaries into "hipsters," who are creative existentialist philosophers seeking constant release in an imitation of a misunderstood image of a black man's perceived orgasmic immediacy, and "squares," who allow themselves to be tranquilized via "psychic blood-letting," in order for them to "conform to that contradictory and unbearable society which first created [their] neurosis."[13-32] He sees the American Negro as the ultimate hipster who has faced danger due to a marginalized existence on the fringes of society, and found a way to survive artfully in spite of it. We observe that Mailer here, in the 1950s, displays the fantasy about blacks acutely and that it is still related to white sexual repression and now based mainly on projection. Mailer describes African American music as the language that allows a connection to authentic feeling:

The Negro has stayed alive and begun to grow by following the need of his body where he could. Knowing in the cells of his existence that life was war, nothing but war, the Negro could rarely afford the sophisticated inhibitions of civilization, and so he kept for his survival the art of the primitive, he lived in the enormous present. . . . Jazz . . . it had the communication of art even where it was watered, perverted, corrupted and almost killed it spoke in no matter what laundered popular way of instantaneous existential states to which some whites could respond, it was indeed a communication by art because it said, 'I feel this, and now you do too.' [13-33]

Whereas one of Salinger's main themes from *The Catcher in the Rye* is hypocrisy, Mailer hits many of those same notes by distancing himself from the mixed messages of the then current popular culture: "stamped with the mint of our contradictory popular culture (where sex is sin, and yet sex is paradise)." [13-34] Mailer contends that postwar society is full of "psychopaths" readily minted in a popular culture that sends continual external messages in which the squares seek immediate conformist gratification. As a corrective, he seeks to reclaim the 'wise primitive' and a desire to rebel. [13-35] Ned Polsky adds a commentary to Mailer's essay in which he comments that with the exception of Mezzrow, the White want-to-be Negro cannot really find a meaningful place in society; he or she is perpetually stuck between the white and black worlds without really belonging to either. [13-36]

The essay is discussed here for two reasons: firstly, it speaks passionately to the sense of being lost in a world of contradiction, invalid rules of engagement, and diffuse double standards that were experienced by many as a part of the postwar reality. Secondly, Mailer suggests that the solution for the white man's problem is to be found in black culture and art—a notion that was later embraced by groups seeking other avenues than the ones paved for them by mainstream culture. The cover of Mailer's essay is a photo negative of his face, making it appear as if he is, in effect, in blackface. And, unintentionally, the essay demonstrates clearly that African Americans were still in the cross hairs of white man's shadow projection—this time in a caricatured, over-simplified, misunderstood, as well as glorified and idealized version, but a projection nonetheless. Mailer was part of a small group of "hip" influential thinkers prior to the British Invasion who indirectly paved the way for black culture, and with it the blues, to eventually be partially embraced, admired, and imitated by a wider white audience seeking their own release from repression and hypocrisy.

Blues Romanticists

According to Lund and Denisoff, who studied the "contradictions and contributions" of the folk music revival of the 1960s, a romanticized view of African American music and culture took over in the postwar period in so-called counter-cultural groups. They outline a gradual development in these groups:

> *In place of the protestant Ethic, they adopted the posture of the 'White Negro,'*
> *a concept coined by Norman Mailer. The 'White Negro' idealized stereotypes*
> *of black behavior and advocated imitation of such traits. . . . For the Beat,*
> *the noble savage of the fifties was the black jazz musician, in time to be*
> *replaced by the folk singer.*[13-37]

After the 1950s, "folk" replaced jazz as the music of the counter-cultural white movement. It was gradually popularized toward the early part of the 1960s with TV shows such as "Hootenanny." Outdoor festivals and celebrations of folk music were especially popular among the younger generation. Folk was a life style as well as a musical art form for "collegiates and bohemians alike." [13-38] In 1965, when Dylan plugged in at the Newport Folk Festival and went electric, many considered it the end of the folk era. Shortly thereafter the era of the Hippies began. Readily available supplies of LSD took rock 'n' roll in a new, psychedelic direction. Music was reflected in, and reflective of, rapidly changing experiential developments.[13-39]

Simultaneously, a faction of the folk movement grew interested in black blues music. Lund and Denisoff speculate that it was possibly more "politically correct" to "romanticize rural blacks than rural whites," as it made it possible to stand on the side of the marginalized. By 1964, the blues craze grew in small circles, and artists like Mississippi John Hurt, Son House, and others were brought to "northern folk festivals, colleges, and coffee houses."[13-40] Lund and Denisoff suggest that "rural blacks" represented a new ideal for white middle-class musicians, an ideal that brought with it the notion of a return to a simpler existence and a similar longing that Norman Mailer sought to describe as the "wise primitive." Lund and Denishoff write:

> *The theme of man removed from the state of nature has recurred throughout Judeo-Christian-Greco thought. . . . all social philosophers and metaphysicians have chosen to idealize an existence prior to primordial man when all was well, and life was simple and free of the 'social nausea' ascribed to us by the existentialists. . . . The European Romanticists, in the wake of Rousseau, lauded the 'noble savage.' In North America James Fenimore Cooper exhibited a preoccupation with the hero of the wilderness.[13-41]*

In folk circles, social consciousness mixed with this longing for the primordial, the unspoiled, and that which was still unblemished by a confounding culture. Lund and Denishoff continue that white college students even "imitated black southern dress and speech patterns," appearing rather insincere and ridiculous to some outside observers.[13-42] To this day, there are white musicians and radio DJ's, rappers and those hip* hopping along, who, through imitation, simply try to sound "black," rather than try to find their own voice or sound by merging influences with their own expression. Ultimately, idealization of black culture merged imperceptibly with the "authentic bluesman." In the mid-1960s, the bluesman was now romanticized by many as someone removed from cultural corruption and seen to be brimming with raw and genuine emotion.

From the days of minstrelsy, whites have imitated blacks to deal with emotional suppression, repression, guilt, and their need to justify the

---

* Interestingly, the word "hip" is from the African language of Wolof, where it means "someone with open eyes" or "someone who is with it," or who is "seeing and feeling it like it is."

subjugation and oppression of blacks. In the 20th century, the projection gradually turned from one of lampoon and ridicule to one of veneration. This projection, now on blacks as *Übermenschen*, showed up in white culture as the jazz cat and bluesman, idolized by young intellectuals and bohemians in the folk movement of the 1960s. However, and whenever, these typecasts have shown up in white culture—whether as demeaning caricatures or as idealized stereotypes—it has been important to realize that they were, and are, projections of white culture's various needs at various times.

The stereotype of the white, Silent Generation male emerging out of the postwar shadow was someone who was compliant, rigid, and silent. He was the square who conformed, repressed, and allowed convention to dictate his existence unquestioningly. Female conformists were folding laundry and drinking cocktails on the porch, as the sun set on meaningful connections beyond keeping up appearances. Jazz cats, hipsters, folkies, and blues revivalists, each in different eras, sought meaningful life experiences without repressed conventionality; and often they sought this by looking to African American culture.

In John Leland's "History of Hip," he argues that hip starts in small circles of people who mutually push and inspire each other creatively. As they are seen and interpreted by others as hip and trend-setting, they gradually, often after overcoming controversy, are embraced by a wider audience. Through this process of integration, the novel trend loses its appeal to the originators. It becomes more commonly accepted—and in some cases even popular. Hipness thus paves the way for cultural developments.[13-43] According to Leland, it was African Americans who set the trends in popular culture, particularly after the decline of European cultural leadership following World War II.

> *Black innovators, barred from the economic mainstream, draw on their African roots to invent forms like tap dancing, jazz, the Charleston, and hip-hop; white performers hijack these idioms for their own rewards; black apostates who get too fancy risk watering down the culture to appease white audiences. These are essentialist formulas, treating certain cultural values as essentially black – usually spontaneity, sensuality, raw emotionality – and*

*others, like control and cerebral rigor, as essentially white. This reading defines
blackface minstrels or the hit parade of pale hip-shakers from Elvis to Justin
Timberlake as simply white boys who stole the blues.* [13-44]

Whites have been addicted to the vibrancy they have found in black
culture for a long time. The dangers of ridiculing and diminishing a group of
peoples by racist caricature are well-established. When whites *romanticize* black
culture, however, they likewise perpetuate stereotypes. After weighing the
strong and silent role models and finding them too heavy, some whites in the
post war era hoped to find access to a more uncomplicated, embodied,
natural, and straightforward way of being by emulating and venerating black
culture and heritage.* These assumptions distort just as do those of the racist
agenda. Emulating the appearance and practices of another culture, without
deep understanding and immersion, inevitably gets it wrong. According to
various studies quoted by musicologists McClary and Walser, African music
and dance are "a highly disciplined set of practices" in which:

> *The body figures not as the desired-yet-dreaded other of the cultivated mind but
> rather as the indispensable medium that links the physical world with the
> spiritual that facilitates the internalization and reenactment of communal
> beliefs. This very different way of organizing the world serves as the basis of a
> complex cultural fabric that is no less intricate, no less intellectually mediated
> than the Hellenic/Christian heritage that gave rise to European cultural
> forms.* [13-45]

African and African American cultures did not emerge from a cultural
vacuum. They were no more intellectually, emotionally, or spiritually
endowed, and neither were they less. The African culture that arrived on
North American shores through slavery had certain practices embedded that

---

* See *Dreams of My Father* by Barack Obama (Obama, 1995, 2004, pp. 123-124). Here
President Obama recounts being horrified at his white mother's simplistic, and overly
idealized notions of what it means to be black while watching the movie "Black Orpheus."

encouraged and supported understanding of physicality, emotions, connections to others, to ancestors, and to spirit. But that does not make black culture superior or inferior. It was, and is, our desire to *judge* others through lenses of projection as good or bad—as pure or contaminated—that distorts the picture. Each culture has within it elements from which others can learn. And elements that are better left behind.

In Norman Mailer's interpretation, black culture was one where living contentedly and being instinctually in tune with the moment was the end-all, since tomorrow could mean unrest, persecution, and destruction. Such living for the "now" was a desired ideal for postwar hipsters, who were feeling that their culture was moving too rapidly, and too superficially. With regard to music in the 1950's and 60's, it was common among seekers within white culture to observe African American performers' rhythmic, perspicacious, and self-assured grasp of musical inventiveness as something largely unavailable, but much desired and emulated by whites, whose musical creativity was hard-pressed to ride the coattails of the onslaught of new musical possibilities constantly emerging out of African American culture.

Blues Revival

Debunking the prevailing delta origin myth of the blues need not devalue the great achievements of all the Afro-American performers one iota – in fact complicating the birth of the blues may increase our respect for their artistry – but it does frame the emergence of so many white blues performers in the 1960's, 1970's, and 1980's differently. If blues music began as a displacement or projection of white moods, hurts, needs onto black oral traditions, then it may be a healthy trend for whites to experience the blues as their own rather than mediated by black others.[13-46]

Charles Keil

Beyond white projections of mythological proportions and a search for a primitivism that was a phantom of the imagination, blues music offered admission into a universe of feeling, moving, and sensing that was, and is, universally accessible. Eric Clapton commented on his discovery of the blues in the early 1960s:

Now I didn't feel I had any identity, and the first time I heard blues music, it was like a crying of the soul to me. I immediately identified with it. It was the first time I'd heard anything akin to how I was feeling, which was an inner poverty. It stirred me quite blindly. I wasn't sure just why I wanted to play it, but I felt completely in tune.[13-47]

Since the 1960s, whites have connected powerfully with the blues, and as mentioned previously, constitute well over 90% of its audience today. They have expanded the art form through their own immersion, study, and new creation. Finding authentic expression as a blues musician of any color often includes years of first studying the blues masters. Here, the feel, technique, and ability to ride on the waves of felt inspiration are internalized. It is then, after this apprenticeship wanes, that the musician finds his or her own authentic expression by merging tradition, experience, technique and sound with inspiration, innovation, personality, etc. This is then broadcast, in a moment of creation, through a give-and-take, cathartic, and almost ritualistic* relationship with the audience. White blues musicians, like all blues musicians, reflect the context-specific circumstances of who they are, where they grew up, and how they were raised. After learning the craft, each becomes able to express universally shared emotions they recognize and with which they resonate.

Many writers of blues literature—e.g., Charles Keil, Leroi Jones, Paul Garon, magazines like "Living Blues," certain contributors to a recent anthology about blues as accessible philosophy edited by Steinberg and Fairweather, etc.—have sought to identify the relevance of blues as a function of *who* plays it. They have also explored its relevance through historical, social, and cultural lenses. For them, the relevance of blues is measured from a vantage point that blues is the music of the disenfranchised and oppressed, of those suffering economic hardship, and specifically of African Americans. This viewpoint did not commonly resonate with blues

---

* We will look at blues as modern ritual in Part III.

boomers. The blues fans who were interviewed for this study did not mention race unless directly asked about it. Some did state that poverty was a prerequisite for "living the blues," but the majority of fans did not apply social, cultural, or economic parameters of the performers as significant in relation to what they personally got out of listening to blues music. It was quite common to want to honor and pay tribute to the originators of the blues, but at the same time to feel that the blues was very much "their" music as well. They stated that blues is music that speaks to common humanity—not a particular segment within humanity. This is Universally Authentic Blues (UAB). Blues boomers stated that blues often creates a bond with blues musicians and other blues lovers, no matter who they were. This sense of universality—the ability of the music to connect across cultural, social, political, and historical divides—was extremely relevant to fans.

However, this does not mean that modern blues fans are unaware of how blues was birthed out of cultural oppression and socioeconomic hardships. These aspects were of great significance. For instance, 82 percent of fans surveyed stated that the awareness of blues being birthed in situations where the originators suffered many hardships added to their appreciation of blues music and the artists themselves—how they made sonic magic out of horrors. At the same time, 94 percent of survey participants agreed that skin color was irrelevant, and that blues is open to anyone. In the interviews, questions about the suffering of African Americans in the shadow of slavery often had fans referring to how they recognized, resonated, *and* empathized with emotions of feeling powerless. They did not express that their own suffering could be compared in severity to that of the original bluesmen and women, but simply that it made them feel a bond. This awareness creates a depth of experience for modern blues fans when they listen to the old masters across time.

The data also clearly demonstrated that they found blues music accessible and relevant for any musician who can play with integrity and honest expression. The discussion about who can "rightfully" play the blues based on their ethnic, social, or cultural backgrounds was irrelevant to the vast majority of fans. Context-specific Authentic Blues (CAB) however, is valued immensely. They listen to old blues masters, and study their stories; they relate their historical knowledge about the circumstances that the music was created in and it adds to their appreciation of the music.

Body-Movement-Embodiment

Blues educator, journalist, and author, Art Tipaldi, observed that the way music makes us feel like moving physically varies by different audiences and times:

Art: In many blues clubs I go to, even the Blues Cruise—the minute bands start playing, people are up dancing. There's something to the beat of the music that attracts this demographic that you're writing about. It's what we danced to in the 60s and I think the beat in the music goes with the shaking of the hips in the same way that, whatever hip hop and rap beat is out there is the perfect beat for the way kids dance today. We went to a wedding in San Diego about a month ago . . . and all the 30-35 year olds were up dancing, and they were dancing a whole different dance than what I remember dancing.

Marie: Sure. And it definitely wasn't polka.

Art: It wasn't polka....

Marie: Laughter

Art: But we were—their body movements were in tune with the beat that was being played by the DJ. Somebody said once long ago that when you change the beat you change the dance. Maybe that's what Charlie Patton discovered in those juke joints in Mississippi, when he started flailing away at his guitar that, as he kept that base string finger pop (beat noises), maybe he found that was what kept women's hips moving. Then you get again Sam Phillips and Elvis. Maybe when hip hop took off, it took off because somebody found a

*beat that went with a new style of dancing. I think for our generation the blues
is danceable music. We just were on that Blues Cruise and probably most
every show, Bonnie and I were dancing to a number of songs, because your feet
are just moving to it, whether it's a shuffle or whether it's a rock and roll kind
of beat. So I think it still has that danceable appeal, and still has that dance
party feel to it.*

Blues fans mentioned that when they listened to good blues, they found
it impossible to sit still. Even if it was to tap a toe or nod in time with the
music, it is often felt in other places than just our auditory canal! Fans
expressed that blues makes them want to *move*! Blues and blues-inspired
music, as it was brought into white culture, opened up the floodgates for
spontaneous movement to music. The blues, and its offspring rock 'n' roll,
brought an outlet for a more spontaneous musical appreciation and
expression. Professor of African American literature and culture, Aaron N.
Oforlea, describes how whites took inspiration from the black community,
who danced spontaneously and unrestrained, in close and sensual ways, and
almost seemed to let the music transport them.[13-48] Once African American
music became integrated in their lives, white audiences were no longer just
inactive and restrained in their response. Rather, they often screamed,
danced, fainted, and let it all hang loose. They allowed themselves to *feel* and
partake in the music rather than just listen to it. African American musical art
forms thus contributed to a dissolution of the body/mind barrier of
emotional restraint. Cognitive psychologist, neuroscientist, and musician
Daniel Levitin writes that it would shock us if the audience at a classical
concert suddenly jumped up and started acting like they would at a James
Brown concert and "whooped, hollered, and danced." He finds that such
embodied and physically active reaction is closer to our evolutionary roots.
He contrasts it to the expectations of the audience in the symphonic musical
tradition, where a more reserved and entirely cerebral and internal response
is expected.[13-49] Levitin further speculates that music in the European musical
tradition for the past five hundred years became increasingly specialized; it
was to be performed by musical virtuosos for appreciative and often
sophisticated audiences. The link to direct embodied involvement lessened,

as this division between performer and participant continued, and thus music appreciation became increasingly sedentary and cerebral.[13-50] In short, the more specialized and premeditated the music and the more controlled the setting, the less we feel the urge to move. The more the music is spontaneous, based on repetitive (predictable) structures and is able to facilitate contact between performer and participant (and in a style that speaks to the participant), the more we feel like moving when we hear it. The ethnomusicologist and anthropologist John Blacking writes:

> *I do not say that we can experience exactly the same thoughts associated with bodily experience; but to feel with the body is probably as close as anyone can ever get to resonating with another person. I shall not attempt to discuss the issue of musical communication as a physiological phenomenon; but if music begins, as I have suggested, as a stirring of the body, we can recall the state in which it was conceived by getting into the body movement of the music and so feeling it very nearly as the composer felt it.[13-51]*

Blacking finds that it is indeed through the embodied connection with music that a particular human *connection and communication* takes place in non-verbal and powerful ways. In the Western musical tradition before blues, jazz, and rock 'n roll appeared on the scene, these kinds of nonverbal communication skills increasingly fell by the wayside. With the merger of the African American and European American cultures that was at the base of both the creation of, as well as the (white) revival of, the blues genre, we see a reintroduction of embodied awareness. "The playful eroticism of Africa," speculates Lomax, was part of the drive that spurred the creativity that flourished, where blacks used their call and response work songs.[13-52] Aaron N. Oforlea finds that Lomax projected his "repressed sexual fantasies" onto the black people he was studying.[13-53] However, Lomax points to elements that indeed were foundational to the appeal of the blues, and that later, when whites merged it into rock 'n roll, appealed so strongly and viscerally to young white American and European audiences. Lomax again:

These blues couplets belong to the powerful undercurrent of African-American eroticism that has come to influence Western culture. Carried on the tide of black popular music, it broke past Western prudishness and has drastically liberated sexual attitudes in the United States.[13-54]

Lomax focuses here again on the sexual element. And interpreting an embodied appreciation and awareness as purely "sexual" is certainly partially a projection. Whether black music liberated sexual attitudes, or simply allowed expression of more liberated attitudes, is an impossible question to answer.

As we round out our historical excursion, we can conclude that blues has merged, morphed, and inspired many genres. But through it all, it has also remained a steady force field available to people of any race in any culture as a way to integrate their experiences of the past into a musical, bluesy "now." This is not just about imitation or appropriation. It is about using a social, musical form that allows those who understand its potential to connect sincerely with others while digging deep: to recognize, resonate, reclaim and reconnect to parts of themselves that they might have forgotten along the way.

In Parts III and IV, we return to the present, and once again connect with the collective voice of blues fans, and how they talked about blues music as life-changing, restorative, and important in their lives.

Part III

The Transformative Power
of Blues

Chapter 14:

Our Blues Story

We will now deepen our look at some of the more life-changing elements of blues music. As mentioned before, we experience emotional involvement with blues music in different ways. These experiences can be broadly categorized into three "levels." We can use these three blues levels to describe and conceptualize that which is otherwise difficult to put into words about our experience of the music, to gain an overview, and to recap some of the elements from Part I:

- *Blues Level 1 (BL1)*: Music as entertainment (play/fun). We described this level in Chapter 3. Blues here produces an aesthetic or pleasing effect by being enjoyable, playful, or captivating. It is used as a distraction, celebration, release – to let one's hair down. It is music to gather around with likeminded others.

- *Blues Level 2 (BL2)*: Universally Authentic Blues (UAB). Music allows recognition and resonance with universal emotions. It is not dependent on time or place. We explored this level in Chapter 8. We can listen to blues from another era, by people from different social/ethnic/cultural backgrounds, and still resonate with the (feelings in the) music. It is not dependent on context. Music is expressed by musicians in the form of a "groove," melody, instrumentation, (and likely also) lyrics. Fans experience a sense of emotional connectedness, catharsis, and emotional recognition through universal emotions evoked through the music.

- *Blues Level 3 (BL3)*: Context-specific Authentic Blues (CAB): The experience is dependent on cultural/social externals, which are time- and context-specific (we will explore this level in Chapter 17). Elements of the style of music, instrumentation, musicianship, and contents of lyrics are broadcast, received, and understood in the context of a specific time, as well as the cultural and social environments that produced them. Understanding its "authenticity" depends on understanding the historical, social, and cultural context in which the music appeared as informative with regard to when, and by whom, the music is performed.

BL1 and BL2 can be utilized or actively sought out depending on need, desire, level of "initiation,"* and the listener's ability (or willingness) to engage emotionally with the music. The level of enjoyment of the particular style of music, level of personal engagement with the music, and the feeling of safety and belonging determine the experience. BL3 acts as a reciprocal historical/cultural/social container in which BL1 and 2 take place and are referenced. Someone from a different cultural experience, or era, than a particular manifestation of blues music, may not understand all elements of the musical experience, as the context-specific elements might not translate fully. The level of historical/social knowledge and/or experience of the era, the artist, and the culture in which it appeared will then determine the fullness, or the depth of the experience.

The blues acts as a simultaneous and integrative vessel for these three levels of experience. The three levels facilitate and contribute to connection and connectedness, as indicated below (Figure 5). All four manifestations of connection (to self, others, higher power/altered state, and ancestors) are possible in BL1, 2, or 3, in two levels at a time, or even simultaneously in all three. The experience, however, will always be based in the context-specific layer, since all audience members, listeners, and musicians are a product of the time and space that shaped their interpretation and understanding of the music. This model of the three Blues Levels affords us a vantage point from which we can begin to describe and conceptualize the various elements of

---

* See Chapter 16 about "Discovery" and "Initiation.".

the blues experience. Blues is not just for a certain group of people. But it can express group experiences that are deeper and clearer within the confines of a specific group (BL3). At the same time, blues from a dissimilar time and cultural group can speak universally to all who are open to it (BL2). And the element of blues music as entertainment and play is built into many blues experiences by default (BL1). These levels, in other words, merge imperceptibly, as they exist interchangeably and fluidly.

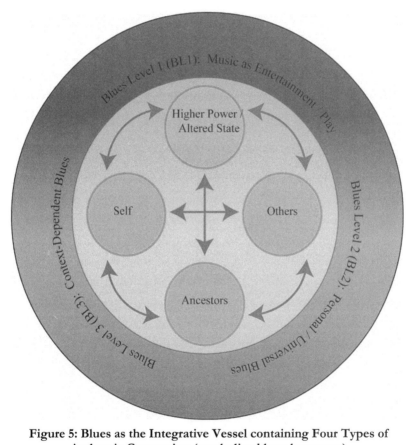

Figure 5: Blues as the Integrative Vessel containing Four Types of Authentic Connection (symbolized here by arrows)

A study about jazz and race in the 1930s and '40s found a similar confluence of leisure aspects as well as personal/universal/collective and social/historical/cultural roles of the music. Andrew Berish writes:

The music provided the soundtrack to daily life, and it accompanied work and leisure, filling home and work spaces alike.*Inevitably . . . listeners found very different personal meanings in these sounds.† The music, though, also registered social feelings and experiences that went beyond the idiosyncratic and personal.‡14-1

Although Berish wrote the above about jazz, all music probably contains these three layers to some degree. But it is likely that blues-inspired music does so to a relatively high degree because it is so dependent on emotional involvement both of the performer and the listener.

In any case, we can observe that with regard to modern blues fans, blues in the 21st century integrates these three levels of experience seamlessly and simultaneously. Together, the three blues levels act as an integrative vessel that holds time, space, personally and collectively felt emotional experiences, and provides ample possibilities for entertainment and fun. With the blues, connection to self, others, spirit, and ancestors can take place in interchangeable ways, depending on the fan's need, level of involvement, and understanding at the time. A blues fan might enjoy the music primarily as fun and entertainment one day (BL1), and the next day feel a deep connection to a specific time in history when the music was created (BL3). The following day, the fan might relate his or her own story to one that is told in the music (BL2). This, at least partially, explains why blues music is never played or received the same way twice. It is always dependent on our inner and outer circumstances. As shown in Figure 5, BL1, 2, and 3 are seamless, interdependent, fluid, and interrelated. The three levels interact continually; in combination, they serve as a container that enables authentic connection to unfold in various ways.

---

* Blues Level 1: Blues as entertainment.

† Blues Level 3: Blues with a specific societal, cultural, historical significance interpreted through the lens of context.

‡ Blues Level 2: Blues as a Universal Experience.

One of the things I have often wondered about is how listening to "sad" music somehow made me feel better. The blues fans I spoke with had similar thoughts, and the vast majority stated that listening to blues music usually acted as a mood enhancer, even if the topic or the feel of the music was sad or about loss, heartache, etc. We will cover this element next.

Chapter 15:

Catharsis and Ritual in Blues

To summarize, blues boomers get the benefit of a decreased stress response by simply labeling a negative emotion, and neither hiding nor running from it. The music can also actively move them beyond this experience of identification/ recognition/ resonance/ accessibility, and, often subtly, into an experience of release and discharge of energy that makes them feel renewed and refreshed afterwards. Fans stated that they are often unaware of why blues made them feel better—or even that it did. This was typically a subtle shift, but a shift nonetheless. Catharsis—moving through emotion to feel a subtle or more pronounced release, purge, or sense of cleansing—is another universal aspect of blues. Catharsis, emotional recognition, and resonance exist outside of a specific time or societal context. They all happen in BL2, the realm of universality. Blues music from the 1920s might provide a sense of catharsis or release to a modern audience when fans recognize and/or resonate with certain commonly felt emotions. Emotions are largely recognizable and easily shared across temporal, cultural, and social barriers.

The power to affect catharsis is part of the healing potential of blues. Jon Michael Spencer quotes Leonard Goines, who claimed that "the music functioned for blacks in the same way professional therapy functioned for whites."[15-1] In a similar vein, in his account tracing the roots of hip-hop to blues, Ralph Basui Watkins quotes Larry Neal as stating that "even though the blues may be about so-called hard times, people generally feel better after hearing them or seeing them. They *tend to be ritually liberating* in that sense" [emphasis added]. [15-2] Psychologist Mark Winborn traces the connection of music and healing in ritual back potentially hundreds of thousands of years to drumming, dancing, and chanting cited in quotes by Plato as well as Roman philosopher Boethius discussing music as the healer of the soul and restorer of balance.[15-3]

Blues is uniquely suited to induce catharsis because of the following musical features:

- Vocal patterns of the blues, as well as the instrumentation, can have a "wailing" quality to it; this style is well-suited to express emotions (and particularly distress) sonically and nonverbally.

- "Blue notes" add to this experience by further increasing the tension and eventual release by offsetting the normally harmonious to be slightly "out of balance," only to resolve back into harmony.

- Simple and/or powerful rhythmic patterns of the blues produce a musical repetitive structure that is capable of inducing a light trance in musicians as well as in listeners.[*]

- Lyrics are often personal in nature and/or speak directly to the emotions by "telling it like it is," and thus enable an emotional recognition through a sense of rapport, kinship, and honest connection.

- The musician sings and plays from a well of inspiration typically covering emotionally charged subjects from personal or vicarious experience. These can be "negatively" charged (fear, loneliness, abandonment, grief, etc.) or "positively" charged (delight, joy, excitement, desire, etc.). With regard to blues making us feel better, even if the topic is associated with negatively charged emotions, it is often because the emotions expressed help us access unresolved or repressed psychic material, and move through it connected to others.

To unpack ritual elements in the modern blues milieu, it is of interest to invoke some of author and professor of sociology, T.J. Scheff's theories, since he specifically studied the role of catharsis in rituals, healing and drama.

---

* This element of blues trance will be discussed in Part IV.

The ritual potential in blues holds various components that all carry with them a potential of cathartic release. Scheff's central point in defining what creates a successful ritual is this: "The social form must reawaken *collectively held distress which is unresolved in everyday life.* The reawakening must occur in a context which is s*ufficiently safe so that the distress is not experienced as overwhelming*" [emphasis added].[15-4]

In the context of modern blues fans, "unresolved distress" was often expressed when interviewees talked about their disappointment with the world; here they gave voice to underlying repression, disillusionment, or disappointment.

"Properly Distanced" Ritual in Blues

Using Scheff's terminology, a "sufficiently safe" social form here is the blues concert, or blues music by and of itself, where ritual catharsis can and does happen. Winborn echoes this sentiment: blues "allows us to identify as fully as possible with feelings in the singer that we might otherwise exclude from our awareness because of the pain involved."[15-5]

In blues music, the concept of "distancing," as it was described by Scheff, has both a literal and figurative meaning. Fans can choose their "distancing" literally by where they choose to sit or stand compared to the location of the stage, and figuratively by how involved and immersed they allow themselves to become in the musical experience. When the data was compiled, it was clear that dancing close to the stage was no indication by itself of a deeper experience. Fans might listen intently sitting in a chair further back in the crowd.   Close and active physical involvement was not necessarily an indicator of a higher degree of a cathartic experience than a more quiet and introspective approach.

For example:

Blues fan: [At concerts or festivals] I tap my hand, tap my toe. If there was a good guitar solo, I might give it a little bit of a hoot. But I'm generally a fairly passive quiet person. I'm not overwrought with emotion . . . so I tap.

Marie: Ok, so now the fact that you're not hootin' and hollerin,' does that mean that you don't experience the music?

Blues fan: Oh I do. I really do. I just don't have to show it. That's all.

Marie: Ah ha.

Blues fan: You know that's just, I'm taking it all in, but yeah I don't have to show it to experience it. I certainly feel it, but I don't have to be hootin' and hollerin' to show people I feel it.

Enjoyment did not need to be physically or vocally expressed, or close to the stage, to be *there*. Other fans felt that when the music "took" the audience, they had to move physically and freely with the experience, and that being at a blues concert could thusly be a freeing antidote to a normally sedentary lifestyle:

Marie: Right. You work in IT [Information Technology] work as well . . . we sit a lot. We do a lot in our heads.

Blues fan: Exactly. And then this is the time where you get up and you're not in your head anymore. It's all in your emotions and your heart and your body. You get to be free. You don't have to worry about whether or not you look goofy. 'Cause there's a bunch of other goofy people standing up dancing too. Every once in a while there's a bunch of good people who actually know what they're doing dancing, but we just admire them. (Laughs)

Since there was no observable correlation between how deeply fans related to the experience depending on how close they were to the stage, it seems clear that the safety of distancing in the blues ritual is mostly figurative. The festival or concert setting is typically a place of recreation (play) and fun, not a place where one goes to consciously delve into hidden emotional material, or where one concerns oneself with remedial thoughts of any kind. It is a place blues fans generally perceived as safe. Most fans mentioned their sense of connection and feeling of safety in the blues "container" as crucial to their experience of being able to let go. The blues concert or festival can therefore "fly under the radar" as a quasi-therapeutic instrument that is "properly distanced," although it carries the potential for cathartic release in the form of laughter, tears, spontaneous shouts, physical movements to release energy, etc. The emotional recognition or resonance that brings it on might be slight or indirect; it may not be directly relatable to one's own latent emotions, yet might still manage to create a physical reaction or indirect abreaction that might not happen in many other places.

Here follow a *few* of many moving and life-affirming examples of catharsis in blues today. This blues fan had just lost his brother and walked into a blues concert toward the end of the show. After the show, he spoke to the musician and said:

'Dude you just killed me. My fucking brother just died. I just put him in the ground and I walk in here and you're singing this, it's like you knew!' And he looked at me and said 'Man I'm sorry.' I said 'no. It's just like when I arrived, and this is your last number, and it's just like holy shit, it goes beyond our expectations or our predetermined things that we're gonna like or dislike and things like that; sometimes it's bigger than all of that. . . . Yes, it was an emotional . . . I mean it's all pretty strange . . . I don't wear all that on the outside personally; as gregarious and open that I am, I'm very shielded because I have to be. That's me. I share everything with everybody, but stuff that matters I don't share with a lot of people. And this was kind of like "oh my God" and . . . it allowed me to also recognize the fact of what I just went through. That's total serendipity in its purest sense.

Interviewees often talked about cathartic experiences as precious and meaningful to them. Often, catharsis happens due to a combination of unpredictable factors, and what might "work" to produce a certain release at a given time might not work again, even under similar circumstances. Catharsis in blues is dependent on many factors, and on which blues level it is experienced. Release is enabled and prompted by the music and the human connection, where it can flood to the surface and discharge spontaneously. These emotional discharges were often described as being so subtle that fans only recognized that they happened because they suddenly somehow felt a bit better. Fans described these experiences in the interviews as chills, laughing out loud, feeling tearful, a shiver, a need to physically move about, tap a foot, dance, jump up and down, wave their arms, sway with the music, etc. Ninety-four percent of fans agreed blues music helped them release emotions, and 92 percent stated they felt the healing effects of blues: what is commonly meant by "hurt so good." This term, hurt so good, could well be interpreted to mean that one can let go of unresolved distress (that is often felt as paradoxical and maybe difficult to describe) in a properly distanced ritual, while feeling connected to others. Here are a few examples of responses from fans when they were asked how blues music has helped them release emotions:

> *Lost my brother—he was 27. When I listen to blues, especially Clapton's 'Run,' it describes exactly how I feel at times. It makes me cry, but it feels good. I guess it's comforting to know we all go through this sort of crap in life. That whole album I can relate to, another song is about how it affected his relationship with his wife. Again, I've been through the exact same thing!*

Another commented:

> *Sad emotions can be made happier as burdens are lifted by expression. Sometimes I need someone to cry with.*

Yet another:

The Blues can lift my spirit, by connecting with a powerful groove that lets me release my problems to God. Through that emotional release, I laugh and feel great.

Many also felt that a sense of compassion with the people who originated the genre could lead them deeper into a cathartic experience:

I think it's emotional for me, the emotional aspect of the blues and the connection to some of the old blues; looking back at what they experienced, the African American experience. The new blues carries on that particular experience and bring it into the modern age. Yeah, emotional, absolutely, I remember watching Shemekia Copeland last year at a concert—oh it just went right to the heart. This one particular tune, she had me all in goose bumps everywhere, oh my. She said I'm gonna put down the microphone now and then sing. Oh my, my, my. . . .

A clear majority of fans described experiences in blues music in which they got chills, goose bumps, or many other sensations when they had a peak moment of experience with the music. Many found it particularly meaningful when it was shared with fellow audience members. They often found it difficult to describe, but some were able to put it into words:

When the audience is all reacting the same way—kind of in awe of what's happening in front of them, with them, and to them, . . . there's just an energy that you feel in either the room—or out in the field, depending upon where you're seeing the music, that you just all kind of know, and it's very hard to describe, it's just an energy that exists. . . . I would say that doesn't happen too often, but, yeah, there are times when I hear something and it just, you know, chills down my spine—like wow that was really incredible! Or you find yourself grinning with a wide grin, not even realizing you're doing it.

Or:

In a live situation when you're playing in front of an audience and you get everybody to feel the same thing at the same time—it gives me chills when a performer can take everybody there. That's awesome. That's what I pay money to see.

Or:

When something clicks I get physically excited. I get goosebumps, or I smile so hard that it almost hurts. I love seeing a band live and you know they're clicking. Something's different that night. They're not just 'oh, let's get this set over with,' they start clicking and they start to feed off each other. That just excites the crud out of me. I go nuts.

Mark Winborn quotes Robert Moore's Essay on *Ritual Sacred Space and Healing* as stating that "ritual has the capacity to transform profane space into sacred space." We can observe here that the bluesman or woman of today can indeed still move a crowd into a state of the experiential, straddling ritual realms of the sacred and profane simultaneously. In his book about urban blues during the blues revival in the 1960s, Charles Keil wrote:

The word 'ritual' seems more appropriate than 'performance' when the audience is committed rather than appreciative. And from this, it follows, perhaps, that blues singing is more of a belief role than a creative role – more priestly than artistic. The preceding discussion of bluesmen and preachers supports this shift in perspective, as does the Saturday-night and Sunday-morning pattern of the Negro weekend. Bluesmen and preachers both provide models and orientations; both give public expression to deeply felt private emotions; both promote catharsis – the bluesman through dance, the preacher through trance; both increase feelings of solidarity, boost morale, strengthen the ideology. [15-6]

This dual experiential role of the blues performer as part trance-inducing preacher and part catharsis-facilitating bluesman in a ritual-like setting also appeared frequently in the study. Here follow a few examples:

A definition of the blues is—I think it's a methodology of people to express their hardships and feel better about it; whether it's through music, dancing, or songs. If you have the blues and you're kinda down, if you're playing the blues you—you're playing music that directly channels to your soul that you turn into a conduit, and through the expression of your soul you can become happy. It takes your focus away from your problems and allows you—it allows you understanding and it allows you clarity. It allows you a good feeling. It opens up doors for inspiration.

Or:

Well it's kind of freeing in a way, right? If you sit around in your little isolated corner and you're feeling these things and you think nobody else understands it—nobody else gets me [and] these horrible things that are happening. But if you get out—and sometimes it's hard to talk about right—if you go to therapy and you could talk about your feelings, it's like you still feel like this is a horrible thing that is happening to me. But if you take that out and realize this happens to other people, this is not just you—you're not just sitting in this little box by yourself—these are universal emotions and other people have felt this way too, its freeing! Because you don't feel so isolated! . . . It's like my son used to say: 'when I listen to angry music I can really get into that music, and then I don't feel angry anymore!' It helps you let go of that emotion, right? So you're not hanging onto it. You can feel it; you can connect with them; you can express it—and then you can let it go.

Or:

It depends on what I'm listening to; it can actually make me feel like I've been cleansed. I don't know. It's a release. It just—it's so hard to explain. It just brings an inner peace. It just brings me to a peaceful place. I guess because I can relate so much to some of the songs; it just makes me feel better hearing it. It brings me to a level where I feel better about myself. There are some songs that just literally make me cry, and I'll sit and cry and cry. Then I feel better. So I guess that's the purpose of the blues.

Here is an interchange from one of the interviews with a blues fan:

Blues fan: If I didn't have the blues . . . gosh, I don't know. I'd probably still be a pot-smoking hippie.

Marie: (laughs)

Blues fan: I wouldn't be able to convey my feelings as well, I know. I probably should be truthful—would not be alive. I know that the blues has gotten me through some pretty tough times. When I'm feeling bad I can put on some good guitar music and it can really take me away.

Marie: So it's a—it's a pretty big deal.

Blues fan: It is. It's like one giant Prozac.

Chapter 16:

Blues as Ritual of Initiation and Connection to Ancestors

Do you remember how you discovered the blues? Most fans do. To many blues boomers, discovering the blues was life-altering in scope and effect. Most fans had some sort of initiatory experience with the blues that clearly delineated a reality of "before the blues" and "after the blues." Blues music might have existed on their awareness radar screen prior to such experience, but without the emotional connectedness to it that they had after the blues bowled them over. The importance of the "initiation experience" from individual blues fans discovering the blues was a very clear and consistent finding. Several participants used phrases such as: "I was hooked," signifying that interacting with the blues was habit-forming for them. Fans often described that when the moment of discovery happened, it was immediate, significant, and quite powerful, but as the below statement shows, a more "roundabout" way of becoming a blues fan was not uncommon either:

> *I have no idea how I gravitated to Blues. All the music I loved early on was Blues based, early Eric Clapton, Allmans, and a friend took me to see Muddy Waters in Raleigh, NC, and I was struck..., but I faded to Jazz, tired of it, and drifted back to Blues without knowing how, or when, it happened. It seemed to happen through Blues Rock.*

Prior to the moment of discovery, blues fans were often aware of the blues, but it didn't "speak" to them and therefore it did not have the significance that it received post-initiation. A few fans were gradually "converted," but most had an almost revelatory discovery, or initiation experience. Chris Barber referred to this moment as his entry into "priesthood." Although for most modern blues fans, it did not have such almost religious overtones. Several blues fans and industry professionals stated they didn't find the blues; the blues found them. Many fans recalled that the discovery was transformative on various levels. This moment therefore affected blues boomers in their private lives, and became a part of their leisure pursuits, or even semi- or fully-professional ones. All blues fans interviewed for this study had a moment in time when they knew that something about this music was different; it spoke to them. Here are a few of their descriptions of their first moments over the blues threshold:

- *"It had me mesmerized! . . . It was like—this is nothing I ever heard before, and it just did something to me. It was like a lifting and I wanted to hear more of it."*

- *"It just hit me . . . I have to have more of this."*

- *"These people have no pretenses."*

- *"It made me feel great; like this was my music."*

- *"It just grabbed my heart."*

- *"It was that rawness."*

- *"But it really started changing my life big time after my divorce. That's when it—that's when I hit it probably heavier and started really getting into it as far as not only listening more, but becoming more part of who I was."*

- *"You know when you're a teenager and you hear that kind of call out to souls or from your soul; it's extremely contagious."*

- *"Wow—there's other music out there—other than what's on the radio."*

- *"I was hooked, ever since then I was hooked."*

- *"It just hit me."*

- *"I just went "wow." It was just so raw and there was just so much expression to it."*

- *"I've had depression problems all my life and music gets me out of that. I don't have to go on Zoloft and all this crap."*

- *"I was just hooked from then on out. I'd go into music stores and ask: 'What do you have that's blues?'"*

Mode of Discovery, Conversion, and Blues Evangelism

About three out of every four blues fans in this study did not grow up aware of blues music, but discovered it later. Roughly half of the interviewees stated that the British invasion—or British bands in general—led them to a discovery of the blues. Artists mentioned most frequently were John Mayall, the Beatles, the Rolling Stones, Eric Clapton, and Led Zeppelin. The rest were evenly split into three groups. One group referred to seeing the "Blues Brothers" movie from 1980, starring John Belushi and Dan Aykroyd, as the moment in time where they became aware of and curious about the blues; a second group mentioned Stevie Ray Vaughan as the musician who first made them curious about blues music; the third group simply mentioned a live music experience with blues music as the moment of discovery. There were a few who also wove into their story of discovery that they found blues music when they themselves started to learn how to play the guitar. Only very few stated they had discovered the blues as children. The vast majority of interviewees shared that their original moment of discovery was through listening to white performers, but that later, fed by curiosity about the influences of these white artists, they connected to the history of blues in African American culture.

Many blues fans play blues as a hobby (a few play semi-professionally or professionally, as well). Although I did not ask specifically, the interviews indicated that a high percentage of especially male blues fans play an instrument. Scott Pantall, my collaborator, commented that it makes sense that blues fans want to try playing blues music themselves, since they seem to get so much out of hearing and participating in it. Several blues fans mentioned the guitar solo as the vehicle that offered them an access point into how the performer felt. Many fans found meaning in their discovery of blues as a nonverbal mode of communication. They expressed a desire to pass the discovery along, because it provides them with something that is profound, yet playful and fun. They did not want to just hold on to the experience, but desired to share it with others: a form of "blues evangelism." Blues fans often thought deeply about why they wanted to play this music for others and thus help them to discover it as well. Blues was clearly more than just good music to them. Here are a few examples:

> *I love the genuineness of blues. The openness and how it relates to life and the soul and the spirit too. I mean people need to know that they're all connected and that there's not just this one person, not just this one group, but hey look we are all in this together. All of us. And blues is for everyone to have and to hold. It should be there to bring people together, and that's what I would like to see it do. Expand more. Get where more people are more aware of the blues, especially the younger generation so that they can feel that, and hopefully help grow in their spiritual growth. It is a way to get along better with one another.*

The *blues experience* was a gift that blues fans were excited to both receive as initiates, and later share with others. Fans typically connected to one another because of their love of the music, the lack of judgment in the blues community, and the general kinship shared with people in and around the music. Jay Sieleman spoke to this aspect of finding commonality on his first blues cruise with a sense of self-deprecating humor:

> *But I did joke to my wife after about 4-5 days that some of the fans on this ship weren't half bad either. And I can be a little standoffish and aloof and picky and offended by whatever—and I found that I was not having the usual problems with people that I normally do. (Laughs) I found myself thinking: 'this guy's kind of cool' and 'this person's not that stupid,' and those kinds of backhanded compliments. I've found that to be true to a large degree ever since, and I've often said that being a blues fan says more about you than just your taste in music.*

Blues fans are initiates on various levels into a loosely defined and permeable group membership. Many spoke about their joy when they had succeeded in passing on the love of blues, particularly to younger generations. For industry professionals like Sieleman, the discovery process was similar. None of them grew up knowing about the blues directly from their upbringing. Their discovery moments were distinct and memorable. The joy of the music they experienced personally formed the core of their blues evangelism: it was what made blues their professional calling. Here are a few notable examples:

Bruce Iglauer:

My real 'conversion moment' was hearing Fred McDowell at the University of Chicago Folk Festival in 1966. His performance reached out to me across rows of seats, slapped me across the face, and said, 'Wake up, boy! This music is for you!' Considering that Fred was an extremely poor and uneducated black man from the Deep South and I was a . . . middle class college student from the Midwest, we had little in common culturally. But the directness and honesty of his music spoke to me so strongly.

Blues singer, Janiva Magness:

Blues music just made me feel like I wasn't alone . . . because I was very, very, very alone as a child and as a young girl. A level of alone in the world: untethered, not connected to any other human being, that is so hard. . . . It made me feel like I was connected to something that was greater than me. And until that point I had not experienced that.

The founder and president of a blues-based record label from Germany, Thomas Ruf:

Blues musicians expressed their state of life, their emotions, their suffering in their music. That was very powerful to me. I was really impressed by the emotional effects of the way these performers expressed themselves and I really could relate immediately—like feel the depths in that music; it spoke to me.

Blues as Ritual Connecting to Emotionally Authentic Ancestors – The Treasure Hunt

I heard that he covered a lot of other people and I looked into the names on the CDs or albums and looked at whose songs they were. That sent me on a quest. That would be the best way to describe it. Documenting every cover song that Stevie Ray Vaughan did. Who did it? Who was the first—what version of that song did he most likely hear? Or find the oldest version of that song I could find on some recording. And so by doing that I found Freddy King, Albert King, B.B. King, of course Hendrix, Albert Collins, Hound Dog Taylor: just this world of people that Stevie Ray Vaughan covered—and Buddy Guy. And so then I started buying those people's CDs, and listening to the music. And I had this list. I had done all this research to try and find out—here's the song, what album is it on? What CD can I find it on?

A large majority of interviewees, as expressed in the above quote, described the notion of what we labeled *the treasure hunt*. This is a descriptor for an exceedingly common phenomenon among blues fans that the discovery of one artist leads them to explore this artist's influences, and how this artist in turn further influences other performers. This in turn leads down a trail of discovery to more and more artists, typically going back to a time progressively closer to the origin of blues music in the Mississippi Delta. Ultimately, nearly all interviewees mentioned fascination with this kind of treasure hunt. When I did not ask about issues of origination specifically, the frequency with which blues boomers talked about the importance of honoring the originators fell considerably. Still, it was clear that the historical connection was an important part of their understanding of the music; they appreciated the fact that it was passed down from originators in the American South, and that it remains recognizably connected to its ancestors, despite its continuing evolution. Here are a few of many examples:

> *My older brother was a blues and jazz fan, who introduced me to the blues through bands like the Yardbirds and the Blues Brothers when I was a kid. I, in turn, began reading and pursuing my own taste in the blues with Hendrix, the Doors and Led Zeppelin, and eventually back to Delta Blues and Electric Blues with musicians like Muddy Waters, Howlin Wolf, John Lee Hooker, Robert Johnson, Bukka White, Son House, Skip James, Charley Patton, etc. The early blues musicians were awesome and fathered the genre for sure but the greats of today are still honoring them and show them great respect.*

Or:

> *I do believe that a certain element of hardship in someone's life helps with their expression of the blues, so in that respect the sentiment of the original blues has gone. However, the influence of these artists and their struggles is open to interpretation today in order to keep blues meaningful in the modern age.*

There was a sense that the blues lineage had given a gift to the world that was unique and precious. Fans felt nurtured by a continuing connectedness, back through time and place, to the people who were instrumental in creating this music. Implicitly this connectedness also provided them with visceral knowledge of the human capacity for overcoming obstacles, and of the human ability to create something out of nothing. For most, it was inspirational that the creators of the blues genre were poor, disenfranchised, and oppressed and still had managed to show a way to persevere emotionally:

> *I just find it fascinating because they were the real deal. . . . They had nothing. They were often so poor and they might have had three strings, and they*

couldn't even ask their parents for a dime because they didn't have any either.
They put strings in between wood planks and tried to make music out of it
and express themselves. . . . I have so much respect for that and what some of
the musicians did later on was—I don't want to say they perfected it because I
could never say that. They took it and they made it their own and they
expressed it in their way, but to me the greatest—the biggest thrill that I see is
the musicians that took the music that was already there, put their own twist
on it, and they discovered the roots and they go back to playing with their
mentors. So you have these younger musicians actually studying and playing
with B.B. King as opposed to just talking about it, and to me that's—it's like
they're trying to reconnect with what gave them the reason to do it to begin
with.

It was common for blues fans to feel a kinship across time and space with
blues musicians of previous eras:

Marie: How is the blues genre relevant to you now as a white person in our
modern age?

Blues fan: Well I guess the emotional aspect is always relevant because the
lyrics are now historical. Those are still relevant, right? It's not like disco
music, where it was a fad or era that's come and gone. The problems and
issues that black musicians had when this music was initiated are still
problems and issues that we all have today. Maybe different orders of
magnitude, but they are still relevant issues.

While blues fans felt connected to blues originators, they were also
careful to underscore that the suffering of these blues ancestors put their own
problems in perspective. Many made statements along those lines:

But I in no way have had to suffer in my life. I've had bad things happen to
me but I wouldn't compare them to the type of experiences early blues
musicians had.

The feeling of kinship to blues originators as emotionally connected
ancestors seems to transcend racial barriers, at least from the perspective of

white blues fans toward black performers.* An example of this can be found in the liner notes to Rory Block's album, *The Lady and Mr. Johnson*, in which she performs 13 of Robert Johnson's songs. The liner notes read:

> *From 1964 until the winter of 2006, I thought Robert Johnson had no surviving relatives. There was a sense of terrible loss and loneliness surrounding his tragic, early death. . . . Imagine my joy when halfway through the project, I learned that Johnson's family had been found, alive and well, in Mississippi. Heart pounding, I dialed the phone, and in a shaking voice I said: 'You don't know me, but to me you're family... I feel like I'm finding long lost kin!' On the other end came a beautiful voice in a deep, mellow tone, and the hair stood up on my neck.*[16-1]

Blues fans were clear that looking to another reality than their own, often could put things in perspective:

> *Well, I think it is because of the constant-ness of the oppression of the blues originators and what they had to go through. This is something they had to deal with their whole lives. It wasn't something like some people who all of a sudden have the blues after having had two days of bad experiences. But the blues is about life as a whole. You know that's how we learn later on as we grow hopefully spiritually as well. You know, the blues becomes more and more genuine as you go, because you're able to incorporate and realize, just like the original black blues players did, that this is about life. All of it! Not just a couple of days, but this is my life.*

The historical understanding and felt connectedness to ancestors afford blues boomers an appreciation of, and vicarious or direct contact to, the good, bad, and ugly of the human condition. So the connection to blues ancestors, in essence, is also an acknowledgment of who we are as emotional, paradoxical, strong, and imperfect human beings. And in the blues ritual this

---

* Whether this kind of kinship is felt from the African Americans toward white blues lovers would be an interesting area to study.

acknowledgment of our own complex nature is possible through an understanding of those who came before. It clearly adds an element of depth of experience. Here the blues offers a history lesson and connection to what went before, but, where learning about history can be boring, detached, and meaningless, blues fans generally expressed that learning about the history of blues ancestors felt relevant.

Why Do We Need Rituals?

I find it interesting that blues boomers, who grew up surrounded with many intangible anxieties and fears, but with unprecedented economic and social wealth and safety, find such connection to bluesmen and women of the past, who were victims of racism and economic hardship. I often heard statements along the lines of: "I think I have it bad, and then I listen to this blues song, and I realize I am really, really lucky by comparison." Simultaneously, blues fans felt a strong connection to what was being expressed. Blues music offers access to a felt bond between human beings that goes beyond color, culture, and social standing. It also offers acknowledgement of the fact that uncertainty and pain are unavoidable parts of life. This matter-of-factness feels comforting and "real," when compared to the prevailing cultural myth that we can insure, buy, prepare, or rationalize our way out of all our troubles. It is clear that blues fills much deeper needs for modern fans than simply being an auditorily, pleasing pastime.

In an essay called *Two Notes on Modern Rituals*, the author, Bruce Lincoln found that there were two main categories of ritual that were important and still significant:

1. Initiation rituals: historically those that would appear at rites of passage: birth, entering into adulthood, marriage, death, etc. These rituals would be characterized by a symbolic action that would signify a new reality. This could be shown in the form of a *symbolic or actual gift* (a mantra, new name, spear, watch, etc.). Initiation into a

new "phase" was also *communally acknowledged*, as the group was changed with admittance of the new member.

2. Rituals regarding invoking ancestors: historically a way of *connecting to the solidarity of the lineage*, bringing in the memory of the deceased into the presence of the living. Rites connect the living with those who came before, and afford a sense of *continuity in the community by fostering a deep sense of belonging* [emphasis added].[16-2]

Both forms of ritual play a role in the relevance of the blues today. Blues, as a ritual of sorts, provides a steadying antidote to some of the effects of our everyday lives that get increasingly fragmented. In the 21st century, we live in a fast-paced culture that our neurology is not evolutionarily wired to keep up with. In a culture shaped by technological and material overload, many options are readily available. At the same time, previous family structures and community-supported ceremonies and rituals are often missing, meaningless, or "over-distanced."* Omnipresent technology increasingly shapes our daily lives. As the 20th century was coming to a close, innovative surgeon, author, and thinker Leonard Shlain wrote:

> *Today, CNN geopolitical bulletins assault the eye like an artillery barrage, flashing and exploding in our living rooms. Talking heads proffer facile explanations that do not satisfy our yearning to make sense of our century.*[16-3]

The personal computer has since moved into our homes in earnest and smart phones abound, further inundating our neurology. This barrage of information, combined with ubiquitous marketing incentives and schemes in all media to sell us easy solutions, has intensified exponentially. In fact, we live in a world that is getting increasingly complex and demanding of our skills, and at the same time leaving us increasingly disconnected and

---

* The term "Over-distanced Rituals" will be explained later in this chapter

disjointed. Modern conveniences designed to make our lives easier often also bring more demands on our ever-scattered attention spans and give us more information to relate to.

We live in a time when we don't even really know what it means to be in community, or what it means to be mentored by wise elders. If we engage in rituals and ceremonies, it is often with a keen eye to what we might gain personally from our participation in them. At the same time, casual internet connections and diffuse social networks are expanding. In fact, there are more devices connected to the internet than there are human beings on Earth. Forty percent of people *globally* state they spend more time interacting online than they do face-to-face.[16-4]

According to thought-provoking research cited by Danish author Tor Nørretranders, although our brain can compute over 10 gigabytes (ten billion bits) per second, we can only *consciously* process about 40 bits of information per second. He states that the "bandwidth of our consciousness is far lower than the bandwidth of our sensory preceptors."[16-5] According to Nørretranders, watching television offers more than a million bits per second—reading, by contrast, about 25. Who knows how many bits inundate our neurology when we have five "windows" open on the computer while chatting, texting, watching videos, reading, etc.? Although I have found it difficult to substantiate Nørretrander's claims, the point he is making is ultimately relevant to this discussion. We really don't know what might be the evolutionary consequences of this constant bombardment of our awareness by flashing virtual realities. And abundant research shows that we are certainly much less able to multi-task than we think we are—our brains are unable to effectively concentrate on more than one activity at a time.

Our everyday reality is complex and filled with information-overload; this can easily create an underlying sense of over-stimulation and confusion. Even if we find ourselves with enough clean water to drink, healthy children, a solid roof over our heads, and enough food to eat, we might suffer in ways that are difficult to express because this suffering is intangible. It shows up as anxiety or depression, and underlying causes are not easy to identify—a diffuse feeling of being overwhelmed by the modern condition combined with an unrealized and unquenchable longing for real human connectedness, ritual belonging, and to quote C.G. Jung, wholeness. Jung wrote about a former patient in a letter to Bill Wilson, co-founder of Alcoholics Anonymous: "His craving for alcohol was the equivalent on a low level of the spiritual thirst for wholeness, expressed in medieval language: the union with God."[16-6]

After the postwar practice of marketing consumer goods to teenagers, the marketing machine began marketing to children— and even to babies. We are in some ways perceived as successful and even patriotic solely on the basis of our ability to be good consumers. Positive and affirming connections to a sense of belonging—to family, community, and a life purpose beyond one's ability to make money—are undervalued and even difficult to find in modern life. There is an underlying narrative sold in ever-present marketing schemes in our culture that we as individuals can buy, drink, drug, or vacation our way to happiness and contentment, as Betty Friedan was among the first to point out. And, as the Rolling Stones' anthem for the Baby Boomer Generation indicated, we still "Can't Get No Satisfaction." Unsatisfied people make great customers. We have needs that never get fulfilled because our actual core needs are rarely, if ever, acknowledged. We are the consumers always on the lookout for the next cheap thrill or easy fix, willing to mortgage ourselves into ever-increasing personal debt to quench an insatiable thirst. And while credit card statements pile up on our desks, we escape into online virtual realities. Here we can perfect our online profile pictures and edit out feelings and actions that are deemed undesirable from our postings. In fact, we can edit our authentic being straight into the realm of pure imagination. Ridicule, bravado, sarcastic cleverness, and gossip are easy to find in online communities and even in political discourse. But how on earth do we deal sincerely with distress communally and personally? We don't really know how to walk through our blues. It is culturally accepted instead to sit in front of the computer posting funny videos of babies, dogs, and cats while trying to swallow the scream that is building catastrophically in our throats. Blues boomers often expressed that although our world abounds with "connectivity," much of it is superficial and not really meaningful:

> *You should see these people like, when I take the bus or whatever, everybody's texting. Everybody's on their phone and I'm just sitting there on the bus watching all these. . . . I'm older but I still got some kick left in me and I want to get out and I want to socialize with people, and now it's like nobody has anything to say to anybody.*

Or:

> *Why do I think that is? Partially because there's a thousand channels on the media. There's millions of channels on the internet. I'm not sure why there's— I think it's a Tower of Babel kind of thing where you have too many different understandings and perspectives. I'm not sure.*

I asked blues fans if they thought people felt lonelier in spite of new technological methods of connecting, and three out of four agreed that this was the case. Many comments here spoke to such loneliness, and some mentioned the blues as an antidote. As an example:

> *Our expectations of what we believe others 'should' give us have become almost impossible to fulfill. I think our brains are overloaded with pleasure endorphins from the immediate and constant interactions with others, even if we're miles apart. I believe this is why the genre of blues is becoming more mainstream, more people are connecting with those feelings of isolation and loneliness than ever before in man's time.*

> *People don't experience community the way people in the 1950s and before did. We are isolated by politics and economic realities. We don't feel safe being authentic.*

> *Everybody is . . . 'interacting' online but not really interacting with other humans in any real way at all.*

A few felt that new technology was actually helpful in reaching meaningful connections:

NBN is the group I started on Facebook in 2010. I see people from all over planet earth 'connecting' through the power of this genre!

The vast majority however felt that human-to-human contact was preferable and missing in their lives:

People are too busy and tired from working/ stress to want to go out and be with people. On my radio show my saying is: Go get the CURE!!! Go see LIVE music!!!

Over-Distanced Rituals

Blues fans expressed that experiencing blues at concerts, festivals, in the car, or at home with a morning cup of coffee offers connection on many levels, and that it feels "real." It is furthermore a ritual that—here paraphrasing Scheff—is properly "distanced" in such a way that collectively felt distress is awakened in a context which is sufficiently safe, so that the distress is not experienced as overwhelming. Scheff further states:

In the area of ritual, I raise a question concerning the poverty of modern ritual. I argue that most rituals in modern society are over-distanced, that is, they are too vicarious, and therefore do not lead to catharsis. [16-7]

Churches, mosques, and temples successfully uphold a traditional function of religion as a provider of ritual, where rites of passage are celebrated: bar and bat mitzvahs, prayer services, confirmations, weddings, memorial services, baptisms, etc. We have weekly, monthly and yearly ceremonies and practices that connect us to seasonal events, God, and communal rites of celebration—singing, chanting, or praying together. These are the traditional places to practice such rituals. And for many of us, they are still meaningful and crucial to our self-understanding and identity, as well as a collective sense of belonging.

But a rapidly growing number of people state that they are floating around without any religious affiliation. Traditional religion is increasingly losing its role as ritual-provider and relevant community-builder. My first experience of religious ritual was through a small Lutheran church growing up in Denmark. Sundays at church, in my experience, were devoid of any meaningful involvement. The minister and his congregation simply seemed to be going through the motions. Sundays at church were painful for me. I saw no joy, no connection, nor any clear reason for the ritual of going to church. It seemed like something we just "had to do." My parents were the same going in as they were coming out (only possibly more annoyed with me as I could never sit still and be quiet enough through seemingly endless sermons). It shaped my understanding of church as a mostly meaningless ritual. Later, I experienced encounters with other churches, in which rituals were practiced with more involvement, and where people were more invested personally and collectively; instead of overhearing the congregants gossiping after the services, I heard and felt a sense of non-judgmental togetherness. I still found the subject matter of the religious experience difficult, but I observed that some religious ceremonies and rituals can have a visible transformational impact.

We have, however, many needs that religious ceremonies and rituals are not designed to fulfill. Therefore, we look to many different kinds of rituals in our daily life. Earlier, I referred to how America historically has been seen as a land of consumerist rituals,* and it is clear that we now, broadly speaking, in the entire Western world have plenty of rituals that are quite obviously ineffective. They often fail with regard to producing a cathartic response, or in providing a meaningful sense of belonging. A quick look at the contents

---

* See Chapter 11 about the postwar years in the UK

of an anthology of modern rituals shows a plethora of them: rituals for comic strips, dancing, architecture, eating, consumption, sporting events, pornography, etc. [16-8] Rituals abound, yet many of them are simply based on individual needs fulfillment.

In the previously quoted essay by Bruce Lincoln, he refers to an anthology of nine writers* who in the 1970s more or less uniformly came to the conclusion that:

1. Ritual is a necessary part of life;
2. Ritual has largely disappeared; and,
3. Attempts to create new rituals or invigorate old ones are problematic.

Lincoln concludes that it is difficult to distinguish which rituals are merely habitual and which serve a deeper function.[16-9] Professor of political science and religion, Frederick Bird, writes that "sociologists tend to view rituals as meaningless routines, as unthinking habituated activities or as overly elaborated ceremonies." He continues that Protestant religious thinkers have been critical toward the more elaborate form of ritual in the Catholic Church, as form over function. Bird finds it important to distinguish between which rituals are truly meaningful and which are simply "stylized and habituated forms of behavior."[16-10] This conundrum is precisely the critical point for this discussion. It seems that we have plenty of rituals in our world, but finding some that are transformative and that connect us to a sense of individual and collective significance can be difficult. We value personal freedom and we can "shop around" for rituals, yet many times this shopping process becomes simply a search for comfort or entertainment. These rituals are impoverished, "cushy," and removed from emotional experience. According to Scheff's theories, these rituals are "over-distanced." They do not evoke a sense of "collectively held distress" that can be re-experienced in a safe and properly distanced setting. It might also be difficult to find settings

---

* "The Roots of Ritual" edited by James Shaughnessy.

that offer a sense of kinship rather than competition. It is, according to the study of nonverbal vocalizations across cultures, and as referred to in Chapter 7, precisely in our pain, desperation, and suffering that we recognize and resonate with one another across temporal and cultural distinguishers. But our culture is ill equipped to really know what that means. We have to look beyond the gloss to experience this sense of communion elsewhere. It is certainly possible. It exists when we donate our time to animal shelters, homeless organizations, adopt a child, or take in a stray dog. Or we can experience it when we feel the embrace of our community if we, or a loved one is ill, and we have managed to step out of both "can-do" and "victim" mentality and instead just invite others to walk an uncertain walk with us.

Yet we are often distracted away from these offerings. Our virtual post-modern experiential shopping cart contains plenty of ritual-like opportunities that don't connect us to deeper layers within ourselves, nor do they typically lead us through them. Individually chosen rituals might be pleasant, blissful, beautiful, and convenient, but they do not contain the grit that is necessarily part of collectively-or individually-held distress. Combined input from blues fans made it clear that our interest in the blues can offer us a way to walk through, and very importantly, share, our joys, delights, and also our frustrations and pain. Through emotional connectedness, it is possible to experience individual and shared catharsis. When we thusly recognize emotional commonality, we also feel a sense of belonging and resonance, and it allows us to find some measure of relief that is not just based on feeling comfortable, or simple needs gratification. Blues connects those who connect to it in discovery, and once they are converted through "initiation," the blues becomes a treasured element in their lives—the gift they want to keep giving by passing it on. Blues offers a ritual connection to emotionally authentic ancestors who walked through destruction, fear, and heartbreak. These ancestors honestly expressed how they fell down—and how they got back up and kept on walking. A blues fans stated this poignantly, synthesizing voices of many:

When you walk in the blues, you never walk alone.

Chapter 17:

Context-Specific Blues

Context-Specific *Authentic* Blues

Although many emotions are universal, we observe that the social and historical circumstances in which those emotions appear and find expression are not. The blues evolves with its audience and can address different needs in different styles, manifestations, and eras. Some blues scholars disagree with this finding. Below are two examples that are almost 50 years apart:

1. In 2012, professor of philosophy, Philip Jenkins, stated that "blues authenticity depends upon group membership," and thus white blues performers, although they may be excellent in every way, sing *"a variant of a cultural expression derived from a very different kind of experience"* than that of blues players and singers.[17-1] When Jenkins uses the word "authentic," he specifies that he means *"authoritative, original, and pure."* [17-2]

2. In 1963, Amiri Baraka (Leroi Jones) wrote: *"Blues as an autonomous music had been in a sense inviolable. There was no clear way into it, i.e., its production, not its appreciation, except as concomitant with what seems to me to be the peculiar social, cultural, economic, and emotional experience of a black man in America. The idea of a white blues singer seems an even more violent contradiction of terms than the idea of a middle-class blues singer."* [17-3]

What blues boomers expressed was largely contrary to such views. They stated that they enjoy a variety of expressions, each on their own terms. Jenkins's conclusion that blues is invalid when performed by outsiders of this original group membership does not, therefore, broadly align with what is important to current blues fans. Jenkins concludes that authentic blues performance is race-, culture- and expression-dependent, and therefore by definition inauthentic if performed by those who do not have "group membership" *as African Americans*. Jenkins determines that because this group has been discriminated against due to ethnic origin, this exact experience is the prerequisite for authentically playing blues. Jenkins, Baraka, and others, e.g., Paul Garon find it largely invalid for races and socioeconomic groups other than impoverished blacks to play blues. If we subscribe to the notion that the blues broadly understood is only valid in one specific social and ethnic context, and mainly set at a time in the past, then we must also be willing to accept that the blues as a contemporary art form is dead, *or depends on continuing racial oppression and poverty*. To basically call contemporary blues musicians frauds and cultural appropriators closes doors to growth, mutual understanding, and appreciation. If we take these statements as parameters for what determines the future role of blues music, it makes it problematic—in fact a guilt-ridden proposition—for white or black middle-class, contemporary, and future blues performers to find *their* authentic voice (here meant as honestly and transparent expressions of their current background, context and situation) within the blues format. The blues becomes a style of music that is off-limits to all but a narrowly defined group, or it becomes an act of pretend. By a wide margin, fans do not want to limit the expression of blues to fixed temporal, ethnic, or socioeconomic frameworks.

Today when we express our opinions about the blues, it is beneficial to carefully define the concept of "authenticity." To wish to honor originators of the blues and to encourage African Americans to partake in the continuing trajectory of the blues is a proposition that was widely encouraged by those participating in the study. But conversely, they also broadly encouraged current and future blues expressions as a big tent approach. Of course blues fans clearly expressed that it is, at the same time, entirely appropriate to talk about authentic blues as a product of the Mississippi Delta, by African Americans who experienced horrendous discrimination, marginalization, and the effects of racist policies and practices. With regard to the parameters of who *originated* the blues within the confines of Context-specific *Authentic* (here meaning "back to origin") it makes sense to look to the blues originators in the Mississippi Delta. Other contexts, however, can likewise allow authentic expressions within them[*]. As an example: a white person who grew up in a middle-class, suburban neighborhood who has apprenticed with blues masters, immersed him-or herself in blues tradition, and who has discovered that technical prowess is not necessarily the end-all requirement for being a masterful blues musician, can certainly play a form of context-specific authentic blues when it is based on his/her own experience, group membership, and emotional connections. Context and integrity here defines the parameters upon which the level of authenticity is experienced. Were this aforementioned white person instead seeking to copy black speech, dress code, musical expressions, etc., the expression would not be authentic to his or her own context, but rather be an act of musical theater.

Readiness for New Musical Expressions

Toward the end of the movie "Back to the Future," Marty McFly is on stage wooing the 1950s audience with a musical approach they have never heard before. He "duck-walks" across the stage while playing the Chuck Berry standard, "Johnny B Goode." In the wings listening to McFly is Chuck Berry's imagined cousin who calls Chuck on the phone and yells into the receiver: "You know that new sound you're looking for? Well listen to this!" The audience goes wild. It is perfect timing for Marty to introduce this new kind of music. The audience's anticipation is met and surpassed by this leap into another kind of musical expression, while a few stand immobilized in confused horror and watch. The gap however, between the anticipation of the audience and the new approach is not *too* great, thus the music is

---

[*] See section about John Mayall

welcomed by the majority of the audience, as it makes the leap from one style into another. Later, when Marty starts playing more psychedelic licks on the guitar and rolling on the floor while playing and kicking his amp—antics from the 1960s and beyond—the room grinds to a halt. Marty then comments, "I guess you guys aren't ready for that yet." It is an entertaining and made-up rendition of what happens when a certain point in musical development has been reached—and the audience is ready to be stretched into a new synthesis of expression. But the musical leap cannot stretch too far.

Blues Evolution

In the wake of musical developments and leaps, some feel a sense of betrayal of expectations, while others embrace and celebrate the newness. Bob Dylan, "going electric" at the Newport Folk Festival in 1965, is one such well-known and oft-referred-to example. While many in the audience were ready to stretch into a new expression and manifestation of the musical form, others were enraged and disappointed, although the reasons for this disappointment differ.[17-4]

As Marty McFly imaginatively demonstrated in the movie, the musical leap has to build on what came before to such a degree that a virtual bridge over the gap between old and new can happen as a fairly seamless blend. It would be difficult to imagine Jimi Hendrix's playing style sprout directly from Charley Patton's musical expression. But through a series of evolutionary developments, likely through the music of Muddy Waters, B.B. King, Albert King, Buddy Holly, Eddie Cochran, Guitar Shorty, etc., it works. It is comparatively easy to observe how this works when we look back in time, but it is more difficult to see this process as it happens. We are attached to our preferred styles of music, and there is often an element of feeling let down when it evolves; we don't like to be denied our expectations. So the delight, excitement, and in blues certainly, emotional appeal in new musical developments must somehow be greater than the sense of feeling let down because of a new direction. Music evolves because musicians infuse the music with gradual developments built on previous musical styles, merged with new influences and inspiration, and the audience ultimately gives feedback that they get more out of the new expression than they did from the previous one.

Blues boomers widely embrace new forms of blues if they meet certain arbitrary criteria, while they are also generally big fans of old styles. It is not an either/or proposition. They mostly see this evolution as a sign of the blues genre's health and vitality. Of survey participants, 78 percent *disagreed* with the statement that "real blues" died after the more rocking versions entered the market in the 1960s. Most comments about this topic were nuanced and supported the continuing evolution of the genre.

> *This is a tough one. Times have changed and most of the blues musicians from the 60s that I listened to are dead. Transitions seem to happen approximately every 20 yrs. 1920s blues is slightly different than the 40s blues which is slightly different from the 60s blues, etc. and technology has changed. The way young musicians hear and 'learn' blues is way different than the 'old' days. Styles have changed from 'pre-war' acoustic country blues, and graduated into an electric urban city blues into even harder 'rock/blues.' Real blues to me is like art; you know it when you hear it, and it touches your very being— like nothing else can.*

One of the main reasons that fans found blues music unique was the notion that it allows each new generation to find their distinct expression within the format and reclaim it for their own time and place. Blues music evolves constantly, both meeting the expectations of what came before as well as stretching the genre to help it thrive, be vital, and relate to new generations. Even as blues evolves into other genres, the blues format also continues to evolve while still being broadly recognizable as "blues." Even if blues fans to a large degree (over 80 percent) are over 45 years of age, they encourage and applaud young musicians who are embracing the art form. Fams broadly celebrate that the blues continues to be influenced by current events and the era in which it appears.

Looking for a model that explains how new eras of blues music can be considered a relative and descendant of what came before, and how each new development includes and transcends its predecessor, we find parallels in Integral Theory. Ken Wilber, who founded it, writes:

> *Reality is composed of various levels of existence – levels of being and of knowing. . . . Each senior dimension transcends but includes its juniors, so that this is a conception of wholes within wholes within wholes indefinitely.*[17-5]

As blues music changes, it advances in a reciprocal dialogue with the tradition(s) of ancestors, current reality, level of mastery/musicianship of the performer, and the needs and wants of the audience at any given time. Charles Keil writes:

> *Although the first blues singers obviously had no planned developments of their musical expression in mind, many estheticians will agree that incipient forms of a style almost preclude certain further developments and encourage others. . . .The 'final causes' of blues development and change of style are of course the predispositions and needs of the blues audience. . . . The blues exist because some men feel called upon to address themselves to certain basic problems in song and because these songs meet a cultural demand.*[17-6]

Keil reflects that historically the blues has filled specific needs at a specific time for both performer and audience, as it both includes and transcends tradition with current expression and needs. Compiled data from blues fans confirms this is not just a historical finding; it is still true today. In this role, the blues musician of any era since its inception is the vessel through which the current cultural joys and concerns can be addressed, allowed expression, and find resonance. Obviously, in the 21st century's internet-connected kaleidoscope of available distractions, the needs of performers and their audience are different than they were for the mostly black blues audiences and performers prior to the 1960s.

continues to be infused with current inspiration, and not simply turned into stale replications of previous eras' expressions. Blues boomers largely were unimpressed with bands who sought to imitate and emulate previous manifestations of blues forms, without *also* exhibiting emotional honesty and accessibility. They were generally not interested in seeing blues performed as an act, where blues players are simply reciting their parts. And since very few of the old blues masters are still alive, they found it important to not just get stuck in contemporary forms that are mere shadow projections of their past vigor. The blues of the second decade of the twenty-first century is an evolutionary product of everything that came before. It would not be possible to have a Stevie Ray Vaughan without also having had Albert King and Jimi Hendrix. Albert King in turn would not have been who he was if he had not started out singing gospel in the family church—if he had not played drums for Jimmy Reed, and later switched to the electric guitar. He built some of his own sound and expression on his love of Blind Lemon Jefferson and Lonnie Johnson, who set the standard for future guitar players/singers. Albert King united inspiration from his personal experiences with the inspiration of who he listened to, and the techniques and sound possibilities that were at his disposal at the time. He integrated and transcended as he went along.

The time- and context-specific elements of the blues are different for each epoch. Figure 6 attempts to show how such societal and cultural context might have changed—in this case, primarily in North America. It demonstrates that the blues performed after the 1960s transition era from mainly black to mainly white audiences, is vastly different from what preceded, with regard to the composition of its audience and to the social and cultural elements that inform and influence both the performers and listeners. The Blues Evolution Timeline attempts to describe probable relevant factors in various decades. The evolution of blues music is important to modern blues fans who embark on the treasure hunt for the thrill of discovering influences, exploring back and forth along the blues timeline.

Fans often engage in this treasure hunt back in time because they initially connect to a contemporary blues singer or performer, who in turn stimulates their curiosity about a particular song or set of influences. They expressed that the treasure hunt, and the search for influences, offers them meaningful, relevant, historical connection.

Blues Evolution Timeline

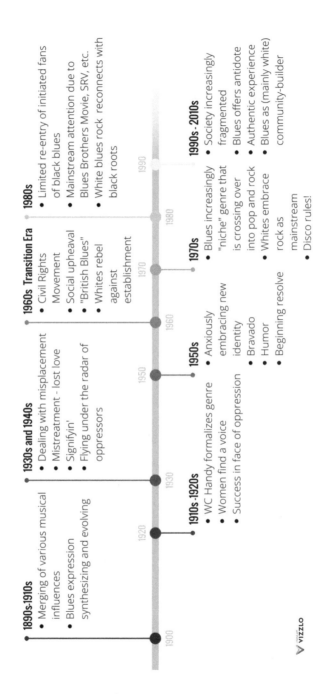

1890s-1910s
- Merging of various musical influences
- Blues expression synthesizing and evolving

1910s -1920s
- WC Handy formalizes genre
- Women find a voice
- Success in face of oppression

1930s and 1940s
- Dealing with misplacement
- Mistreatment - lost love
- Signifyin'
- Flying under the radar of oppressors

1950s
- Anxiously embracing new identity
- Bravado
- Humor
- Beginning resolve

1960s Transition Era
- Civil Rights Movement
- Social upheaval
- "British Blues"
- Whites rebel against establishment

1970s
- Blues increasingly "niche" genre that is crossing over into pop and rock
- Whites embrace rock as mainstream
- Disco rules!

1980s
- Limited re-entry of initiated fans of black blues
- Mainstream attention due to Blues Brothers Movie, SRV, etc.
- White blues rock reconnects with black roots

1990s - 2010s
- Society increasingly fragmented
- Blues offers antidote
- Authentic experience
- Blues as (mainly white) community-builder

Figure 6: Blues Evolution Timeline

The blues evolves because artists synthesize inspiration with elements of tradition to a degree that allows the genre to be recognizable yet doesn't violate the law of musical progression by attempting evolutionary leaps that are not yet supported by current, musical evolutionary scale. Any new composition in the blues format has the potential to build on tradition and influences, synthesize current emotions and inspiration, and move the blues format forward into the future.

Blues boomers were also generally thrilled with new interpretations of blues standards from the past. They were often enthusiastic about the notion of the same song being performed by different musicians from different stages of the Blues Timeline. This was part of the historical connection to blues ancestors as well as the treasure hunt for them: to pinpoint how a familiar song gets a new "flavor" depending when, how, and by whom it is performed:

> *They are not the originators of that song, but when you hear that same song and you trace back its roots and who originated it, and all these artists that have contributed to it, it just adds richness and a flavor that you don't necessarily get if you just listen to the modern music.*

As group memberships change, so do other forms of expression incorporated into the music. As an example, the practice of communicating in veiled modes through signifyin' was an important secret code for black people to safely mock, or talk behind the backs of, whites, who would otherwise harm them if they sensed any kind of noncompliance or defiance. When we discover elements of signifyin' in our modern treasure hunt, it is now mostly of relevance as a historical reminder of menacing shadow from the past: a reminder to never forget. It becomes a part that helps us understand more of the whole. This insight from comprehensive study was crucial to many blues boomers:

It's more than just 'he's a guitar player.' You have to say well 'what are his trials? What are his life experiences? Who is he influenced by?' And it becomes a personal pursuit.

Fans frequently stated that it was inspirational, meaningful, and important for them to study and listen to old blues masters from before the 1960s. They talked about doing so as if they were visiting with beloved grandparents. This immersion taught them meaningful lessons about the human condition and afforded a kind of emotional access to a time and a place from the past. A small portion of blues boomers preferred only listening to blues music from certain historical eras. This was the music that spoke most powerfully to them.

When we are moving in the layers of CAB, we discover that what was relevant to a person in 1920 has a different meaning to someone in other times. For example, sexual and domestic abuse, racism, and continuing veiled, yet empowering expression when performing publicly, were important issues for listeners of Ma Rainey and Bessie Smith's risqué lyrics in the 20s. However, for a blues fan who listen to it today, the lyrics might take on varying layers of meaning depending on historical insight. Superficially, the songs might appear to be fun and entertaining but as the historical context opens up through study and immersion, a much deeper connection to the material is possible. Additionally, on a universal level (BL2 - UAB), audiences might relate to free expression of physicality, talking oneself out of feeling victimized and using humor to disarm to defy societal conventions boldly, etc. However, the time- and culture-specific context (BL3 - CAB) adds extra layers of relevance for audiences and performers of particular eras, as it does for listeners who delve into historical explorations as a part of their enjoyment of music from previous eras.

The sound and make-up of blues music thus changes depending on who, where, and how it is performed. Is it a black, white, upper, or lower class individual? Is it performed in the Deep South, in India, or in New Jersey? Is it performed acoustically or amplified? Blues music is assimilated and interpreted by an audience that, just like the musician, is shaped by their time, place and space. A contemporary, middle-class, white American or European, Baby Boomer audience will have a different social/collective mindset in which to absorb and interpret blues music than, say, a mostly black audience in 1950s Chicago, or 1930s Mississippi.

Deep Context: History of Origin

While most fans enjoyed a historical exploration of the blues, many felt an emotional connection to the originators. They stated wholeheartedly that we ought to honor the originators by making sure their names were mentioned when contemporaries played their songs, and that royalties were paid in full to whomever they were due—or to their descendants. But, what else can we do? The idea of honoring originators of the blues on a deeper level is fraught with difficulty as the following exchange exemplifies:

Marie: Is it important to you that we honor the originators of the blues genre and if so how do we best do that?

Blues fan: What do we mean by honoring them? I don't understand what that means.

Marie: You tell me: Is it important that we honor the originators of the blues genre?

Blues fan: Sure. Yes of course it is. How, what, why, where does the origination start? So do we need to go back to Ghana? Yeah, yeah, ok, what—is it Buddy Guy? Is it Howlin Wolf? Is it Charlie Patton? Is it the unknown blues guy who sang one song in Memphis that someone else heard? Is it W.C. Handy? If we could identify them or whatever, I'm just not quite sure. Of course it's important to honor them.

Blues influences stem from a complex and many-facetted historical context. If we are to address the concept of authenticity in blues by examining what might be its origin as a pure and unadulterated expression, then we will indeed have to look significantly further back in history than to the end of the 19th century in the Mississippi Delta. Seen from this perspective, and within the concept of "relevance," the very notion of "purity" is problematic. It is precisely by the *merging* of influences that the blues as an emergent musical style has thrived, expanded, and remained relatable. There is tension between what musicologists consider important, and what is significant for blues artists and fans. Fans were largely content to experience relatable and universal aspects of blues music (BL2), and to pepper their interest in the music with a historical treasure hunt, but academics often have another stated goal. According to an article in the *Journal of the American Musicological Society* by Alexander Rehding, the history of musicology has often focused on the quest for origins in search of "resonances of purity, simplicity, authenticity, and stability."[17-7] Musicologists seek to "heed this pure essence—'the original elements of music."[17-8] Through their analyses, they seek to deduce and rewind back to inception. Their stated goal is to exclude and circumnavigate impure, or non-original, influences from other traditions. According to Rehding, the musicologists' focus on music's purity, mixed with strict musical rules about what belongs in a certain tradition, leaves little room for forward-moving *artistic* experimentation.[17-9] It is useful within the *academic* tradition to seek to find original, undiluted musical components that, through analysis and categorization, unearth new information about the historical trajectory of the music. Rehding concludes that a strict definition of musical expression might satisfy musicologist criteria, but, in fact only works retroactively. While Rehding discusses a particular quest of German musicologists in the 20th century, I believe the discussion is also relevant here: a narrowly defined understanding of the inception of blues music—equaling purity of origin—thus depends on, and must be defined by, interpretations of the parameters applied to define such emergence. Art and academia here work on opposing directional tracks in their understanding and appreciation of musical tradition. Art carries us into the future through innovation and exploration; academia describes our musical past through retroactive analysis.

Blues music is, and has always been, an expression born from amalgamations of many influences. Yet discussions of its origins often take, as a starting point, the birth of the blues on American soil by infusion of African influences that survived the onslaught (and attempts at eradication) from European American culture. But the multi-cultural origins of these African influences in turn, are not often part of the discussion: an internal African slave trade had been operational for centuries prior to initiation of the trans-Atlantic slave trade. In the seventh century, armed horsemen kidnapped and raided areas across the Sahara.[17-10] There is evidence that some of the foundational elements of blues music stemmed from the resulting merging of cultures—that some of the musical elements of blues were forged in the mold of slavery *in Africa* through the capture of slaves, who were held by their African captors centuries before European and American slave trade started. Blues researcher Paul Merry writes:

> *A growing body of evidence . . . suggests that the true origins of blues music might be from the parts of Africa touched by Islam. You only have to hear for yourself the traditional music of the Tuareg people of North Africa to appreciate its uncanny correlation with some of the earliest recorded rural blues. Coincidentally, these Berber nomads are also famously known as the Blue Men of the Desert, due to their indigo blue robes. . . . Tuareg warriors had traditionally hunted down and traded in the black slaves since Roman times.* [17-11]

Muslim music not only influenced musical expression in Africa, but was brought here indirectly by Africans who had internalized some of the musical traditions of their Muslim captors, and directly by some African slaves who were themselves Muslim. Paul Oliver writes in *Savannah Syncopaters*: "Such Muslims, devout, learned, and given positions of responsibility on the plantations, undoubtedly stood out from the rest."[17-12]

Some musical components of blues music—perhaps the sliding pitch, the call and response component, as well as the blue notes—might thus be traceable back to these Nomadic tribes that bought and sold African slaves for centuries before the Portuguese began the transatlantic slave trade in the

1400s. It follows that the musical backdrop for the blues developed as an accompaniment to cultural mergers and influences that took place centuries before the blues was named and marketed, and even before Africans arrived on North American shores. The fact that white culture was, and is, influenced and greatly inspired by a black musical tradition represents a continuing evolution, since black and white cultures increasingly interrelate and integrate. It is also natural, of course, that this African tradition was inspired and influenced by the European-American tradition it landed in, including the church music that helped inspire the Spirituals, classical music, European and Appalachian folk songs, show tunes, military music, etc. WWII brought African American music to European shores, and Britons brought it back in new ways. The music continues its continual process of synthesis and evolution wherever cultures meet today.

Slavery is thus an important context-specific element in the understanding of blues music. The heavy hand of slavery has weighed down the human race for thousands of years with its brutal and autonomy-destroying practice. It continues today. And for all the horrors connected with the practice, mutual inspiration also happens in its wake. Although this is a horrific and repulsive type of inter-human exchange, new musical and artistic input and assimilation still takes place wherever, and whenever, different cultures intermingle. Attempting to seek "pure, authoritative, and original" musical traditions that are untainted by outside influences is therefore a fool's errand unless we choose an arbitrary starting date and decide that this is the date of inception. Otherwise, how far back do we need to go to get such pure expression? It is impossible to speculate. Musical traditions have mutually inspired and influenced each other for millennia, and will continue to do so, no matter how they were, and are, brought together.

When we look at the history of the blues in North America, it is obviously forged in a dialectical tension between European and African cultures on American soil. The tension stems primarily from how various civilizations, and here primarily the British, European, and American, historically have treated native populations, and populations that were "dissimilar" to themselves. This is the backdrop upon which the blues shows up today with an almost exclusively white audience. I asked the interviewees whether they personally felt guilt about the atrocities perpetrated against African Americans in the name of slavery. The vast majority did not. They felt appalled at what had happened, yet most felt that they were not responsible for the actions of theirs or others' ancestors. Many expressed relief and joy about developments toward more equality, and celebrated these advances. Some expressed an attitude that we "cannot change the past—but we can do something about the present and the future." For instance:

> *I'm more responsible for my own actions and my own responses to people . . . and that my children were not raised with that kind of prejudice. That's the responsibility that I feel towards it. I know it was passed down from generation to generation—some of this bigotry, and I just want to make damn sure it doesn't go to the next generation, and that is where I feel responsibility.*

Several of the interviewees who did not feel guilty about the historical issues surrounding slavery felt that their ancestors, too, had experienced similar oppression. One of the blues fans I interviewed has Austrian-Jewish as well as Mexican-American Catholic ancestors. He talked about his grandfather being a sharecropper in the US, after narrowly escaping Pancho Villa. On the Jewish side of his lineage, his family had likewise experienced discrimination:

> *I would read about Buddy Guy growing up or B.B. King or Albert King and hear the stories about how they grew up sharecropping and how hard that was and it's like, 'I get that.' I mean, I never had to do that kind of work, but I know their stories. They're my family's stories. And on my dad's side, his dad showed up and they lived in New York City . . . and it turns out he couldn't get a job during the Depression. Nobody would hire a Jew. . . . That was when our family name got changed, so he could find work. So it's those kinds of stories, stories about being discriminated against and overcoming—that's the personal connection to blues music for me.*

Missing from the narratives among blues boomers, when they talked about the oppression that their own relatives had suffered as ethnic minorities, was the fact that whether they belonged to Jewish, Eastern European, Mexican, or other minorities, they were not sold into chattel slavery. The practice of indentured servitude, as was seen with the Irish population, was typically a temporary—albeit still horrific—practice. It was not a lifelong practice that was *automatically* inherited by the children of the indentured. Any impoverished and disenfranchised demographic group has been, and continues to be, exploited by the wealthier classes. However, it is paramount to exercise caution when talking about indentured servitude and slavery as having an equally devastating legacy. Discrimination and bigotry against African American groups went much further for much longer. They were targeted and kept separate simply because of the color of their skin until the 1960s, and the social slide and economic aftershocks in the African American community continues to this day. Segregation created a wound in the US that affected the descendants of former African slaves proportionally much more profoundly and lastingly than other ethnic groups—except the Native American population. A small minority of blues boomers felt directly responsible:

> *Yes, we are guilty as hell. . . . It's so disturbing when you hear racist comments or innuendos about things—or people's body language speaks a thousand words sometimes. It's disturbing to know, and almost embarrassing to say, 'yeah I'm a white man.' I'd rather say I'm a red man. I'm a Native American. . . . But, uh, yeah I can—yeah, I sense with them that white man has a long way to go. Not all, thank goodness. We have some good people out there. We are all human. We're made of the same thing, of the same spirit.*

Underlying the issue of race and blues today is the history of slavery and ethnic oppression. It is context-specific, and here, blues boomers uniformly expressed their disgust about the practice. Some fans felt that blacks leaving the blues is indicative of indirectly wanting to send a message to whites:

It is one of the questions my friends and I that go to blues festivals always ask ourselves. ... It is very rare to see African Americans at these blues festivals and blues events. And we always ask ourselves why? Because this is in theory their music that we've just co-opted for ourselves. And ... I would love to understand that more, but I do think we've co-opted a style, and we identify with a problem . . . . I'll say to some degree it bothers me that very few African Americans show up at these events. . . . It's either they have no interest in that style of blues; they don't want to reward what they may consider a bastardization of their music. Or maybe it's just not marketed in their communities? I don't really know.

Chapter 18:

Post WWII Reality for African Americans

Why *did* African Americans Flee the Blues?

In order to answer this question, it is useful to take a brief, partial look at African American history of the 20th century and beyond. In WWII, African Americans got the "privilege" of serving alongside whites. This was possible due to new policy implementation. Just a few years earlier, in 1937, the American Army War College (AAWC) had concluded that African American soldiers were unfit to serve in the military. This decision was based on findings from WWI, when a black division served under Southern white officers who found the experience unworkable. At the same time, during WWI, another black division led by the French army had done exceedingly well. The French army had enthusiastically requested more such African American divisions. But this request was ignored in the conclusions of the AAWC, which was instead based on Southern white officers' testimony. The conclusion read (cited by Stephen E. Ambrose):

As an individual the Negro is docile, tractable, light-hearted, care free and good natured. If unjustly treated he is likely to become surly and stubborn, though this is usually a temporary phase. He is careless, shiftless, irresponsible, and secretive. He resents censure and is best handled with praise and by ridicule. He is unmoral, untruthful and his sense of right doing is relatively inferior.[18-1]

This ignorant finding, based on bigoted officers' testimony, was obviously cloaked in pseudo-logical, bigoted nonsense. It was conveniently ignored when the need for troops intensified in WWII. Even before the United States entered the war, there was a need for all the manpower possible to help with production in war-related industries. The Fair Employment Practices Commission (FEPC) implemented US Executive Order 8802, which decreed that employers were no longer allowed to discriminate based on race or religion. The Executive Order proved useful when the United States actively entered the war after December 7, 1941. Suddenly the supposed "inferiority" of African Americans to serve in the war was, at least temporarily, a non-issue for lawmakers. In the 1930s, racism was clearly not just expressed in Hitler's Germany. Historian Stephen Ambrose is quoted as saying: "Soldiers were fighting the world's worst racist, Adolph Hitler, in the world's most segregated army."[18-2] A sense of double morality permeated the issue. Racial inequality understandably made the American claim of democratic ideals sound hollow to many African Americans.

Therefore, African Americans were initially hesitant to jump on board the patriotic bandwagon and enlist. Lauren Rebecca Sklaroff states that "With the failed promise of World War I in the minds of black Americans, and as American discrimination proved as pervasive as ever, many black individuals were hesitant to support a largely undemocratic nation."[18-3] Still, by 1944, 150,000 African American troops served in the United Kingdom alone.[18-4] Black divisions were largely kept separate from white ones, but total segregation was not always possible. There was some effort from the State Department to avoid racial tension in various ways. One of those methods was the creation of an all-African-American variety show to be broadcast abroad on the American Forces Radio Network. It was thought that this show would help diffuse the topic of "racial inequality."[18-5] This was the same radio show that Chris Barber and many other overseas civilians listened to during WWII, and that blew their minds. It featured popular black musicians, comedians, and actors. Other than affording black servicemen their own show on the radio, it also introduced authentic black music and culture—beyond caricature and minstrelsy—to many white servicemen.[18-6]

Servicemen were carefully segregated when possible. Yet, since the United Kingdom did not have laws of racial segregation, black and white troops encountered one another in social settings. During leisure time spent in clubs and bars, black soldiers were right there next to white fellow-countrymen. Tension often ensued, mostly from white American soldiers who were indignant about having to socialize in integrated settings.[18-7] White servicemen worried about how this experience of racial commingling might later affect racial sensibilities back home. It was also very provoking to them, for instance, when they saw white (English) women socializing openly with black men.[18-8] In 1944, the first group of African American nurses, "despite early protests," also served in hospitals and attended white soldiers.[18-9]

In an attempt to ease the tension and create a temporary fix for the problem, General Eisenhower ordered servicemen, with no regard to the color of skin, to "work together, train together, live together in order to attain successful teamwork."[18-10] In other words, since social contact was tension-filled, it was easier to put the tension aside when involved in hard work and when all depended on each other for survival. However, "working together" did not mean that black and white servicemen intermingled. Each group had distinct functions (e.g. blacks loaded and unloaded cargo, whites practiced disembarking from landing vessels).[18-11] While military leaders could issue and reinforce orders, when the men were at work on the base and when it was deemed advantageous to the campaign, enforcing the orders in social settings was complicated. Tensions continued, yet racial barriers were inevitably breaking down.

During the course of the war, about 1 million African American troops served in the military.[18-12] Having served alongside their white fellow soldiers and gotten a taste of societies without racial segregation in Europe and the United Kingdom, those soldiers later reported their experience to their families and friends upon their return home to the US, where segregation was still enforced. It is clear that this experience directly or indirectly inspired many to become active in the fight for racial equality. The Civil Rights

Movement in America in the 1950s and '60s thus gained momentum from African Americans who had served in the war.[18-13]

After the war, black soldiers returned to America and were expected to once again fall in place and accept their separate but unequal status. The FEPC was terminated on a national level, and enforcement of its rulings was left up to the states which were simply *encouraged* to support racially inclusive policies. The United States Employment Service (USES) declared that: "The . . . post-war program for service to minority groups must, therefore, be based upon persuasion and education."[18-14] The lack of federal insistence on fair and equal employment practices was therefore largely ineffective. Such "persuasion and education" did not happen broadly in most states, and the FEPC's fair hiring and employment policies were enacted only by a few Northeastern states. After the war, discriminatory hiring practices were again commonplace in many parts of the country. When whites were openly favored in the hiring procedure, nothing was done to penalize such action. In 1951, for instance, a corporation advertised that it had "good jobs for men." However, when black men sought employment there, they were told by the head of the Alabama State Employment Office that the company was interested in "white applicants only." When the matter was brought up with the Federal Employment Board, they determined that "no action should be taken on the matter."[18-15]

African American Suburbs

It is relevant to mention here that it was common in the postwar climate for many blacks to move from Southern states to Northern cities (the African American Migration). In turn, many whites moved from cities to the suburbs (a move known as "white flight"). Associate professor of economics, Leah Platt Boustan finds that there was a direct correlation. In fact, 2.7 whites moved out of the city for every one black person moving into cities from the (rural) South.[18-16] Between 1950 and 1970, the population in suburbia swelled, doubling in size to 72 million people.[18-17] According to history professor,

Andrew Wiese, who specializes in the history of suburbanization, about 1 million African Americans managed to build a home in the suburbs between 1940 and 1960. Yet, this was *clearly* not a typical scenario. Blacks who penetrated the equity-building landscape of middle-class suburbia were often met with acts of terrorism from white neighbors who saw black families as a threat to their attempt to climb the social ladder of (white) society. Charles Abrams, the man who created the New York Housing Authority, wrote:

> *Homeowners, homebuilders and mortgage lenders seemed convinced that people should live only with their own kind, that the presence of a single minority family destroys property values and undermines social prestige and status. National and local real estate organizations were accepting these assumptions as gospel, as were popular magazines, college texts, and technical journals.* [18-18]

Even more troubling was the fact that official regulations were created to favor whites, by bending loan and mortgage rules to help the white population and keep others out. Both the mortgage programs of the Federal Housing Administration and the Veterans Administration subscribed to these discriminatory practices.[18-19] The government enforced racist policies with its support for suburban segregation. Wiese writes:

> *Government, too, was deeply supportive of racism in the housing market. Through the late 1940s, white property holders vigorously enforced deed covenants that restricted the sale or rental of property to 'Caucasians only,' and American courts upheld the practice. Moreover, the chief federal agencies responsible for housing followed standard real estate industry practice in discriminating against African Americans and other minorities.[18-20]*

African Americans were not allowed to secure federally supported loans to buy houses in the late 1940s. They remained in public housing arrangements in the cities. The ones who tried getting a loan to buy a piece of the American Dream—even those who could purchase a home outright with cash—at a time when it was affordable—were often prevented from doing so by other discriminatory practices. Housing prices rose rapidly and by the time racially biased laws were changed, and African Americans were allowed these loans, housing prices were prohibitively high. While white suburbanites were able to build equity in their homes, use this equity to invest in college education for their children, and establish a safe, middle-class lifestyle, this was often not an option available for the black population. The ones who had escaped the scarcity of rural living in the South were often stuck in dead-end urban poverty. Sociologist, Charles Abrams, wrote that the FHA adopted policy was based on racial laws that "could well have been culled from the Nuremberg Laws."[18-21]

Today, we see the direct result of these policies. African American families possess the least wealth seen since the Great Depression. A 2014 article published by the Pew Research Center finds: "Wealth inequality has widened along racial, ethnic lines since the end of the Great Recession." The article states that "the racial and ethnic wealth gaps in 2013 are at or about their highest levels observed in the 30 years for which we have data."[18-22] The Pew Research Center article is based on numbers from the Federal Reserve's Survey of Consumer Finances and it finds that white families nationwide have more than *13 times* the net worth of black families, on average, and this is the largest gap since the 1930s. This certainly gives us food for thought for our supposedly "racially desegregated" and "equal opportunity-providing" society.

African Americans Leaving the Blues – and Finding It Again!

Due to increased mechanization of farm labor in the South and emerging jobs in northern industries, black and white sharecroppers gradually left the South. Black blues musicians took their music with them and as a result blues music changed its sound, as musicians allowed their new realities to merge with urban inspiration. In the 1950s, Chess Records in Chicago promoted artists such as Howlin' Wolf, Muddy Waters, Little Walter, and Etta James.

The blues now sounded more edgy, electric, and was created out of a "city" environment compared to earlier styles of country blues. The recording industry called all kinds of African American music "Race Music." This term was a catch-all phrase that did not distinguish among genres such as ragtime, blues, jazz, or gospel, as we do today. Okeh Records, Emerson Records, Paramount Records, and others promoted this music. These record companies discovered that African Americans were a lucrative audience. The music on their labels did not typically have a white audience beyond certain kinds of jazz (Ellington, Armstrong, etc.). By 1949 the music was re-branded by Billboard Magazine as "Rhythm and Blues" (R&B). This term later came to encompass a variety of contemporary (mainly black) genres (e.g., *soul, funk, hip hop, rap*). According to musician and author, Dick Weissman, by the 1960s, artists like Muddy Waters and Howlin' Wolf were increasingly seen as out of sync with younger black blues audiences. By the mid-1960s, whites, in turn, more broadly discovered blues artists. In fact, B.B. King did not get his first major hit until 1970, when "The Thrill is Gone" became a crossover hit, and the majority of record buyers who made it a hit were white.[18-23]

By this time, African Americans no longer saw the blues as a genre with relevance to their lives. Younger blacks distanced themselves from their past by embracing a new reality in which they did not have to rely on the blues' veiled modes of musical communication. Young blacks got a voice as the Civil Rights movement marched on, beginning in the 1950s and gathering steam in the 1960s. In the North particularly, they no longer needed the quiet and indirect ways of remonstration that was necessary for their parents. They valued the "expressive lifestyle" of speaking their mind directly and sometimes forcefully (as through the Black Panther movement, for instance) as opposed to the "depressive strategy" of former times.[18-24] They thus often interpreted the blues as irrelevant, dated, depressive, and inefficient at speaking to their needs, wants, and current situations.

As mentioned previously, the indirectness of blues music had been forged at a time in which direct protest was not possible, for fear of repercussions and punishment. English professor Robert Springer writes:

The bluesman generally feared to bring more trouble on himself than he already had, especially in the South, and this was an important factor in his attitude towards 'writing' a song on a controversial subject . . . In the blues one must listen for protest between the lines. [18-25]

In 1975, Nat D. Williams, who was interviewed for a study by Springer, is quoted as saying:

The black man just couldn't express what he wanted to say; in order to give his master some assurance, he mixed what he had to say: the words served the purpose of keeping the whites happy, [they] were for the whites' benefit very often. [18-26]

To blacks growing up in the 1950s, 1960s, and beyond, the signing of the Civil Rights Act in 1964 and the Voting Rights Act in 1965 meant that they had legal rights—they could officially speak more openly. The language of indirectness and discretion therefore became a symbol of an earlier time when they had to live in constant fear of repercussions—now at least this fear was lessening or transforming. As new and timelier musical styles emerged, the blues was no longer needed as a musical, emotional release valve for the oppressed, and having ever needed such became a gruesome reminder. To young blacks, this music felt like the music of the victimized, and they sought to distance themselves from it.

The blues was largely mute, or very indirect, with regard to politics. Paul Oliver writes that the blues is silent when it comes to most political causes including the Civil Rights movement, Black Muslims, Black Power, etc. And when it comes to commenting on Jim Crow laws and other "political" issues, the blues mentions them only sporadically.[18-27]

In a 1976 article called *The Regulatory Function of the Blues*, Robert Springer further comments that the blues came to represent a "near" taboo to young blacks. Focusing on the future held more vitality and hope:

The blues is a way of coming to grips with daily existence . . . it is a way of expressing the way things are . . . . But for [young blacks] thinking about the future is more vital than singing about reality, and the past is nearly taboo. 18-28

Springer writes that blues historically allowed blacks a kind of "escape in fantasy from repressions imposed upon [them] by society," and it played a role in "social control" allowing the blues to be used as an escape valve to release pent-up tension through music.18-29 Springer here uses the term "social control" as *having an outlet that prevented blacks from discharging aggression in ways that would incur repercussions from whites.* It is no wonder that African Americans sought to distance themselves from such musical styles at that time.

"Happy" blues, the danceable and joyous expressions that were also a big part of the blues universe that allowed tension release, was taken over by new musical expressions. Soul music (a mix of gospel, blues, and jazz) became the "official vehicle of the new black awareness and to some extent, avant-garde jazz on the East Coast and in the big Cities." 18-30 Of course many other genres followed in their wake as well. These new musical manifestations were emotionally more removed from reminders of the past. Writing about his time as a young white blues enthusiast in Chicago in the 1970s, Bruce Iglauer recalled that he experienced young blacks calling blues "Uncle Tom" or "Slavery Time" music, and/or they saw it as the music of the uneducated and hopeless.18-31

In most places in America, blues moved on after the 1960s largely without a large black following. I believe many of the (older) black blues artists who remain today, with few exceptions, are sadly unappreciated and/or under-paid. They often find themselves playing to mainly white audiences who treat them kindly, yet who might resonate more enthusiastically with white blues artists. There might be a shared "group membership" now in white blues that leave the originators of the genre feeling as if they are visitors in their own land—at least with regard to audience demographics and monetary compensation.

After I finished the research, I spoke with a good friend, Joe Louis Walker, about this conundrum. Walker is an African American musician, born in 1949 in San Francisco "in the projects." For him, the blues is many things. Mainly it is a social construct. You can "play the blues," or you can "live the blues," and he points to the harsh economic and social conditions that are at the root of "living the blues." He asserts that when you live the blues, you do not *choose* to play it. You have no way out. The blues, then, becomes a way of life, not a musical expression. Walker has every pedigree and credential as a bluesman. He has played in the White House, played on a Grammy-winning album with B.B. King, has a lifetime achievement award from the Blues Foundation in the USA, and has many other accolades. Still, he finds it difficult to attain financial success as an African American blues artist. Throughout our discussion, he expressed the tension he feels between knowing that black people invented this music, and that white people seem to have an easier time getting known for playing it. At the same time, Walker feels real joy about sharing this musical landscape with humanity, no matter their social class or the color of their skin. And he gives a few hopeful shout-outs to the young, incoming generation of black (and white) blues players. Below are some excerpts from our conversation:

JLW: We're in 1955 Mississippi. You go to the hospital, they fix you. The other guy goes to the hospital, they fix him. I go to the hospital, and they let me bleed to death (laughs). I think I got the blues. I think you seen the blues, and you said: 'Hey listen. You know what? I don't know if I want that blues like that right now that Joe's got, but you know what? I don't like the unfairness in it, and I don't like the BS in it, and I'm gonna dedicate my life to changing it.' That's what Bloomfield did. That's what John Paul Hammond did. That's a big difference. It's a difference between having to play the blues, and growing up and being the blues. . . . But in a way when you get guys like me, Billy Branch, Lucky Peterson, Kenny Neal in a room, it's invariably gonna come up 'Hey man. I wish we had it a little bit better. Why is it that so-and-so and so-and-so and so-and-so just picked up a guitar two days ago, and now they are on the cover of this magazine? Well, but they get known for the blues. We never heard them play the blues! We never heard them play anything . . . You catch my drift?

Marie: Yes I do.

JLW: Ok, so now; this is the situation: So when you say that the blues encompasses us all and we all suffered like that wise man said, yes we do, however it's a little bit of a difference, when you know that you've created something, and you know that you've done something—and all you want is a chance not to have to go through what your daddy went through in hard time Mississippi. But you say: 'Ok. I got a way to get out of here. Everybody tells me I'm Johnny Be Good. Playing a guitar like ringing a bell, but unless my name is John Lennon, I can't get my song played! John Lennon making more off my song than I am, but God bless John Lennon for being good enough.

Marie: Well you know what? It's the darndest problem to have. These are the originators. These are the people that came up with this brilliant methodology to not just play music, but to move through emotions and connect with other people. This is powerful stuff. This is possibly, I mean, after 2000 years of repression of the body, this music came in and—in my way of seeing things— it opened up our humanity again with this incredible gift. And so what is the best thing that we can do to honor this and pay homage?—I mean obviously the blues has gone worldwide. I was in India, and there were Indian people playing the blues. . . . You can go on YouTube and you can see it, and you can be a part of it. So how do we deal with this? What's your suggestion to honor this, and to give back?

JLW: I think number one, what you're doing is great because you ask the question. It's a huge part of the blues because it's—it really speaks to not only—it speaks to our living situation, our political situation, as we are now. As it spoke to before . . . suddenly it got away from being somewhat political, or speaking to the sign of the times, and it's a lot of it now is one guy doing two verses of: "I Lost my Baby" and 78 verses of guitar solo and one of: "I found her."

(Both laugh)

Marie: Wearing a sharkskin suit? Yeah, yeah, yeah.

JLW: And looking like Little Walter, and blowing a harmonica out of his little – and that's great. That's—I call that imprinting gone wild. That's ok.

Marie: (Laughs)

JLW: But it gives people a purpose, doesn't it? It gives people a purpose, and that's great! But what you're speaking about, and I'm speaking about, is the big picture. And I'm very, very cognizant of how I speak when it comes to that situation, because it can be mistaken. So, sometimes I preface it with: I lived in a house with Mike Bloomfield, Buddy Miles, people like that and so many different cats, and being the youngest guy in the room. So when I speak, it's a composite of all these people. But Michael's thing was to try to make it fair for his heroes, because he knew it was never fair. It was always screwed up. The business was just total pirates from Chuck Berry, Smokey Rob- you name it. You know. You're in the business. So he's trying—and the same thing with the English guys. They wanted to make it right. They even recorded their hero's songs to hope they got the money, which they got part of it, but I guarantee that Chessman got a big part of it, and the publishers and what have you. I've met so many people that have made so much difference in our lives: Bonnie Raitt to Mick, they all want their heroes to be treated fairly. I mean that's the first thing Bonnie said when she got those Grammys.

Marie: And you know what? Almost every fan I talked to as part of my research mentioned how important it is that when white people play the blues that they acknowledge, 'Hey this is a song that so-and-so wrote. This is where it comes from. Go listen to these guys.' All of them said how important it was to them that this was paid forward. That there were royalties paid to these people. It is part of the consciousness out there. But that still doesn't make it fair out there. It's still not right.

JLW: Well you know, how does a Kenny Neal, or Joe Louis Walker, or Lucky Peterson fix the problem? How do we fix the problem? We gotta get on somebody's blues cruise and we're 13,000 down the list, and I mean no disrespect. None. Zero. Or we play a festival, and some kid who used to come and see me when he was 14 is now the headliner. And that's OK. That's no problem. But they're telling me how great he is, and that's no problem either.

And I've been—I've played with Earl Hooker. I've played with Matt Guitar Murphy. I've played with people that just, your mouth drops.

Marie: I know your résumé, thank you very much. You're a very impressive fellow.

JLW: But you know what I mean? And so you say: 'Ok, number one: Music's inclusive,' so you don't get exclusive. You know: 'Oh man. Woe's me. I gotta problem. Everybody's got a story.' Like you were saying, everybody's got a story, but the story of these blues is, it's social studies, and if you look at the old guys who invented it, and the reason they invented it: the cathartic thing. Knowing that they weren't gonna be paid for a good day's work. And even if they were, they were gonna get ripped off. Blah, blah, blah, blah. Whatever. And so they invented this here stuff that nobody wanted to play. The guitar wasn't tuned half the time, but it felt so goddamn good, and then everybody wanted to play it. . . . And so you get all these young guys, white, black, whatever, and they're playing it, and they're becoming gazillionaires, and the old guys are saying: 'Whoa. Why can't I make any money?' Now the old guys are dead. Now the guys, like me joke: the old guys are me now. And it's the same fucking thing. I don't like to talk in terms of black and white that much, but I'm a realist. I'm not a politically correct fucking dude. I'm a real cat. You think that here's this music that we—that's largely invented and promoted around the world by us—and between Robert Cray and Gary Clark [Jr.], there hasn't been a young African American blues star. Does anything about that seem right? No, it doesn't, because there's been guys with a hell of talent, so you gotta think that maybe, what is it? Is there a glass ceiling? What is it? What it's doing, is that it's showing young guys, like me when I was young, that I can't be the next Stevie Ray Vaughan. I can't be the next Elvis Presley, but I can sure as hell be the next Buddy Guy, B.B. King, or Chuck Berry. And that's all that entails. Right now going on worldwide, a bunch of young people playing the guitar are from Africa. They are—one of the biggest ones right now, Selwyn Birchwood. I played on his record. Jarekus Singleton. If you look on all the Best of 2014, both of their names come up. There is a big resurgence in blues for young guys like that, because they've grown up seeing people like me. People—not just Buddy [Guy] and them, but people they can relate to—that aren't necessarily hugely famous, that they can relate to—playing music. Like Selwyn, he doesn't mention Stevie Ray Vaughan, not that he doesn't like him, but he mentions Sonny

Rhodes. How many guys you know mention Sonny Rhodes? (Laughs) But Selwyn looks like Hendrix. He doesn't play like him. So in the context, I think that guys like that are drawing younger African Americans to the music, and also the bottom line is you can make a trillion dollars doing a rap record and not pay [any dues]. You do it in your kitchen. You gotta spend a lifetime to play an instrument. You gotta know how to play an instrument, and there's gotta be instruments to play.

Marie: But it's coming back. It's coming back. The younger generations, they see people like you, and they relate in another way. Unfortunately we're still segregated in some ways. Unfortunately there's still incredible unfairness, but there is—there is a trend towards not seeing color so much. And at that point this becomes about that which you're talking about with the guitar. It's an expressive quality. We can express our humanity through this medium that can't be done on a computer. It can't be done with just a beat and a voice. It can't be done in some of those other ways. You need that singing guitar to do it, and at that point it's not about the color; it's about how do we express that which accesses, and unlocks, these sides of ourselves in a way that is just free.

JLW: Well it's mostly not about the color. I just gotta say, because this is still America. It's still the world but it's—here's the good part: Guys like Selwyn Birchwood, Matt Schofield in England, Little [Derek] Trucks. They grew up in a world where they don't want to hear that BS. None of them do. So you have a generation of kids come up and hopefully they will be our leaders in this country. They don't give a shit if two guys fall in love together. They don't give a damn if me and my Jewish wife walk down the street. So the older generation is sort of gonna die off, and if they don't they're gonna have to change. And record companies are changing, because they're sort of becoming almost redundant, but the ones that are surviving are seeing that blues is a big ass tent. I mean huge! It's the one thing I swear to God, where I can be sitting right next to somebody from a totally different political slant, who grew up with a silver spoon, blah-blah-blah-blah-blah, and they're asking me what guitar did I play on my 13th record? What strings did you—? [Laughs]

Marie: But more than that too. They can also stand there and they can hear somebody sing their heart out and they can have—they can cheer up and they can look in each other's eyes and know that at that moment, it doesn't matter. We're all united in that experience.

JLW: And that's the power.

Marie: That's the power right there.

JLW: In another—the allure of the blues and the guys who invented it and all the guys who are trying to keep it going, but mainly the guys who invented, the guys who had a hard time, is that when guys like Bloomfield, guys like John Hammond, guys like Walter Trout*, when they came to their heroes and said: 'Hey man. I want to do this. I'm sincere.' They got more support than a lot of them got from their own parents. And that's the legacy that I got. I've had so many kids in my band. White, black, you name it, girls, boys. And you know what? A lot of them went on further, and I'm so glad that the blues allowed me to be able open that door for them, 'cause they're gonna open the door for somebody else. But to me that is the real power of the blues: all those guys— and they could've been bitter as hell. Muddy Waters could've been—B.B. King—just on and on and on and on and on. And you gotta hunt to find two or three of them that were really pissed off all the time. I knew Albert King really good. He wasn't pissed off all the time. He was real supportive of Stevie Ray Vaughan. I knew Freddy King very well. He let me play his guitar. He wasn't pissed off. But when it came to the blues, if you sat and talked to Albert—all you gotta do is watch Stevie's In Session[18-32] to see how much they really liked each other. I think the world of someone like that, who could go through all that, and still turn around and say 'You know what, you're sincere and you are like my son.' Like Muddy called Bloomfield his first son. He called Johnny Winters his second son. Mick [Jagger], no Mick was second son. Johnny's third son.

Marie: It's powerful. It takes that separation out and I know it's still there, because it's not fair out there, but it's important to go the other route and say:

---

* Walter apprenticed with John Lee Hooker, Big Mama Thornton, Lowell Fulsom, Deacon Jones, Finis Tasby, and many others before he joined Canned Heat and John Mayall's Bluesbreakers.

'Here is something that allows us an experience of utopia, where these kinds of separations don't exist, and what that feels like.' That, to me is genius.

JLW: It is. It really is, and it just transcends everything; it disarms the baggage.

Young, black musicians are beginning to once again embrace the blues as an art form from their cultural heritage. Their audiences are still mainly white baby boomers, but maybe this will gradually change. An African American artist like Fantastic Negrito claims his music is a reaction to a mindless pursuit of wealth and prestige. His musical career is about turning his back on being concerned with "what sells." He states on his website:

'Fuck what's hot now, what moves me?' Negrito turned to the original musical DNA of all American music: the Blues. Adversity, including a near-fatal car accident, primed him to channel his biological and musical forefathers: the blues musicians of the Delta.

Fantastic Negrito attracts younger and racially mixed audiences. He and other African American artists that play and sing the blues today bring hope that the blues genre will evolve to broader and broader relevance as black artists reclaim and re-connect to a new sense of meaning and synthesis of expression: a truly powerful blues revival in the 21st century.

Context-Specific and Universal Dialogue: Race and Resonance

The blues can, as Joe Louis Walker said, disarm the baggage. It has the ability to tell it like it is. It holds within it a potential to unite rather than separate. Here we might begin to find a space where we do not need an excuse for, or condemnation of, the past. The blues teaches us that if we can recognize our own pain, we can also resonate compassionately with the pain of others. The blues holds within it a potential to create an experience of our commonality. This understanding can certainly lead to a more engaged and proactive participation in debates around inequality and social injustices.

Blues clearly builds muscles of compassion and breaks down perceived barriers between people in different circumstances. This feeling of resonance was expressed often by blues fans:

> *Yes I mean we all feel it. . . . I don't have to live in the deep south in the 1920s to understand what those people—I can never fully grasp what they went through—I can never fully grasp the emotions and the feelings—but I have a feeling I understand, at least in part, what they went through. So . . . I don't have to go back and live in 1920s Louisiana to understand what they're going through. . . . We can all identify in some way.*

While we can never fully understand the suffering of another, we can observe that blues music is able to engage our humanity in a field of compassionate resonance:

> *I think a lot of people connect to the feeling of it. They probably have something in them they feel. They'll probably learn that language sooner or later, if they listen to it long enough, or they get involved in it. Just something in their background—they like it, or they connect with it. Or they may have had bad times in their life and not understood what was going on. Then you start listening to other people's stories in the blues.*

As whites embraced blues music in the 1960s, and African Americans largely abandoned it, blues became an access point of protest for some whites. For them, the plight of the black man, marked by suffering, stood in contrast to a more protected and conventional white suburban upbringing:

> *My particular home town was white suburbia; people were very well off. Everybody was working: very well off suburbia—the 2.3 children, the nice manicured lawn. I was born in that generation, during the baby boomer times life was wonderful. All of a sudden, this San Francisco movement came and*

the hippie movement, and we all decided, no, this isn't for us—or so we thought—because I was white middle class: nothing to protest; everything was good. But in my mindset, it just didn't feel right. Nobody was appreciating the arts. They were all into making money, and buying houses, and raising the family into this wonderful utopian society that we grew up in in the late 50s early 60s. . . . But we all had rebelled and a number of us, in my home town, about 13, called ourselves hippies, and yeah picked up on the music and ran with it as a form of protest too, because again African American music—wow it was just the devil's music in some minds, certainly our parents' minds. 'What are you listening to that nonsense for? You should listen to Henry Mancini! That's the music I grew up with.' And show tunes, yeah literally! . . . Black music to me was rebellion. It was against the standard, it was against the norm. To me it was rebellious and rebelling against the parents, and rebelling against society. Because the mindset was still there: the African Americans were oppressed during the 50s and 60s . . . . Watching all this go down on TV on national news . . . , let's support through our association with music! If nothing else, we can certainly be supportive of the civil rights music movement. If we can't be there, we will support through music and it will be a form of rebellion as well.

A few fans expressed clearly that it was almost as if the blues had provided a window into a more "real" world than the suburban Utopia. This was not a typical response. It was however typical to find a depth of fascination in learning about the history of the blues masters of times gone by, and that this immersion deepened appreciation of the music. Art Tipaldi spoke to this multifaceted aspect of African American tradition that drew him to the genre:

The more I read about it the more I wanted to hear the earliest blues I could find. The more I wanted to listen to the blues that was recorded in the 20s by Charlie Patton, and Son House, and Mississippi John Hurt, and Blind Lemon Jefferson, and so many others, because now the blues made sense. Not only as music that came out of this oppression and suffering but also as music that was a relief because, like I say to people sometimes: 'hey the blues really was just party music in the beginning too, and it was a chance for people to blow off steam and dance their tails off for the whole night in these juke joints in Mississippi and throughout the South!' But yeah, going back and starting to read the history of the music I was able to put some more detailed stories with some of the names I had been hearing and I was exposed to so many other names. We all know the myth of Robert Johnson selling his soul to the devil—well it's quite a realization when you discover that Robert Johnson was so far along on the history of the blues. If you asked the casual blues fan many people would say 'Oh he's the man who invented the blues.'

Marie: Oh gosh no.

Art: And you realize 'oh gosh no!' He might have been 3rd or 4th generation coming along. So it helps to read the history and to understand the conditions. Then you start to realize that, in addition to this music being a healing music, in addition to this music being good time party dance music, it was also music of protest, and that there were subtexts within the music and things were being said in the music for these black oppressed sharecroppers that they couldn't say face to face to their white oppressors. Then you start to hear some of these songs so differently. Samson Pitman's 'Cotton Farmer Blues' is all about getting screwed at the end of the year by the ledger that The Man keeps and songs about Mr. Charlie, and even songs about whipping a horse where the man might have been singing about getting even with the oppressive overseer, and the horse became the symbol for that, so then you start to hear these songs in a whole different—[laughter]

Marie: Whole different lights and layers of the treasure hunt if you will keep sort of getting one more rich with meaning. The signifyin'! Once you find that little tidbit and you start going into that—

Art: That's right! You could teach a history course. A history of America in the 20th century through the blues and what it teaches and what it chronicles. Just what you said.

Marie: Yes I agree. That's actually a question that I had later that you already answered [laughter] but back to this notion that there were these horrific conditions. At a seminar that I was at not too long ago the speaker at some point was an African American lady who is a board member at an Urban Habitat Program, and she had just been on a trip back to West

Africa and had connected with the places, where the black people were held before the slave ships came and took them away. She was weeping telling this story about almost being able to feel her ancestors and their fear—and the way the women were treated particularly. . . . She was very, very emotional about it. At the end of her talk, a man stood up and he said: 'I stand here as an Englishman hearing your story and the guilt of my ancestors is so overwhelming to me that I would like to offer you $100,000 for your cause. Would you please accept that?'

Art: Wow.

Marie: It was a very, very intense moment obviously. She happily accepted the money for her center helping at-risk youths. Did you ever connect to such a sense of white collective guilt about our ancestors' deeds regarding their treatment of black people as property, the horrors of slavery, etc?

Art: Huh . . . um . . . that's hard to say. I don't know if I've ever been witness to an event like the one you just described, but I have been—I have certainly seen that in—portrayed within documentaries about slavery and I have been to a certain number of conferences. Especially educational conferences where someone might speak to those horrors either as a guest speaker or someone in the audience and people in the audience will rally around that person with emotional support or—but I can't pinpoint something like that.

Marie: Ok so maybe. Has any sense of—maybe guilt is a strong word— but a sense of sadness about what happened? Has that been a factor in your participation with the blues?

Art: Oh absolutely. Because so much of the music is tied into . . . the history. when I was teaching, there were times when I would be very moved by video or documentaries that I was seeing. I can remember certainly the Scottsboro boys. The case of the 9 boys who were accused of raping white women on a train in Alabama in 1931, and just the whole treatment of them certainly affects you. The killing of Emmett Till in the 50s—[he was a] young black boy in Mississippi who was found at the bottom of the Tallahatchie River for whistling or speaking to a white woman. What was the other one? I used to show a video about the civil rights movement . . . as African Americans in

1962-63 were walking to a vote. They were in a parade and little children were carrying American flags. Little six-seven-eight year-old children—I can vividly see sections of this video where American white police officers are ripping the flags from these children's hands.

Marie: Oh.

Art: And the reaction right there is the same reaction I had the first time I saw it in this news documentary and my students felt the same way. Like: 'oh my god,' and there's this one of this sheriff—I'm doing it with my arm—he's got the flag in his arm, and he's swinging his arm from side to side and the little child is holding on to it and being swung from side to side until he finally rips it from her hand. And they're collecting American flags from African American children whose parents are going to vote. So those kinds of things! Documentaries—PBS documentaries on slavery—which have been excellent, all make you understand—there was one just recently on about abolition called The Abolitionists. It all just makes you understand from a historical point of view, what some of those—just such a small amount of horrors. And you can extrapolate to what an enormously large amount of horror that African Americans first as slaves and as freed slaves went through, and still went through until they were given voting rights in the 60s. There are a lot of historical events that really reached deep into the meaning of the blues and the music.

Marie: So that was sort of a connective tissue, learning about the history between you and your understanding of the blues.

Art: Yeah, again that's not the first thing you do. That comes later. The first thing we all do is we all dance to the music and go: 'Wow this is really cool music!' And then you start to read the story of the music, then you're watching something like I said—it might be a PBS documentary on civil rights—and all of the sudden, you can connect the dots yourself from the music to what you're seeing. You're not necessarily reading a book about how the music was part of that movement, but you can see it and you can think about the music and your own experiences with the music, and you can extrapolate and put the two together.

Interest in the blues can give a whole-brain understanding of context-specific history: where our logical faculties study facts and events as written about in history books, the music adds a more creative and emotionally felt element. When we connect the dots, as Art Tipaldi discussed, a more complete understanding of historical *events* and of *the people* who came before us becomes possible. The blues adds a soundtrack that can allow us to resonate with universal emotions felt by people who experienced them, and also a way for us to connect to a specific era and the events that took place at that time. But as mentioned before, this resonance also carries the risk of us thinking that we know what it was like to walk in the shoes of those who are oppressed. And we won't, and we can't. It is possible, however, to resonate with suffering, even if circumstances are completely different. And many fans felt compassion and rage about the African American plight when they delved into it, and some felt moved to speak up and act. The blues gave them an enhanced perspective on what it is like to be disenfranchised in this world. It was not uncommon either for them to mention that they learned something themselves. As an example, here Thomas Ruf, talks about his discovery of blues music, and what particularly resonated with him:

Marie: *What was it about this music that hit you like that? That spoke to you?*

Thomas: *Well a lot of it was the social consciousness. . . . These guys were poor but they found a way to express it and use this music to pull themselves out of their misery. Take them out of their poor surroundings and put them out on the road, make them leave and go someplace else and travel and find a better life.*

Marie: *And how did that resonate with you?*

Thomas: *Well, I guess if you know all my biography, it resonated in the way that I sort of did the same thing. I started to travel the world following a blues band. That was my ticket to starting to travel, getting to see the world, and*

*getting to meet people. Learning how to communicate with people, because it
was impressive to see how these guys could communicate and relate and make
people smile and make people start talking to them. I learned a great deal.*

Thomas was referring to his travels working with Luther Allison and seeing
how the man, the music, and the approach of a more direct, embodied style
was transformative. He told me a story about how he experienced the blues—
via Luther Allison's appearance in Germany—and how it could communicate
across language and ethnic barriers:

*Thomas: I then promoted my first show with Luther. I was working in
the . . . church youth club at the time in my hometown. I got to get the city [to]
give me . . . the city hall, which I still don't know how that happened because I
was only 18! I couldn't sign the contract—but they would let me put on the
show! I didn't know anything about security, or how to put on the show. I just
put up posters and did what I thought at the time to do. And in some kind of
way it worked. About 300 people showed up and it was an amazing show!
What really impressed me was what happened after the gig. Luther came to
me and told me that they wanted to eat after the show—and that was
something new to me. This band wants catering—or food? Or all this stuff
that go along with it—so I didn't know what to do. Because in my home
town, there was nothing open after like 10 o'clock: everything was closed. It
was a very small town so I called this old lady that was my friend. She sort of
was the outsider in the little town. I guess that's why she liked me, and I liked
her. Also she came from a whole different kind of background. This old lady
had this bar that was also a restaurant in my little village, so I called her up
and asked her if she could stay open. I explained that I had this band—this
concert—and they wanted to eat, and if she could cook something? She said:
'Yes,' and promised to keep her joint open. After the show—about midnight
—we bring Luther and the band to this . . . bar and to this old lady . . . and
the window shades were down! The bar was already closed because it was
after-hours. But there was still something happening inside, there were some
people inside, and there were these old Black Forest musicians performing in
there. Like three musicians with a fiddle and these instruments that they
have . . . the Black Forest folklore music and they were doing waltz music in
3 . . .*

Marie: ¾ beats

Thomas: And then Luther got so excited that we were eating there, and after we were done eating, he jumped up: Grabbed his guitar and jumped on stage and smiled at these guys, and these guys were like 75-80 years old, really old German men. Nobody spoke a word of English. Luther didn't speak a word of German, and he just started jamming with these guys. I just realized that this black man is probably the first black man that these old Black Forest guys ever saw.

Marie: Right.

Thomas: Because where I grew up there weren't too many black people around. . . . And they started to jam! They found a way to communicate and have fun together. And then the old lady, who owned the bar, she came out with a cane with the double head on top. She got all excited. She joined in there—started to push the cane up and down in time with the beat and so on. It was really incredible. It was the very first time I think my business was rocking. I had money and payment, so business interaction was rocking, and it started a connection that went on for a very long time.

Marie: Still going.

Thomas: . . . I just realized that if you used a language like the music, or like the blues, you can really cross borders and cross barriers and communicate— even with people that you don't share the language with, or people you don't share the background with. You don't share the same ethnic holidays or religion. You have nothing in common, but still you can communicate: get through and make them . . . like you and you like them. It was a beautiful thing. It was just very beautiful.

Marie: That's such a unique story you have because you really—I know those places in the Black Forest with the musicians you describe, and this black man coming in there with this completely different way of being, what did he do in that room to them?

Thomas: They all lit up. Everybody in that room lit up through that presence and through the power of music . . . everything was loose (laughter). Thomas: They started jamming like crazy. He inspired them to play harder and louder and better and faster.

Marie: (laughter)

Thomas: It was hilarious in a way, but it was great. It was a very memorable night. Everybody who was there will never forget that. That was really incredible. And it kind of set the path. I wanted of course to meet this guy again and do another concert the following year, and it wasn't the last either. Many, many were to follow!

Later, Thomas commented on the elements of blues music that attract blues fans *today*. He reflected on the felt sincerity, the transparency, and the lack of glitz and glamour found in blues history:

Thomas: Historically, I guess it was an art form of very poor people. This is something that attracts a lot of white middle class white people of our type: that they respect the music for coming from very limited sources. There's not—it's not music of the fancy guitars and the shiny clothes and all this. It is bare bones. It's the kind of music where you really have to be born to play it. There's nothing you can really fake. There's no . . . false motivations. Your motivations have to be pure, because if your motivation is to become rich, or to become famous, or to become whatever, you will be looking for something else. You will not be looking into a career in the blues.

I related to Thomas the same story I had told Art (and all the blues fans I interviewed) about the Englishman offering $100,000 to the at-risk youth organization and asked if he ever felt an element of guilt about being white, and how our ancestors exploited black men and women. Thomas answered that he feels that guilt can be inherited, yet there is not much we can do about it. Having grown up in Germany—in the post WWII climate—he was used to dealing with implications of ancestral guilt:

Thomas: I want to compare this to the way I felt about being German. When I started to travel outside of Germany as a young man, I realized what I never had before—of course I learned about the Holocaust in school, and about Nazi Germany and all—that there was the problem with my ancestors, like you said, I got to travel to these countries and I learned about the problem. I could feel the distance in how a lot of people treated me: 'Oh it's a German guy.' And so I was a German guy among the Americans. The German guy among the Americans and the French. And I could feel that we were—that we were liked—yet a lot of people were still skeptical and started making comments and jokes. This also happened when I started to work professionally with people who were Jewish from Brooklyn. They started to make these really terrible Nazi/Jew jokes. They really got me, and tried to corner me, and tried to make me turn red and stuff. But I could never feel . . . the emotional connection of feeling guilty, because I always felt that I'm really sorry about how it was before. I have . . . compassion, and I feel sorry about the stuff that happened, but I don't feel sorry in a way that I feel guilty because I'm a German. Because I feel this has nothing to do with what I did in my life. That really I cannot relate to that in terms of building guilt feelings for me personally. I understand that guilt, and that it is a burden that will last for generations, not just the one generation, but more generations to follow, because it was just so huge. But it was nothing that I can take personally.

Bruce Iglauer talked about the notion of the blues historically as the music of the oppressed. He bemoaned the lack of more mainstream knowledge and awareness about the genre.

Bruce: Most Americans (of all colors and ethnicities) are very unaware of the history of the blues, the creators of the music, the culture that blues sprang from, and any knowledge of the current blues scene. We don't need a blues museum for blues fans; they're the ones who already know about the music. We need blues awareness to be injected into mainstream culture. I wish that more mainstream pop artists - like what Bonnie Raitt and Eric Clapton have done - would present blues artists as opening acts on their tours. I wish that television producers who present live music cared more about blues. Ultimately, though, it will be an artist who will be the 'bridge' to bring awareness to the tradition, perhaps someone like Jack White. We blues insiders are less equipped to do that, sadly. So this isn't an answer, because I don't know the answer. I do know that blues tends to be perceived as 'for blues fans only' and not as a music that speaks to a mainstream audience (except perhaps in the form of flashy 12-bar guitar solos). That perception must be overcome.

Marie: Have you heard the phrase "keepin' the blues alive?" If so, what does it mean to you personally?

Bruce: I hate this phrase because it implies that the blues is virtually dead, like the Monty Python character in the plague sketch who says: 'I'm not dead yet!' The reality is that the only way that blues will avoid becoming a museum piece (like New Orleans jazz or big band swing) is if it is made relevant to contemporary audiences. Old styles of blues are, in a sense, 'dead.' Who under the age of 40 dances to a shuffle? Who cares about plowing behind a mule? The only way for blues to remain a living art and culture is for blues to adapt itself to a current audience both lyrically and rhythmically, and at the same time maintain the elements of tension and release and honest, true-to-life and angst-filled storytelling that have been intrinsic parts of blues all along. So, should there be blues with hip-hop beats and lyrics like: 'I woke up this morning and my hard drive crashed'? Yes, that's exactly what I mean. I am the recipient of two "Keeping the Blues Alive" awards, and I would much prefer they were called "Carrying The Blues Into The Future" awards.

Iglauer also addressed the blues as an art form that requires some personal involvement; it is not just "background music" to have a good time to, but rather music that offers potential for deeper engagement.

Bruce: In general, I think that hardcore blues fans have a sense of joint 'ownership' of the blues. So I like being among knowledgeable blues fans who can appreciate a live performance with a lot of soul and intensity, and who really feel the music. There are a lot of fans for whom blues is a party music and nothing more, and who aren't interested in the history or tradition, just in the good times. I have a harder time with those fans, who often seem to want to go to a show to take pictures of one another and post them on Facebook. Having a party with blues is fine. Having a party with blues as background music doesn't make me very happy. I still enjoy sitting around with other hardcore blues fans listening to recordings and talking about them, and I prefer to go to gigs with real blues fans who love the tradition. I think a lot of us

blues fans think we've found the Holy Grail of music and nothing else
compares. I suppose other niche music fans feel the same way, but I don't care!
In my heart I believe that blues is the most important, most emotionally
fulfilling music ever. And I'm sticking to that opinion!

Iglauer echoes the sentiment of John Ruskey that the blues should not be considered solely entertainment. According to Iglauer, it requires veneration in how it is appreciated that elevates it from being sheer glossy, superficial entertainment. But I think he is saying something else as well that aligns with what blues fans stated en masse: that the blues requires authentic connection rather than the kind that is propagated in a superficial (mainstream) "selfie" culture. It might be difficult, though, to know when this connection is authentic or not. How do we determine that someone who is laughing and taking selfies at a blues concert cannot five minutes later be deeply engaged with the music, and have deep knowledge about it? And if they don't, is their enjoyment of the music and the social scene less valuable than someone who treats the blues with more serious consideration?

In my interviews, I did not come across blues fans who solely enjoyed the blues as a vehicle for having a good time. Many blues fans are indeed attracted to the levity and fun times at concerts, festivals, and shows, but they are also engaged in other elements of blues for varying reasons, and this engagement often includes a fairly solid understanding of historical, social, and cultural elements of the origins of the blues. They also largely appreciated more modern and contemporary manifestations of the music, which was similarly very meaningful to them. Knowing blues lineages and being able to cite lyrics from the 1930s are not the only ways to engage with the art form. Each blues fan or industry professional I interviewed had their own interpretations of why blues music was important to them. But one key element remains: it was important to them, and they all expressed experiencing an emotional engagement with the music.

It would be interesting to go back to the times of early bluesmen and women and hear their take on what the blues meant to them. My guess is that, for artists, it was a way of making a bit of money that didn't entail backbreaking labor behind the mule or cotton gin. My guess is that it was first and foremost because the music provided entertainment that their audiences danced and swayed to on Saturday nights. It was also a way of connecting and bonding—a way to find solace, escape, and have fun. It was a way of articulating that which could not otherwise be spoken. The blues then had many of the same functions that it has today. But it is not too much of a stretch to say that blues audiences in the 1920s, 30s, 40s, and 50s mainly enjoyed the blues as a means of entertainment. They were not judged by blues authorities if they did not know the history of the blues or didn't appear to take it seriously. Some might say: "They lived the blues—they were blues history," and yes, but in some ways, so are we today. We live, create, listen to, and partake in the modern blues experience. And just as it does today, the blues did something else then: it flew under the radar and spoke to deeper layers of the psyche. I am sure some of the early listeners had a more superficial relationship with the music. They came to be seen, flirt, and be held in community. Others might have listened more intensely and been able to really "travel" in time and space as they let the music take them. But I don't think any of them sat down and analyzed the deeper meaning of the music as it played. I don't think any of them treated the music with a sense of serious contemplation. That was likely counterproductive to what the music was all about. The blues functioned as a community ritual: a place to straddle the sacred and profane in an environment that allowed release and free expression. The blues has a dual nature imbedded in its make-up. Ralph Ellison writes:

> *The blues speak to us simultaneously of the tragic and the comic aspects of the human condition and they express a profound sense of life shared by many Negro Americans precisely because their lives have combined these modes. This has been the heritage of a people who for hundreds of years could not celebrate birth or dignify death and whose need to live despite the dehumanizing pressures of slavery developed an endless capacity for laughing at their painful experiences. This is a group experience shared by many Negroes, and any effective study of the blues would treat them first as poetry and as ritual. [Leroi] Jones makes the distinction between classic and country blues, the one*

being entertainment and the other folklore. But the distinction is false. Classic
blues were both entertainment and a form of folklore.[18-33]

Whether entertainment, folklore, ritual, poetry, or something else, the blues might be interpreted too protectively by both Leroi Jones and modern blues aficionados alike when they seek to pigeonhole its expression. The risk of doing so is to unwittingly contribute to an interpretation of the blues as an irrelevant dinosaur rather than treating it as a living entity with a beating heart. Even when the intention is to keep it alive and relevant, the underlying agenda might be to afford a certain reverence toward it, or to interpret it through a purist's lens that might deem certain kinds of lyrics or various musical elements as "not bluesy enough." It might be prudent, as we seek a relevant role for blues music into the future, to exercise caution when we interpret certain elements of new blues as irrelevant with regard to what constitutes "real blues." Modern blues "protectors" might hold the notion of "adherence to tradition" the same way some fundamentalist religions refuse to incorporate views that are seen as heretical. But enforcing this puritan view of the blues carries the risk that it straps new blues expression into a dogmatic, backward-looking straitjacket rather a framework in which new inspiration can sprout and grow. Fans generally expressed that their appreciation for the blues develops over time, creating deeper and deeper engagement and enjoyment. It does not, however, develop as a result of forced, intellectual, or rational thought processes or theories about whether rock guitar solos, hip-hop elements, certain kinds of attire, language, or rhythms, etc. are "allowed." It either hooks fans or it doesn't. We cannot expect growth of the blues as an artistic genre if we presuppose that it can only grow within certain intellectual parameters. When blues music connects powerfully and emotionally with an audience, then it obviously serves a need.

Can the blues go mainstream without losing its integrity? Arguments could be made for both sides. The data showed that there is an element of something counter-cultural or slightly rebellious in blues music that blues boomers connected strongly to, which per definition places blues music outside of popular culture. When it comes to determining if the blues contains elements of subtle or indirect means of protest even today, we have to consider what we are protesting and why. For some blues fans, it might be protest to even go to a blues club rather than a country club. The definition of this protest—or desire to explore outside the realm of convention—is as individual as we are. For some, elements of protest, social justice, and connection to blues music work in concert as a meaningful portal to history. And for them, identification with, and understanding of, African American blues music, offers an indirect element of protest against their own more protected, but also often more emotionally suppressed, backgrounds. One might say that at a time when African Americans no longer needed the veiled and indirect modes of expression embedded in the concept of signifyin' to survive emotionally and physically, it became an element that whites latched on to. Through their love of blues music, they could indirectly—or properly distanced—access emotional transparency and find release that was otherwise hard to find. These elements of blues that invoked slightly counter-cultural protest *combined* with emotional transparency became powerful methods of release that flew under the radar of social convention— but now for whites. And if the relevance of the blues thus became important and emotionally sustaining by largely filling these needs for members of white culture, it makes further sense that it lost much of its appeal to most African Americans. Especially when we factor in that blues music was tied to an oppressive historical reality in which an entire group of people, their people, for way too many years, was stuck with no way out.

Nonetheless, whatever may be the color of our skin, our social standing and cultural triggers, each of us is trying to come to terms with the inherent dual nature of who we are. This innate ambiguity creates a sense of ambivalence that our culture does not teach us how to deal with. We are, however, taught how to idealize and vilify, and this is how we are taught to see ourselves and others: as heroes or villains, or as winners or losers. If we choose to leave this mindset behind, and instead look beyond these distinguishers, the study of blues fans indicates that there is a bigger gift inherent in the blues: it can bridge duality by furthering understanding of the fact that we all contain the lover and the scorned, the abuser and the abused, the victor and the vanquished. The African trickster deity, Èsù-Elegbara, who is symbolized in Yoruba folklore by the crossroads, shows up in our lives, and in the life of the blues. Here we are invited to visit with confounding paradoxes in our lives, such as why do "bad" things happen to "good" people? When we sit at the crossroads of our existence, feeling the tension of uncertainty—when faced with disease, death, and detriment—the blues invites us to simply visit with how we feel, and gives us the potential to dialogue, describe, connect and be real, rather than to judge, hide, and deny. However, when we decide to board the train of our enculturation and dissect our emotional experiences into bits, the inherent centrifugal force of such scrutiny spins our understanding of it into parts again: vanquished OR victor, abuser OR abused, right OR wrong, weak OR strong. We are conditioned to seek absolute and finite answers to our emotional makeup, and often find these answers inadequate to describe and explain how we feel.

The blues doesn't play by those rules. The blues provides musical and lyrical ways of describing emotions that open us to acceptance of the complexity of our emotional nature. One can say that the blues offers us a gift given through the African American experience that helps us reconnect with ourselves through finding resonance with others. It encourages us to explore our paradoxical nature instead of condemning it and to seek out solutions that are process-oriented, flexible, and that change and merge as our emotional realities adapt through internal and external dialogue. First and foremost, through a love of blues music and its history we may learn some of the hard lessons of our past and walk forward with a desire to change injustices, because we understand a little more about the agony and long-term imbalances in their wake.

The blues is many things to many people, but blues boomers indicated that, at its core, blues music encompasses possibilities for discovery, acknowledgment, validation, and experience of connection precisely at the paradoxical crossroads of our lives where it hurts so good. There is a sustaining and sustainable power inherent in the blues that extends beyond delivering awesome musical enjoyment. And thus, the blues can still change the world: one person at a time!

Part IV

Blues Healing:
Now and in the Future

Chapter 19:

The Healing Potential of Blues

Pat was a mystical person and came from a world of mysticism. He was deep beyond his music . . . to his spiritual connection to the music of the universe. Geniuses like that are messengers from god. They have that gift, that connection with the source of the divine. I believe that about these great ones. They aren't just great by accident. They're tuned in like a radio to say or do or be anything—just a transmitter of invisible airwaves passing through them.[18-34]

Pat Hicks (GIT founder) speaking about guitarist, Pat Martino

I love watching musicians really "get into the music." As they let go, the music takes flight. At this point, I typically surrender: I, too, start to move with the music. If I am at home listening, I might temporarily feel slightly transported by the music in other ways. It is not just blues music that has this effect on me, but typically it is music that wouldn't exist if the blues hadn't been there first. Blues fans told me again and again that *this* is one of their favorite experiences with the music: allowing it to wash over them, and, for a moment, forget time and place.

In this final section, of exploring the relevance of blues music today, we will navigate and investigate the more mysterious elements of it: those that are the most difficult to describe. The focus here will be on how blues music facilitates experiences in more ethereal ways, such as in light, trance-like states. It is in this realm of the experiential that blues has the potential to reach beyond our five senses and engage a synchronistically enabled, virtual warp drive. Blues music can help transform our perceptions, at least momentarily, in a (slightly) altered state of awareness. Such states can be healing; they facilitate connection, authentic communication, and access to rituals in which we feel restored and renewed. Many interviewees sought to describe how blues helped them step out of their everyday M.O.:

> *It's just a relief from everything. It's a relief from your obligations. It's a relief from your roles, your society roles. It's a relief from all of that. It is just . . . stepping outside of your day-to-day into a different place, and just feeling— letting yourself feel! And I, personally I am not—my ambitions are on a pretty even keel most of the time, right? I don't bounce back and forth a lot, like some people do. And that's fine. That's a good thing, but there are times when you just need to not worry about anything else, and just feel it. And that's where I can do it.*

Situation-Specific Healing

Of course, blues is first and foremost music, not medicine. But blues music does contain elements that are restorative, soothing, and healing under certain circumstances. Accessing a healing power in blues music is dependent on the individual's perceptions, feelings of being safe, ability to be in the moment, level of initiation, and openness to experiential realms. The relevance of blues music as a healing modality is thus situation-specific, context-dependent, and individually gauged, even when it is shared communally. Blues music is unpredictable. It depends on many internal as well as external factors to produce a certain outcome for an individual or group. Ethnomusicologist Gilbert Rouget cautioned that music *per se* does not create trance states; rather, it only "socializes" it, makes it visible, and facilitates a certain emotional "climate."[19-35] In other words, a certain musical expression, lyrical application, or rhythm, by itself, does not automatically create or bring on a light trance state; *it is dependent on many different external, contextual, and social factors, as well as on the readiness, and willingness, of the participant.*

Blues boomers surveyed and interviewed found that blues music occasionally has the potential to bring on a slightly altered state of awareness.

They did not know how it happened, and a few even stated that they would prefer not to know, which is indicative of the reverence and mystery surrounding the blues. A remarkably high percentage, namely 91 percent (although only 71 percent of European blues fans) agreed that listening or participating in the blues can be an almost spiritual experience. Eighty-four percent agreed that it's all about the guitar, and that blues guitar can speak things that words cannot.

When asked why they are blues fans, and to pick among 21 statements, as I referred to previously, the one most frequently chosen was that the blues moves them emotionally, followed by the statement that the blues feels less commercial and more authentic. The third most frequent response, however, was that the blues is good for their soul, but they were just not sure why. Fourth in frequency was that the blues seems more organic and "real." The fifth most popular response given was that blues is just in their blood. Clearly, as numbers three and five indicate, part of the mystery of blues music is the fact that it can be observed as "doing something," yet that "something" is difficult to describe without using the language of the mystery ("blood" and "soul"). Ninety-two percent (yet only seventy-four percent of European blues fans) found they had experienced the healing elements of the blues. Likewise, eighty-four percent of all blues fans surveyed stated that they felt less anxious and hopeless after listening to blues. It was clear from the data that blues music provides relief from what blues boomers expressed as a sense of disappointment with our current world, and it mitigates feelings of worry and anxiety.

As we dug deeper into the interviews, we found that blues boomers fell roughly into three groups along the continuum of healing potential with regard to the degree of impact with two smaller groups and a much larger one.

For all the groups, the music obviously provided is primary function of musical enjoyment, play time and entertainment. In addition, for one of the smaller groups, the blues was hailed as a literal lifesaver and was appreciated for extreme, personally experienced, healing potential; here fans asserted that their engagement with blues music helped to keep them alive or sane. For the vast majority, blues offered a moderate healing potential (although it was not typically talked about as such). Here blues offered them perspective on their own and other's lives, respite, emotional recognition, and resonance in community. For the other small group, their engagement with the music simply offered slight mood enhancements.

Blues boomers did not refer to any single, dominant way in which the blues offered healing. The form of healing varied from fan to fan, and from situation to situation. Several mentioned that the blues had entered their life at a time of crisis and helped them cope. After that initial experience, they valued the blues as an invigorating force and subsequently drew on its healing potential. Others felt blues was just slightly restorative, incorporating it as part of their daily rhythm. Here are a few examples of fans talking about being healed by the blues, in different ways, and to various degrees. First from one of the smaller groups, where fans stated that blues music was a literal life-saver to them:

> *The blues makes me happy. It's like a drug, like an endorphin rush. I haven't done drugs in many years, but I can tell you that the feeling is the same. I was in a really bad stage after a death in my family, and one of my blues buddies came to me personally, and we got to be really close. And had it not been for him, the blues, and that guitar, I wouldn't be here today. When he couldn't think of words to say to me, he'd sit down and play the guitar for me, and when we couldn't function with that anymore, we'd put on our dancing shoes, and go to a blues concert. I literally would not be here today without the blues, because I would not have met him. I would not have known that guitar, and I wouldn't know that feeling. . . . The blues saved my life. It took me through times, and it's still taking me through times that words and medication can't.*

Here are two examples from the majority group:

> *I've had depression problems all my life and music gets me out of that. I don't have to go on Zoloft and all this crap. I started going on a tangent, to go hear live music . . . and I run off by myself and spend 3 days at a festival.*

And:

> *To me, the blues is more relevant now than it ever was. And especially emotional when I play myself. Because to me, that's my only real escape from the daily grind of what you have to deal with, with honor, but then to be able to go play—and blues is the only thing that you can play that has a genuine—that you can let that out. Just like the old guys did. That's how they let that out. They got on those guitars, and they wrote those songs, and they sang them with all their hearts, and that's how you get it out. You let it out that way. So yeah, blues now is more relevant than ever. Because it's—it's the one thing that takes you into another plane. Takes you on another—that next higher dimension—if you will. Where you're connecting on a much higher level, you know, to the spirit itself.*

And finally, here is a representative response from the second smaller group of blues boomers, who simply found it provided a nice musical lift in their lives:

> *It just makes me feel good. Get it out. . . . We're all dancing, and singing along, and dancing, and people were dancing—well there was no place to dance in the place—but at our seat and just—it was definitely magic at that moment. So it depends. And it's . . . it's the kind of music that gets me toe tapping, and is brilliant at lifting me up.*

Devil's Music -
and the Healing (Altered) States in Blues

Some neuroscientists point to the beneficial qualities of "being in the moment," as experienced in meditative states. This is demonstrated in the work by Rick Hanson, Richard Davidson, Andrew Newberg, and Mark Robert Waldman. Through hypnotherapy, the healing potential of hypnotic states is also well established. Trance-like and even psychedelic states of consciousness have been instrumental in healing in native cultures all over the globe, tens of thousands of years before psychology concerned itself with the health of the human psyche.[19-36] When blues fans enter into an altered state of awareness, they typically do not experience big, earth-shattering alterations of perception. Blues offers, instead, relatively minor journeys into the experiential that seem to add a welcome break from everyday reality. It happens in imperceptible, subtle, and mysterious ways. But it is clear from the study that this "embodied and almost spiritual" aspect of the blues was valued and appreciated immensely.

The fact that light forays into slightly altered states of consciousness happen when we let go, and let the blues take over is undoubtedly a part of the reason why blues music historically was labeled "Devil's Music." It offered a ride into a territory that was seen as the sole domain of the church— the sacred—but with an added dimension of spontaneous and often sensual physicality. The blues could be freely experienced on back porches, in living rooms, at dances, and in juke joints, and did not depend on preachers, tithes, a congregation, or formal religious supervision or guidance. One might say that our engagement with the blues can facilitate experiences in which we can merge our minds and our bodies, our thoughts and our emotions, and our spirituality and our sensuality. The blues offers an ordered musical structure in which we can claim, and find expression for, the chaotic elements of our lives. As such, blues music is a powerful force that, if we allow it in, can help us express, unite, transform and heal.

When misunderstood however, blues has historically been viewed as instigator of, or a catalyst for, lawlessness, demon worship, promiscuity, and chaos. The blues defied religious dogma, and this struck deep fear into the hearts of those who felt they needed to conform or make others conform. Blues temporarily transported, freed, and lifted people out of their troubles— threatening the very domain organized religion had traditionally monopolized. Those who labeled the music as being that of the devil strove to be seen as rule-abiding and conventional themselves; they did not want to create trouble, appear rebellious, or disobey authority. For many black people, after generations of slavery and with Jim Crow looking over their shoulder, going against convention wasn't just undesirable; it was dangerous. For people of the suburban mindset living in the postwar climate of the 1950s, it was easy to view the music that broke color barriers and allowed people to feel transported "out of their heads" and into their bodies, as "of the devil." This music was unpredictable—it did something to those who let it take them over. Therefore, citizens seeking respectability, both white and black, at various times through history, have joined in a fear-and-smear campaign to repel the spirit of the blues and blues inspired music, especially when their children were involved.

But what happens when we experience a slightly altered state of awareness through our enjoyment of blues, or blues-based music? What is a "blues trance" anyway? The compiled data were clear: it happens! Therefore, in order to understand and explain the phenomenon, I looked to other research on the subject. In *Music and Trance: A Theory of the Relations between Music and Possession*, Ethnomusicologist Gilbert Rouget proposes: "Trance is always associated with a greater or lesser degree of sensory over-stimulation – noises, music, smells, agitation—ecstasy, on the contrary, is most often tied to sensorial deprivation—silence, fasting, darkness." [19-37] However, David Aldridge and Jörg Fachner counter in their book about music and altered states that there are "many different and, in part, contradictory definitions of the term 'trance' (from the Latin *transire* for 'passing through') or 'ecstasy' (from the Latin *exstasis* for 'to be out of one's head') in the literature.[19-38] According to Rouget's definitions, slightly altered state of consciousness that can be induced by blues music would certainly be considered "trance" and not "ecstasy," since it is not brought on by sensory deprivation, but rather by immersion in a universe of sound. However, according to the Latin definitions, ecstasy, as well as trance, are both fitting descriptions for this phenomenon. The sensation of musical immersion in the blues can be cathartic, as in *moving through* emotions, and ecstatic, as in being in a transcendent state, where, for a moment, time and place cease to have meaning and one is "out of one's head." According to descriptions by blues fans, such experiences often occur in combination. In the following however, I predominantly use the term "trance" although according to the Latin definitions, both trance and ecstasy certainly are appropriate descriptors for what fans described as happening in their engagement with blues music.

In his book, *Music, the Brain and Ecstasy*, Robert Jourdain points to the transformative potential inherent in the experience of ecstasy. It can be pleasant and profound. He writes:

> But ecstasy can be more than extreme pleasure, more than merely raising gooseflesh. Ecstasy melts the boundaries of our being, reveals our bonds to the external world, engulfs us in feelings that are 'oceanic.' A defining trait of ecstasy is immediacy. . . . Ecstasy happens to our selves. It is a momentary transformation of the knower, not merely a transformation of the knower's experience. [19-39]

In the interviews, blues fans talked about these kinds of experiences to a considerable degree, as we will see in the following chapters. They did not use words such as "trance states" or "ecstasy" but rather descriptors such as "slip out of myself," "merge with something greater than myself," "sense of timelessness," a "lifting," "state of euphoria," or "spiritual experience." These all shared the common element that they were pleasant and somehow just *slightly* beyond normal everyday awareness. To start, here is an example:

> Just the feeling—the gut feeling going directly into a state, I guess you'd call it, that I go into personally when I'm listening to good blues music—I go into a state of euphoria. It raises your emotions up, and down, and sideways, forward, and under. . . . It can take me up, it can take me down; it can

take me around the corner and bring me back. It's just an emotional state I go into. . . . That's my source of relief. Many have gone through depression, but people learn how to play the blues, it can really bring you around. Gives you a way of telling, or talking, to somebody that normally you just wouldn't do.

The immediacy that Jourdain talks about was frequently referred to as well. The musicians can take the crowd with them on a journey into uncharted territory of musical experience, where the simple structure of the blues acts as a basic requirement for a shared exploration into everyday, as well as, occasionally, mystical realms. A few blues fans made very descriptive, dismissive comments indicating that talking about blues music in this way was "pretentious psychobabble." Many comments however were very clear about the fact that many fans used blues to rest "in the moment," and that it could transport them. Here are but a few examples:

I become a conduit for the music.

[I] get lost in the music.

It takes me away to a place where I'm just listening and not thinking of all the garbage going on around me.

Well-performed, passionate blues music can dictate your emotions like no other genre. The music can take your mind and your spirit to places that only you can be led to. This can be a very healing, often spiritual, process.

In our modern world, such experiences might be relegated to the realm of the religious, and therefore, when they happen spontaneously in the very secular setting of a blues concert, we may not be prepared to recognize or value them for what they are. And some might also be uncomfortable about the thought of spirit moving outside of established boundaries of conventional religion. These spiritual qualities of a slightly altered state of awareness are subtle, although they hold potential to be deep. Blues boomers verified that these types of experiences were important to them. Here again, it is important to caution that all of these elements often exist side by side, and separating them is only meaningful for the purpose of description. In the following, we will briefly explore the following elements of blues as they emerged in the modern blues fan's experience:

- Mystical Language
- Immersion
- Co-Creation
- Tension and Release
- Improvisation
- Rhythm

Mystical Language

Initiation (see Chapter 16) is an important factor as to whether someone will be able to experience the more ethereal elements of blues music. Many blues fans enter into appreciation of blues through a portal of the experiential. This component of musical experience is difficult to describe, much like the emotional "language" that we covered before. Mystical "language," however, is even more difficult to describe because of its illogical or nonsensical nature. Again, even if we have a hard time verbalizing these experiences, we can certainly observe and describe them circumstantially. There are a few experts in the field, and first, let us visit with one of the most accomplished in the study of a kind of language that makes no rational sense. He is one of my teachers, and I consider him to be a stunningly brilliant and visionary, yet humble and unassuming human being.

For a lifetime, professor of philosophy and psychiatrist, Raymond Moody, has studied the "language of the unintelligible" from various vantage points, and with great devotion. He states that this kind of language simply does not make sense within our normal parameters of understanding. He has observed that his students of philosophy wish to take "corrective action" when they find themselves saying something that is nonsensical, even as they explore the topic of unintelligibility. They quickly want to "reconsider and modify and reformulate until their words convey definite meaning," or they simply get "flustered and give up."[19-1] In a consensus reality, as per Charles Tart's definition, shame or a sense of isolation is often attached to not making sense because one breaks the implicit rules of common "enculturation."[19-2] By adulthood, therefore, nonsense is often relegated to nursery rhymes and children's books by authors such as Dr. Seuss and Lewis Carroll. Or it might appear in poetry. Moody states that "nonsense enters into every human life. And if they reflect, almost everyone can bring to mind events in their lives in which it played a significant role." Moody claims that nonsense has "far-reaching psychological and [beneficial] medical implications."[19-3] Likewise, he finds that nonsense is a language used to describe thoughts and experiences when we are in a hypnagogic state between wakefulness and sleep, and that is a language we use when we are under severe, or life-threatening, stress. Moody quotes G.K. Chesterton's observation—made in reference to Lewis Carroll, who was a "serious and conventional" man in daily life— that "the idea that lies at the back of all nonsense— [is] *the idea of escape*" [emphasis added].[19-4] Further, he refers to Aldous Huxley's remark: "Nonsense is an assertion of humankind's spiritual freedom despite *all the oppressions of circumstance*" [emphasis added].[19-5]

Historically, themes of both "oppression" and "escape" are well established in the blues. Again the blues meets us at a crossroads, where we lack words to describe the process of the language that works, because it often surprises us by its oxymoronic qualities: "It hurts so good," for instance, makes no rational sense. Below is a brief interview excerpt with B.B. King talking to Tavis Smiley about his mother:

King: Oh, she was—with a strap or something? Oh, she could beat you nicely.

Tavis: Yeah (laugh). Beat you nicely.

King: I would say that…

Tavis: That sounds oxymoronic, but I take it. She could beat you nicely.

King: I don't know what that means. What's that mean?

Tavis: You can't beat nobody nicely, but I take your point (laugh). I know what you're trying to say. I get it. That's what I love about the blues. If you listen, you know what they're trying to say.[19-6]

Here, Smiley implicitly talks about the language of the blues as saying much more "if you listen," with a few simple words uttered at the intersection of realities, at the crossroads of human experience. The listening here takes place somewhere beyond the analytical faculties of the intellect; we intuitively know what "beat you nicely" means, but rationally, it makes no sense. It transcends our rational thinking faculties for a moment, and we resonate emotionally with what was said beyond the words that expressed it.

Next, we will briefly look at how blues lyrics support entry into a lightly altered state of consciousness that temporarily and metaphorically allows escape. Dr. Moody refers to the pre-Socratic philosopher Parmenides' description of ancient techniques for accessing states beyond the everyday:

> *[Parmenides was a] mystic and shaman-like figure who knew about visionary techniques for otherworldly journeys. These included prehistoric methods of transforming consciousness through shaman songs. These songs wove together nonsense syllables, meaningless refrains, and intelligible language to create a combined effect. Shamans sang such songs, supposedly, to propel themselves to the spirit world.[19-7]*

Some well-known blues lyrics use a similar combined effect. In Robert Johnson's song "Love in Vain," we see the use of intelligible language, "I followed her to the station with a suitcase in my hand," combined with a poetic (albeit not meaningless) refrain, "All my love's in vain," a mix of literal and figurative speech with regard to the lights, and the ending nonsense syllables adding a wailing and haunting quality: "Ou hou ou ou ou. . . ."[19-8] Another example is Huddie William "Lead Belly" Ledbetter's adaptation of the earlier work and prison gang song, "Black Betty." Here we have the meaningless refrain: "Whoa Black Betty, Bam-ba-lam," mixed with intelligible language: "Black Betty had a baby," and the nonsense syllables: "whoa-oh, Bam-ba-lam." When we listen to Lead Belly perform this song, it is easy to hear how he also uses his voice and the lyrics as a percussive instrument that adds an almost hypnotic quality.[19-9]

The tradition continues in modern hip-hop music, in which artists use a similarly percussive language and lyrical formula. As an example, in Missy Elliott's song, "Work It,"[19-10] we see the meaningless refrain uses nonsense syllables (language in reverse), combined with snippets of intelligible language in the verses: asking for water, getting to know someone, get nails and hair done, etc. The music video accompanying this song likewise combines surreal and real scenarios.

Jimi Hendrix understood the mystical value of unintelligible language and incorporated it in his song writing, which of course resonated with the psychedelic era of the late 1960s. In the song, "The Wind Cries Mary,"[19-11] the meaningless refrain is accompanied with poetic language that makes no rational sense: "And the wind screams/cries Mary." In the third verse of this particular song, we also see a possible shout-out to Robert Johnson, where the blue light on the train now has turned into a traffic light that turns blue, and still signifies the meaning of loneliness. In this instance, Hendrix carries on a well-documented tradition in blues of borrowing lyrically from the oral tradition that in effect acted as what music professor, Ralph Eastman in an article in "Black Music Research Journal" refers to as an interchangeable "large storehouse" in the singer's mind.[19-12] However, Hendrix does not have unintelligible syllables in these lyrics.

The use of unintelligible syllables and nonsense language is an element that is less common in lyrics of contemporary blues performers. If modern blues uses less of this kind of mystical, rich, mix of unintelligible and rational language, it might explain another reason why many blues fans keep finding themselves drawn to the music of the masters: the lyrics of old blues often speak to us in subtle, emotional, and unquantifiable ways. When fans described why blues spoke to them, they often used statements that relied on mystical, metaphorical, or paradoxical language. They described experiences that are "in their soul," "in their blood," that "hurt so good," that blues allows them to "slip out of themselves," or that it provides a "lifting." This is all language that is not logical in traditional terms, yet makes perfect sense when used at the crossroad of rational and felt elements accessed in the blues.

Chapter 20:

Rhythm, Immersion, and Co-Creation

Immersion

In his doctoral PhD thesis in neuroscience, Michael De Pretto writes that music and movement are "irremediably linked"—that, in fact, giving "life" to a musical performance depends on the very subtle qualities of "the groove and the expressivity given to the melody." He writes that trying to improvise B.B. King is something most aspiring guitar players will attempt. Although, according to De Pretto, B.B. King is "not a very good guitar player," he states that the novice player will quickly discover that though the notes might be exactly the same as what Mr. King plays, their attempts sound like a "pale copy" (Pretto's pun—not mine).[20-1] Here Pretto reiterates, from the ivory towers of academia, what Michael Bloomfield expressed from his vantage point as a blues apprentice about his inability to make the notes speak meaningfully like those of the old masters'. The effect and skills of a brilliant blues musician, like Mr. King, cannot necessarily be captured or quantified in technical terms. There is another level of mastery needed than simply playing the notes to communicate meaningfully in this mystical, musical language. De Pretto states that one of the ways to achieve this immersion into the music is through movement and rhythm.

Movement and time (in this context expressed as rhythm) are linked in our bodies and in our world in general. In order for us to measure time, we have to distinguish between "before" and "after." We interpret time as moving forward, because we can measure it in movement. This is part of our interpretive lens that we inherit through our cultural understanding. According to quantum science though, time is relative, simultaneity is relative, and whether the observer *expects* a particle to behave as a wave or as a particle affects the outcome. It makes sense then that the ears and experiences of the beholder in all musical expressions similarly color our interpretations of it as well. This is difficult for us to grasp, when we are in our normal analytical states of mind. We want measurements for "good music," "authentic music," "high-quality music," etc., yet we need to come to terms with the impossibility of finding consensus in such endeavors. We want to create standard measurements for musical quality and genre specificity, yet find ourselves bogged down in arguments about how to determine which qualifying parameters to use for our classification efforts. However, when we enter into an experiential state—a state of emotional immersion into the current moment of time—our analytical mind takes a backseat and a more "relative" mindset takes over. We experience, as many fans stated, that time stands still. In this vacuum, the music takes on a partially automated timing that is felt and not thought about. According to De Pretto, this sense of timing is, for the vast majority of people, at least partially dependent on external cues to stay on track: a synthesis between internal and external stimuli is needed in order for us to connect with the rhythm. The rhythm thus becomes a sort of manifestation of connectedness to self and others. Throughout time, these experiences of rhythmical connectivity have been prized as healing and restorative when used in shamanic traditions, religious mystical traditions, and musical experiences.

Musicians experience a sense of timelessness and let themselves go in the music. Mezzrow describes what this moment in time feels like, when you have trained enough to let your schooling step aside, and get taken over as if by the music itself. It is from this state of transcendence that the musician can step into a field of immersion:

> *I decided to break all the chains off me and let myself go. I started to improvise . . . forgetting all the written music we'd rehearsed. . . . And then, Jesus, I fell into a queer dreamy state, a kind of trance, where it seemed like I wasn't*

in control of myself anymore, my body was running through its easy relaxed
motions and my fingers were flying over the keys without any push or effort
from me – somebody else had taken over and was directing all my moves, with
me just drifting right along with it, feeling it was all fitting and good and
proper. I got that serene, crazy kind of exaltation that you hear religious
people sometimes talking about and think they're cracked. And it was exactly
down to a T the same serene exaltation I'd sensed in New Orleans music as a
kid, and that had haunted me all my life, that I'd always wanted to recapture
for myself and couldn't . . . the ageless language of New Orleans, thumping it
out loud and forceful. [20-2]

Although Mezzrow was a jazz musician, the blues format is perfect for this kind of immersion, as it has such a simple format and structure that the actual technique needed to detach from the "mechanical aspects" of playing is less complex, and thus it is a well-suited vessel to attain this state of trance or detachment. It is in this state that transformative elements of the experience enter the equation. This may of course explain why so many musicians in the jazz, blues, and rock genres particularly, were (and are) users of mind-altering substances. It is well understood that cannabis as well as other psychedelic drugs alter the perception of normal awareness, as well as of time. Larry Sloman, for instance, describes this in his book about jazz musicians and marijuana use:

Because the chief effect [of marijuana] is that it lengthens the sense of time, and
therefore they could get more grace beats into their music than they could if they
simply followed a written copy. . . . In other words, if you are a musician
you're going to play the thing the way it is printed on a sheet. But if you're
using marijuana, you are going to work in about twice as much music in-
between the first note and the second note. That's what made jazz musicians:
the idea that they could jazz things up, lighten them up. [20-3]

Lightening or jazzing up the feel of the music by marijuana use is a way of achieving a state of consciousness where the groove is more "felt" and the sense of time becomes less about "thinking" and more about immersion. However, being in such a drug-induced state in and of itself does not create magical music for the listeners, even if they feel complete unity with the music at the time. I remember well an all-night music session during my high school years after having smoked marijuana. The session lasted many hours and felt, at the time, like the most profoundly creative musical creation. It was recorded, and to say that I was disappointed when I heard the product, after sobering up, is an understatement! In order for the ensuing musical creation to be of quality, it is necessary for the musicians to have internalized and mastered technique, experience, and finesse to be able to allow their analytical faculties to take a back seat, and enter the experiential universe of immersion. A measure of talent is beneficial as well, of course. We can observe that an altered state of awareness was sought intensely by both Mezzrow and Bloomfield, as well as scores of other musicians seeking immersion into the music. In this state, several musicians talk about an experience in which they feel as if the instrument "plays them," rather than their playing it,* or that they are simply a channel receiving the music, as if from somewhere else. There are, of course, many (and in my opinion better) ways of achieving this kind of immersion in music that do not require psychedelic substances. The experience can occur naturally when musicians are in a relaxed state in which they feel synergy with fellow musicians and the audience—when they are "in the zone" while playing. Thus it is easier to "get off the train" if challenging psychic terrain is encountered en route versus being stuck on the hallucinogenic express. It seems likely that immersion in music is related to a concept of relative, felt, and experienced time rather than exact, intellectual, and analytical time. Immersion is thus closely linked and related to the concept of "groove." Groove is of course inseparable from the concepts of "time" or "rhythm." We will get to that shortly.

---

* Helen Bonny—an accomplished concert violinist and the creator of the Bonny Method of Guided Imagery and Music—had a mystical experience in which she felt the violin played itself, and found the audience likewise transfixed in the moment. This level of immersion experience may not happen competently until a level of mastery with the instrument has been achieved, since it requires a level of technical ability that allows the performer to abstract from it to allow a kind of automation to take over. It also requires a sense of unity with the moment—becoming part of it to the point where it is not thought about, just felt.

Access to Performers and Co-creation

The shared experience, in which immersion takes place, is felt also by audiences. It seems to be furthered by the fact that blues musicians generally speaking make themselves accessible to their fans. Fans often mentioned that they appreciate that blues musicians are typically very inclusive and down-to-earth. Art Tipaldi described this relationship with the performers, and their capacity to form bonds with fans on and off the stage, describing a sense of warmth and universal acceptance that reach beyond the artists and extend into the blues community at large:

> *I think the friendships and the camaraderie in the blues world might be unlike any other musical genre. Let's start off with the friendships with musicians where the fans of this music, the devotees of the blues, can become best friends with the performers so very easily. I don't know that that happens in any other genre. For some of these genres you can barely get close to a tour bus to wave as the performer leaves or get an autograph.*

Many fans found this to be true and shared experiences such as this one:

> *I mean the first blues festival I went to, you could go over to an autograph booth and say hi and get them to sign something. I mean that was unheard of—at least in my world—it was unheard of! I think that is part of the attraction that there is not that much of a barrier between you and the artist. You could talk to them. . . . There's that, I mean there's a relationship there's a . . . I don't know what is that word? Symbiotic? We feed off of each other.*

Walter refers to some concerts as "magical." There is an intangible "something" that happens on these occasions. He states that he feels the engagement with the music intensely, and his sense of being immersed in the experience can be near-total. Other than this element, it is difficult to analyze what makes such nights different from the artists' standpoint. But clearly, fans indicated that whatever "it" is, it can be felt by the audience as well. I have observed it from the wings, and I've been in the audience when it happens. It is as if the separation between the stage and the audience vanishes. Typically it will not have anything to do with the venue size or capacity. It seems to happen a bit more when people can stand in front of the stage rather than sit in a more orderly fashion in their own seats. Having the audience close and attentive typically creates a more intimate and connected space. Having the sound system operated without feedback or other distractions and a friendly staff at the venue also seem to play a part in creating enough of a relaxed atmosphere for it to feel like a safe container. Fans gave many examples of this type of experience.

To emphasize the mutuality between artists' and audiences' experiences, here follows a description of this kind of co-creation, as I have often experienced it from my vantage point in the wings of the stage:

Walter will look at the audience, play, joke, and create rapport. After a while, the music might start transporting him further and further "out" (into "space"—trance) and/or "in" (into self-immersion). As he clicks into this state, he sometimes refers to it as if he is simply a transistor radio—a receiver and transmitter—that does very little other than to simply get out of the way. The music comes *through* him and seems not to be *of* him. The audience senses this shift in consciousness; of course, if somebody were to yell "fire," or a well-meaning audience member started wailing out of tune on a harmonica, the spell would instantly be broken. This is an example of how a light trance state can happen under certain circumstances: when the audience is open to it (initiated), feels safe, is able to just let go of the desire to analyze, and instead simply rests in the moment. It is well established that artists seek this type of experience (i.e., Mezzrow, Bloomfield, Helen Bonny); but this study shows that fans seek and attain a similar, although vicarious, kind of experience. When it happens, the audience takes part in the creation process. All of the components I mention below do not have to be present simultaneously— there are various levels of the co-creative experience. Here is an example of what might happen:

The musicians play, sing, and start "clicking" with each other (they are immersed in the moment and the music). They know intuitively where the music is going. Beyond listening, they connect deeply: they feel dynamic changes and rhythmical breaks as if they are almost telepathically connected to the movement of the music. On occasion they start playing like one organism. This in turn "hooks" the audience, who feel that the band is starting to "levitate." Audience members consequently increase their involvement; they hang on every word, follow every note, and experience a near-total engagement with what is being played. As this occurs, they might experience a sense of being lightly transported. The energy from this collective experience of involvement and immersion then feeds back to the band, who in turn respond by feeling their connectedness to one another, and to the audience—and thus inspiration intensifies. It becomes a cyclic exchange of energy between audience and band.

The simple format of the blues structure, which allows improvisation without having to "think" about chordal structure and rhythmical complexity, is a component that seems to make the blues particularly suited to these kinds of collective experiences. Blues music is not performed from a score. It is not read and interpreted, and thus it bypasses first having to be translated intellectually. It is generated from inspiration that rests on a simple, internalized, and felt structure. This opens the door to an infusion of inspiration, immediacy, and certainly for spontaneous collaboration between band members—and a shared experiential and nonverbal dialogue and/or energetic exchange with the audience. Blues fans spoke enthusiastically about such experiences:

> Just the interconnectedness as a group identifying with what's happening on stage, and just feeling that vibe of the music together. The audience, and I'm sure you've experienced this yourself, when the musician is just getting down and kind of going off the reservation, doing their own thing, and the audience is feeling it, and they are just going with it, and at the same time, everyone just knows that this is the time to cheer or clap. Or you know the musician has achieved something here, where they've connected with us, and we want to appreciate them for that, and the musician reacts backward back to the audience very appreciative, because they know, what they did just connected with that audience.

Although the band plays the music, it is a co-creation of sorts because the musicians are carried on a wave of collective involvement that inspires them and creates a collectively sensed experience. At the moment when the musicians feel a loss of "self," they give themselves to the experience. And here they share it with the audience that similarly, by its involvement in the music and willingness to be in the moment, co-creates this common field of awareness. The study shows that blues need not reach this level of involvement and transcendence to be perceived as enjoyable or restorative. But when the musicians reach the transcendent state of light trance, it is cherished by musicians and listeners alike.

Clearly, there are varying levels of this experience. It is most effective when the music comes from, or manages to access, a collective source. Scheff refers to it as "collectively held distress," but it can also be collectively held gratefulness, awe, or *joie de vivre*. Blues boomers were in broad agreement that this type of experience is most accessible when musicians abstain from egoic demonstrations of flashy technique that seek to elevate the performers above the audience. Rather, it is the sense of commonality in shared emotional authenticity from "soul to soul" that fosters these co-creative moments in time that, naturally, can only happen in community during a live music experience. This helps to explain why three out of four agreed they prefer live over recorded blues music:

> *Marie: So when you're in these types of live events, either at festivals or in venues, what's the main thing you get out of live music versus recorded music?*

> *Blues fan: The emotion seems to be right there for me. It's easier for me to just sort of slip—I don't really have a good word for this. It's almost like I get to a meditative state where I can be listening and just slip away from myself. Make the problems go away. . . . It's a very—a metaphorical—yeah. We have lost so much as a modern people. We've forgotten how to just slip out of ourselves. . . . That's one beautiful thing about this kind of music . . . that you can do that.*

When fans wanted to describe what it was about blues music that could bring about an "almost spiritual" experience, their language to describe it varied; about half used language that signified a human experiential connection to the music, such as "soul," "in the moment," "emotional," and "hallucinated on music." The other half used words describing a more ethereal experience, such as "spirit," "collective consciousness," "universe," "connect to higher power," and "goes into another dimension." Here is an example of a fan who was more cautious in his description of what this experience felt like:

> *Well, it does overcome you right? I mean I'm not taking off into different worlds or having these emotions that I wouldn't normally have, but at the same time it does—there's a certain song or certain time or certain note that when somebody performs it, it does take you someplace. But it doesn't take me to another world. Because there's a causal emotion there you know that gets in your heart type thing. . . . I mean I'm not a religious person, but we do go to church, and there are certain times where you come out of there feeling just a little bit different than when you went in.*

Most of the interviewees described live blues experiences as particularly powerful when it came to creating these slightly different states, where communication happened both with the audience as well as performers in the creation of magic in the moment. Blues musicians, throughout time and still today, may fill a function that is not unlike that of a shaman. It is the ancient role of an individual who, by entering into a transformative trance, can bring people together into co-creative states, build a sense of commonality, and foster transformative experiences.

Being in the Moment

Blues boomers mentioned frequently that immersion—and thus the potential for co-creative experiences—happened when they could let go of external distractions, including thoughts about the past and future. Of those surveyed, 94 percent found it important that the music be "spontaneous magic in the moment." Many fans talked about the importance of letting go:

> *What happens is you become enrapt in the moment, you're not thinking about the past, you're not thinking about the future, so it's difficult to worry, and your brain is actually focused on the moment. . . . You can't go to a show and be texting. You have to be present.*

This might explain one of the reasons why Bruce Iglauer finds the "selfie culture" potentially counter to the enjoyment of blues music: it takes away from the moment. Fans frequently talked about "being in the moment" as crucial to feeling connection. This blues fan, who also plays the blues himself, also mentioned the importance of momentarily letting go of an analytical state of mind:

> *When you play a song you are experiencing that moment of emotion, that feeling that you are having—or connection. It's that very moment and that is why you have to let it out. It's not something that you can play from a page, or a tablature, or off this record, or that record. No. It's that moment.*

Chapter 21:

Tension and Release

Distress and Discomfort as Entry Points into Experience

Charles T. Tart argues in his book *States of Consciousness* that, although all spiritual systems ultimately seek a sense of unity or "transcendence of duality," our consciousness remains dependent on the paradoxical and dual nature of reality: "pleasure cannot exist without pain, hope cannot exist without despair, courage cannot exist without fear."[21-1] In Edward L. Berry's essay *Shakespeare's Comic Rites*, he likewise frames an analysis of the appeal of his plays through the ages by describing their universality. He finds that comic plays and rites of passage share a trait: they "share a common evolutionary form—a form in which *periodic forays into chaos lead to new kinds of integration*" [emphasis added].[21-2] Humans are attracted to the elements of tension and release!

Yet our culture is obsessed with telling us that we can avoid pain through a constant state of self-gratification. Advertisers know how to appeal to our pleasure-seeking disposition by selling us the idea that we can *buy* lasting comfort, security, and well-being. And we are easy targets, since we are evolutionarily wired to be pain-avoiders and pleasure-seekers. According to neuropsychologist Dr. Rick Hanson, our brains are constructed to be like "Velcro for unpleasant experiences and Teflon for positive ones."[21-3] In other words, we are wired to be on alert and constantly scan our environment for potential threats, leaving negative thoughts to fester, while positive experiences and feelings slide off our awareness radar. This mindset was very helpful when we were on the plains fending off wild animals and enemy tribes to survive. What wired us perfectly for life in nature, however, can be detrimental to our mental and physical health in a technologically advanced culture where threats to our lives typically do not pop up around every corner, but where large and small disasters from far and wide are continually displayed on our screens.

Since we are wired to scan for danger, it is safe to state that overuse of the 24-hour news cycle can be an unfortunate stimulant for our inbred wiring. Hanson teaches how, based on research in the field of neuroscience, we can deliberately learn to counteract this innate tendency. Hanson cautions further that it is important to not suppress or repress actual negative experiences or feelings: that learning to work with our neurology in no way means suppressing how we feel, but rather consciously observing and slowly re-programming how we deal with difficult memories and negative thought patterns.[21-4] But we are not typically taught how to find such emotional equilibrium, and as a result, we are often stressed, anxious, and distractible. We are affected by a lifetime of having repressed or denied our emotional realities. Many suffer from lasting effects imbedded in their psyches from having grown up with parent who was an alcoholic, or who was mentally or physically abusive, overly strict, or terribly inconsistent. Some suffer from, or live with someone suffering from, PTSD, depression, or other mental scars – conditions that cast long, diffuse shadows over their lives. We can temporarily diminish our pain with medication or alcohol, or distract ourselves by kneeling before the consumerist altar. Advertisers study our neurology intently to seduce and tempt us every chance they get. They seek to offer easy, short-term solutions that keep us running on hamster wheels of frenzied search for relief, when our entire being is screaming out in longing for emotional wholeness that we will never attain by dulling, distracting, or diverting our attention away from dealing with underlying, unwanted, and repressed emotions.

Hanson's research shows we can learn to "take in the good," to focus on the positive without repressing our pain and in the process experience health benefits—mental as well as physical.[21-5] That sounds good, but most of us, however, don't know how. And even if we do, we still find ourselves in a sea of old habits, hurts, cultural triggers, and unnamed perceived expectations. We are afraid that if we express our pain, we will be isolated and ostracized. It is difficult to find socially acceptable outlets for certain cathartic responses. According to Thomas Scheff, we instead "accumulate massive amounts of repressed emotion, bodily tension which is always present but usually not recognized."[21-6] Scheff claims we then become tense, distracted, and isolated, which is in accord with research cited previously.

Blues fans overwhelmingly expressed that engagement with the music offers the potential to address the tension build-up in their lives, while feeling socially accepted and connected. None of them however stated that they deliberately seek out blues music to experience distress or discomfort. Of course not! The purpose of our engagement with the music is primarily to experience fun, play, fulfillment, enjoyment, and entertainment. We don't seek out unpleasant emotions, unless we are forced to do so. The reptilian parts of our brain are wired to avoid pain, at any cost, and social convention supports this. Many fans stated they didn't quite understand it, but the blues usually made them feel good. Even if it was "sad music" about "sad topics," it somehow lifted their spirits.

Ritually liberating and cathartic effects are supported musically by the tension and release in the chordal structure: tonic, subdominant (increasing tension), dominant (most tension), back to the tonic (release). Like a musical ebb and flow, the blues pulsates, vibrates, and soothes our 21st century high-tension, neurologic wiring. When asked how blues helped relieve stress, one survey respondent answered:

The chord structure of Blues is "one"-"four"-"five." That "four" adds just a little tension, and then the "five" relieves it. Sort of like that stress relieving exercise, where you tense and relax muscles in a certain order to relieve stress and relax.

Most blues fans, however, did not specify that they were aware of this particular connection between tension and release, only that blues made them feel good. Much of the healing mystery of the blues works "under the radar."

Tension and Release – Giving into Experience

Robert Jourdain finds that all music is "emotional." It works by allowing us to anticipate expected emotional tension and release. We experience the pleasurable restoration of emotional equilibrium when the tension in music resolves into the anticipated release. Jourdain claims that uncomplicated music delivers simple structures for tension and release to take place in anticipated ways that fill us with a sense of pleasure and order. Music that is too complex, on the other hand, does not bring about release in this way. Here our brain "thrashes about trying to find order where there is none."[21-7] According to Jourdain, and I believe this has some merit, it becomes more of an intellectually pleasing pursuit, but may not offer a viscerally satisfying experience. In blues music, our anticipations are consistently met with a continual, simple, and oscillating chordal structure of tension and release. The "blue notes" add more tension, yet we are always brought home for release and order. The lyrics might support the experience of "tension." For example in the legendary blues song by Robert Johnson, "Hellhound On My Trail," where the lyrics very descriptively tell the story of how bad luck blues is falling down on Johnson like heavy hail from the sky. The lyrics state that the singer is haunted by pain and misfortune to such a degree that there must be "hellhound" on his trail. The stage is set for increasing tension—exemplified by the mention that nature (hail, wind) is conspiring with the mystical forces, and no amount of hoodoo or staying on the run can prevent the the relentless wind from increasing. The solution to this no-way-out scenario is presented as escape: the company and love of a woman will soothe body and soul and make all ills disappear.[21-8] I imagine women listening to Johnson's delivery might have felt inspired to try to be such a safe haven for the night.

Listening to music releases endorphins* which activate a natural analgesic, or pain-numbing effect. Jourdain describes a study in which an endorphin-blocking agent was given to a group of music listeners. When the listeners could not experience the endorphin rush triggered by the music, their enjoyment of it was diminished remarkably compared to the control group who had a normal endorphin response. It seems likely that there is a direct link between music appreciation, involvement, and enjoyment and these hormonally activated feel-good loops of anticipation and reward.[21-9] Since endorphins are not released from purely "feel good" activities such as having sex or eating chocolate, but are also activated naturally when we work through discomfort (to which anyone who has experienced "runner's high" will attest)†, the tension and release aspect of the blues is likely also a contributory element in this endorphin release. Thus, to experience release we must also face the element of tension, whether on a conscious or unconscious level. Our lives are, in fact, enriched by experiencing tension when we are able to move through it and find release. This is partially where the blues works its magic: in its counter-cultural ability to address and reawaken our "collectively held distress," to move through it, and offer release for those who play it and for those who listen and participate by their engagement.

---

* Endorphins and dopamine are chemicals that act as neurotransmitters that very roughly speaking are involved when we "feel good." Endorphins can produce a slight pain numbing response, and dopamine is involved in reinforcing behavior and being rewarded for it. In very simplistic terms: endorphins are naturally produced "opiates" and dopamine is our bodies' inherent "stimulants."

† See Csíkszentmihályi Mihály's excellent work about the concept of experiencing a state of "flow."

Improvisation

When you listen to guitar lines and vocals like a hawk and if everyone who's playing gets it and listens to the nuances that are there—because the music is really straight-ahead and fundamentally very simple—it then takes it to another height where it then becomes a feel between the players. This is why blues is so infectious and has never gone away. There's a spontaneity that happens if you listen as you're playing. What it demands of you is that you listen intently.   Mick Fleetwood[21-10]

Blues improvisation is a nonverbal musical language that bridges cognitive and visceral realms, and offers another entry point into the experiential. It also helps to connect musicians and the audience, as it facilitates both a sense of immersion into the music and connectedness to the moment.

Many blues fans in this study said they connected to blues as a "raw," unpolished, and spontaneous style of music. They marveled at how blues offers a musical language of improvisation expressed in spur-of-the-moment creativity on stage, as well as in the composition of new blues songs. Blues lyrics are often created from elements that are parts of other songs,* and the musical structure is typically a simple one upon which "riffs" and melody are super-imposed. Existing melodic elements or riffs get recycled and put together in new ways as part of the creation process.

In musical composition it can be difficult to distinguish between what constitutes copying, stealing, and what simply constitutes paying homage: borrowing and synthesizing old with new innovation. "Borrowing" influences is inherent in many, if not all musical genres. It is certainly a central component in the blues tradition. This is a discussion that can get contentious: what constitutes original work using borrowed elements, and what constitutes stealing? A particularly difficult element in the discussion

---

* See "Mystical Language" with regard to Blind Lemon Jefferson's, Robert Johnson's, and Jimi Hendrix's use of lights on a train as one example of this otherwise well-documented tradition.

about blues composition and tradition in this context is, of course, based on the fact that once the genre transitioned from being an exclusively African American phenomenon, whites also borrowed elements from the blues tradition. It became a part of the problem of whites profiting from unpaid black contributions, which rightfully opens dreadful historical wounds and activates all sorts of painful reminders.

Intellectual property rights are often up for interpretation. A University of Irvine Law School research paper examining this issue finds that musical borrowing is a documented part of classical music as well as pop music—and, of course, ragtime, blues, jazz, rock 'n' roll, etc.[21-11] The paper concludes that "copyright frameworks should recognize that creativity and innovation are often associated with borrowing. Copyright frameworks should thus be applied in such a way *as to not inhibit such borrowing* [emphasis added]."[21-12] It is clearly a legal no man's land, and an area that can be ripe with (legally sanctioned) duplicity. But there are also elements of borrowing that further creativity and are, in fact, beneficial to continuation of musical creativity.

When artists "let go" and improvise, they allow inspiration to flow through them. For instance, when Walter plays a solo on the guitar, there will be distinguishable influences from varied and interchangeable sources: Mike Bloomfield, B.B. King, Roy Buchanan, Jimi Hendrix, Albert and Freddie King, Muddy Waters, Keith Richards, Chuck Berry, etc. Each of those artists, in turn, created their own sound through such borrowing, modeling, internalizing, etc. He might even decide he is going to do a solo in the style of, say, Chuck Berry, and use a particular guitar vernacular, employing signature licks from this particular artist. However, in order for him to really improvise, and not just copy, the solo must also synthesize his own inspiration, signature style, and guitar "voice," with connection to the moment, the band, and to the audience. No two solos are ever alike, or they will no longer be spontaneous creations—they will instead be premeditated. The music must "breathe" in the moment and be alive and communicate directly each night. Walter, in fact, is so tied to the spontaneous approach that he often "freezes" when music has pre-arranged parts. He does not appreciate having to play the same part the same way twice more than is necessary for melody recognition.

Musicians who improvise must be able to listen beyond just obvious elements of music, such as time signatures and chord changes. To truly communicate in the improvisational realm, they also must learn to pick up on nonverbal cues communicated in the music, whether strictly on feel or in subtle gestures, with a nod, body movements, a raised eyebrow or simply a non-specific sense that the music is now transitioning. This communication happens in the co-creative field, as the musicians (and the audience) "click" with the experience and provide collaborative feedback.

As mentioned before in other contexts, the survey found that 94 percent of blues boomers find it important that the blues is played spontaneously using improvisational methods, ensuring that the music is different each time the same composition is played; that is one of the ways that blues musicians create magic in the moment. And those interviewed for this study echoed this finding:

> *I'm a big jam band fan but you get that in the blues too, I mean they'll just go off on a nice little riff, or nice solo, and just take you away. Brings you right back down, you know. I just love a good jam. I really do.*

Or:

> *What do you feel? Almost like you have to let it flow straight from your soul into your fingers and just let it go. . . . And it's never the same twice . . . because every moment is different. So when you play, the improvisational factor is so important, because that represents the dynamic of time and blues is not static. It's dynamic. It's what's happening. . . . You feel the flow of the emotion and feel the groove.*

A younger boomer blues fan in this study mentioned that it was the confidence of players like Jimmy Page, specifically, and Led Zeppelin in general, that put him over the edge as a blues fan. He found a sense of confidence in their musicianship that allowed them to improvise and "go with the music." Interestingly, he likened this ability to improvise competently to an earlier tradition for virtuoso classical musicians to play their own music in concerts, including spontaneous and improvisational elements. In *The Agony of Modern Music*, Henry Pleasants writes that until about the time of Beethoven, composers found improvisation "fashionable." Pleasants writes that it "was one of the standard features of their appearances as soloists. Certainly many of their compositions should be thought of as the written record of an improvisation, refined by critical afterthought." [21-13] Later, as a more formal and fixed interpretation of the composer's expressed understanding became central to the performance, improvisational elements disappeared. Pleasants continues, supporting our claims of collective experiences in the blues and jazz tradition: "Improvisation in jazz is, to be sure, *more of a communal proposition.*" [Emphasis added.]

At some point, blues musicians incorporated the use of longer, improvisational instrumental solos, superimposing them on the firm and predictable chordal and rhythmical structure. Artists like Lonnie Johnson brought jazz-style improvisation into the electric city blues format. Improvisation took on a new significance in the transition to electric blues, as more extended guitar solos become integrated into Chicago and other styles of blues (Buddy Guy, is a preeminent example). In the 1960s, blues in America was gaining notoriety as an ethnic part of the folk movement. Here musicians fused inspiration with other ethnic influences, e.g., the Indian Raga and Arabian music that were based on instrumental improvisational elements. The psychedelic movement, of course, took this trend one step further into the experiential.

The anticipation of tension release became more acute as these longer solos included wilder experimentation and more tension-inducing components. In a study entitled *Neurobiology of Sensation and Reward*, David Zald and Robert Zatorre found that longer musical progressions that delay a state of resolution intensify the listener's anticipatory expectation of emotional reward. The soloing in improvisation-based blues music does just that: the soloing musician delays the tension release by the insertion of "more notes before a resolution, slowing the tempo . . . before providing the expected outcome."[21-14] Zald and Zatorre likewise mention that the dopamine* reward from listening to music is greatest when hearing it for the first time.[21-15] There is a reason, then, that fans talk about blues music as "one giant Prozac" or "feel-good" music. It seems very likely that endorphin release is activated in the constant possibility of working through tension musically and lyrically. At the same time, improvisational elements secure gratification delays by the insertion of notes, delaying the tension-release, and adding surprising and ever-changing newness to the musical experience. Through its relative minimalism, blues fulfills musical expectations as well as surprises, as soloing and spontaneous musical and lyrical components offer constant newness leading to likely dopamine surges, served up as super-structures of improvisation taking flight. Blues boomers often mentioned guitar solos as important components of their enjoyment:

> *The guitar music just speaks to me. . . . You know how, even in the solo music you have the guitarist playing, and it—the pauses between the notes . . . it's not a steady beat. There are pauses and gaps or you have the impromptu thing that's going up and down. It's not as structured, I think, is part of the appeal.*

---

* We can observe that dopamine here is involved in the expectation of outcome and slight surprise at delay and eventual resolution. It would be interesting to conduct a bi-disciplinary study in the realm of neuropsychology and musicology to observe how dopamine and endorphin release get activated in participants by listening to blues music with listeners pre-screened into two groups: those who are "initiated," and those who are not.

Chapter 22:

Connected in Rhythm—Grooving

One of the elements that connected fans powerfully to blues music was its repetitive rhythmical structure: the simple and much-revered beat that emerges organically in blues, when it is played "right." Blues musicians mention the need for "street," "grease," or "grit" in the rhythmical structure. It cannot be too perfect and "clean." When the musicians—and particularly the drummer—get the beat right, it almost becomes an independent entity. Since many fans play the blues themselves, they often became almost reverent when they talked about the beat, the groove, or the sensed quality of what we could call "not exactness":

> *John Lee Hooker. He doesn't go past the fifth fret. He just stays down next to the neck, and I think his main instrument isn't the guitar. It's his foot. He just starts stomping, and he gets this rhythm going and plays behind it. That's one of the magical things that I teach all my students: . . . the beat isn't something you create. The beat isn't something you make. The beat isn't something you produce. It's something you follow. It's something you bow down to. It's something that is bigger than you are. It exists, and you tap into the beat, and then you follow the beat. You can play along with the beat and that's how you make music. It's that feeling of not forcing something, but playing along to it.*

Many echoed that a simple and repetitive beat allows access to "something bigger." Some felt that the rhythm can help facilitate emotional connectedness to the music:

I guess it's because of the way it affects your insides. How it moves you. You know something about the grooves. Something about—just almost beats with your heart, if you will.

The experience of it "affecting one's insides" was not uncommon. A few mentioned specifically that they also felt that the looseness of the blues format, combined with a certain earthiness was important:

Honestly . . . pop music and country music is more structured and formalized, and rock 'n' roll music and blues music—you let it take you somewhere and it doesn't necessarily follow those rules. I don't necessarily like jazz music, but the same can be said about jazz music. . . . But I think the jazz doesn't appeal to me as much because it doesn't have that bass rhythm to it, and I like the bass rhythm.

It is certainly striking that 95 percent of fans agreed that the rhythmic "grooves" in blues music are important and that they "go with" the pulse of the music, often forgetting time and place.

Let's Groove

The word "groove" has two uses in music. The first has its etymological roots in Old Norse languages, where it referred to a "pit" or "small furrow or river bed." This sense of the word is reflected in music terminology when we refer to grooves of a vinyl LP: the music "jumps out" from the grooves. However, since the 1930s, the word emerged as African American slang synonymous with "being in the zone," "in the pocket," "being in a state of flow." According to Charles Keil, some ethnomusicologists use the term "entrainment" in place of "groove."[22-1] He also jokes tongue-in-cheek that "let's entrain" does not really sound—or work right; "let's groove," however, makes the point!

According to Robert Jourdain, we perceive rhythm with our brains and then translate it into motor activity of the limbs (tapping of the foot, clapping our hands, tapping our fingers, waving our arms, etc.). He states that even though we might feel that we perceive rhythm with our bodies, that it is not the case. Instead, we create "kinesthetic imagery." Jourdain claims that rhythmical awareness is not a simple matter, but rather one requiring complex brain activity. Babies and small children do not have the rhythmical ability that comes with more complex neurological development. It follows that so-called "primitive" cultures that engage in polyrhythmic drumming ceremonies are musically very advanced. According to Jourdain, it is a misconception when people talk about rhythm as "of the body." He finds that "they are simply talking about the pleasure they gain by representing rhythm in their motor systems." [22-2] It is undisputed that the polyrhythmic patterns of certain Native cultures' drumming are exceedingly intricate, requiring complex neurological development. Mere brain activity may explain how such rhythmical patterns are created, maintained, and communicated, but there are some who doubt the completeness of seeing rhythmic experience solely as a function of an auditory, brain-centered experience.

Psychiatrist Stanislav Grof has studied healing potentials of altered states of consciousness for many decades. He mentions eight ancient and aboriginal techniques for inducing trance states. For the purposes of this discussion, I will refer to three of them here:

Sound technologies (drumming, rattling, use of sticks, bells and gongs, music, chanting, mantras …);

Dancing and other forms of movement (whirling of the dervishes, lama dances, Kalahari Bushmen trance dance, hatha yoga, tai chi, chigong, etc.);

Sensory overload (a combination of acoustic, visual, and proprioceptive stimuli during aboriginal rituals, extreme pain, etc.). [22-3]

The ancients used techniques of sound, dancing, and sensory overload in ritual settings to produce altered states. Grof wrote elsewhere that our Western culture has lost connection to the wisdom of such dancing, chanting, and use of repetitive rhythmical sounds to enter into healing states of consciousness; indeed, he deliberates we have largely lost the ability to appreciate and value ceremonial realities working in tandem with material ones.[22-4] Using music as a gateway to altered states of consciousness, according to Grof, requires the listener be more than simply a spectator: "It is essential to surrender completely to the flow of music, let it resonate in one's entire body, and respond to it in a spontaneous and elemental fashion." [22-5] This is absolutely in accord with findings from this study, where fans stated that they did not want to be distracted by too much analytical thought or be in the company of people with whom they did not feel safe to let go mentally and physically—whether that meant toe-tapping or full-body movements; they wanted to fully experience the music.

Michael De Pretto, as referred to earlier, wrote in his PhD thesis about "how the brain deals with rhythmical behaviors." He discusses Carl Gustav Jung's experience in 1925, when he observed tribal drumming and dancing in the Sudan, and felt that the participants reached trance-like states. Jung was concerned that he himself might lose control (of everyday normal awareness). De Pretto quotes Bolton, who in 1895 found that repetitive rhythms did indeed produce a trance, but speculated that more "civilized" people had largely lost the ability to let such experiential states overtake them.[22-6]

This view was in accord with that of W.R. Newbold, who also wrote an essay in 1895, published in *the Naturalist*, in which he relegated trance, hypnosis, telepathy, and other such states of "automation" to the realm of children, stating that it was not of any use for "civilized man." Newbold found that such states of consciousness were only of use to people who did not have more "civilized" methods of communication; they were "eked out of the primitive language of gesture, and held to bind our ancestors of the cave or the tree in, as yet, inarticulate community."[22-7] He concluded that "we can hope to explain these hitherto unknown phenomena, and bring the laws of mind in line with the laws of its material basis, the brain."[22-8] In the late 1800s, when Kellogg wired the foreskin shut of unsuspecting boys, and applied carbolic acid to the sexual organs of young girls, cultural and psychological traits of indigenous peoples were commonly seen as belonging to the realms of the "primitive" and "superstition." Thoughts, individuality, and the mind became synonymous with order and modernity. On the other hand, emotions, collectivity, and being attuned to the body became seen as the root of anarchy and archaic crudeness. Knowing what we know today, it is possible to step out of the either/or proposition in order to recapture elements of "primitive" life, and *combine* them with the virtues of an aware, rational, analytic mind. We can consciously *choose* to use the gifts of our humanity more fully. And the blues offers such a bridge for us to groove along while integrating emotions, experiential realms, collectivity with individuality, rational decision-making, and autonomy. Modern commentators and researchers have begun to recognize that a reintegration of forgotten modes of embodied communication in conjunction with clarity of thought can enhance our understanding and enjoyment of our shared humanity. When we experience the phenomenon of grooving together, we master this process without even thinking about it. We will get back to this point shortly, but first we will briefly look at how musical sound waves affect our physical being. In *Musicophilia – Tales of Music and the Brain,* Oliver Sacks proposes "rhythm turns listeners into participants, makes listening active and motoric, and synchronizes music and minds (and since emotion is always intertwined with music, the 'hearts') of all who participate." [22-9] Gilbert Rouget ponders the ability of rhythm and bass to induce a slight hypnotic state, finding that although rhythm is certainly picked up through the sense of hearing, it can— under certain circumstances—also be felt. When music is sufficiently loud, the wave forms are significant and can vibrate the abdomen, as well as the skin on our entire bodies. We thus literally "bathe in music. . . . Music is then perceived as movement being realized in space. This is even more true when it is made simultaneously with dance, or to make people dance." [22-10]

Our bodies pick up and resonate with music. This resonance is not just about mere auditory perception; there is an actual embodied connection. Just as our auditory nerve fibers pick up vibrations and send this information through the cochlear nerve to the brain, our bodies also "perceive through the skin:" another component of this more experiential, embodied, and primal sound experience. This component explains, why many mentioned the bass notes, and the experience of the lower frequencies of the music as crucial to their enjoyment of it. Rouget quotes Alain Roux describing a pop festival that could be heard "three kilometers away:"

> *This amount of power acts directly upon the body and creates a feeling of participation that many people never attain even during the sexual act. There is no resisting it except by flight. . . . The sounds of the electric bass (infrasounds) produce vibrations localized in internal erogenous zones of the abdomen . . . The repetitive melodies and perpetual thrumming instantly produce a light hypnosis.* [22-11]

It is not clear if the sensations that vibrate our skin and erogenous zones of the abdomen are first sent to the brain, as Jourdain proposes, producing a light trance, or whether there is a physical activation that helps induce the feeling of being transported even before signals make it to the brain. It is obvious however, that this type of experience, resulting from sensory overload, is abundantly accessible, particularly in more amplified forms of blues music. As the following example illustrates, music can certainly be felt even when it cannot be heard.

Walter's first paying gig as a sideman was with a band was in 1970 for a group of deaf people. The band set up and was ready to play, and the room filled up with people. First the audience ate a sit-down dinner in perfect silence, while communicating excitedly via sign language. Then a representative explained to Walter and the band that it was now time for them to play—and they were requested to "turn everything all the way up!" The bandleader asked if some of the audience would be able to hear a little, assuming this was the reason the volume had to be turned up. But the representative explained that if the band played loudly, the deaf people could feel the vibrations through the floor and in their bodies. The band then played at ear-splitting volume and a grand time was had by the deaf dancers, who simply *felt* the music. Once Walter got over the disappointment that nobody could actually hear the music, he too could immerse himself in the onslaught of vibrational intensity.

A hypnotic or lightly altered state of consciousness is enabled by various factors that do not all need to be present simultaneously. Contributing factors can be auditory/sensory overload or felt vibrations, as well as rhythmical repetition. Bass guitar and kick drum infrasounds are perceived by the body as well as by the auditory cortex. In the mid-1960s, Paul Butterfield's Blues Band instructed listeners to "Play it Loud" on the back of their debut album sleeve. They seemed to sense that part of the appeal of their music was its ability to physically vibrate their audience. Music is a whole-body, whole-brain kind of experience, and blues can be a perfect vehicle (Figure 7). Whether loud enough to vibrate the abdominal cavity or not, the rhythmically repetitive aspects of blues music have always been a central part of the musical form, whether it was stomped on a wooden floor, tapped on a box, beat on strings, or later produced by drums and bass. In country blues, sensory overload is produced less by volume than by repetition.

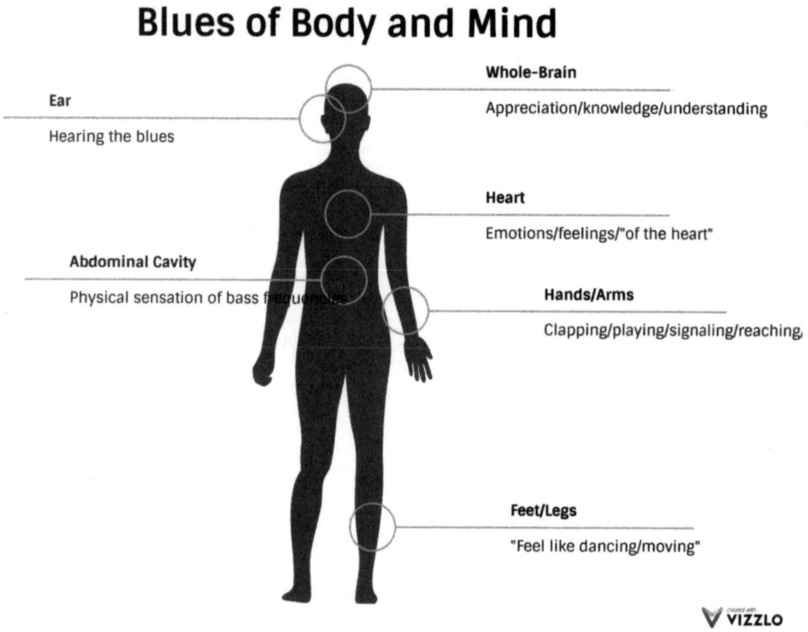

Blues of Body and Mind

Whole-Brain
Appreciation/knowledge/understanding

Ear
Hearing the blues

Heart
Emotions/feelings/"of the heart"

Abdominal Cavity
Physical sensation of bass frequencies

Hands/Arms
Clapping/playing/signaling/reaching,

Feet/Legs
"Feel like dancing/moving"

Figure 7: Music as Whole-Body, Whole-Mind Experience

Rhythm can transcend mere meter and measurement to become a groove—and this is where a reciprocal dialogue between consciousness and automation happens. This is not an easily defined factor, as it is discerned largely by "feel." Therefore written attempts to describe and define what constitutes a "good groove" are not plentiful. Music producer Bobby Owsinsky describes it as "dynamic breathing" between instruments, and finds that a groove, in order to work, is "created in tension against even time. . . . In fact, if the groove is too perfect, it feels stiff.[22-12] Since the mid-20th century, Charles Keil, as quoted before about groove as entrainment, has been intrigued with what components make a groove. His definition likewise centers on the slight "Participatory Discrepancies or PD's" that "are measurable differences or discrepancies in attack and release points along a time continuum."[22-13] He states that the groove is a paradoxical quality in which the musicians are "in synchrony with each other," yet at the same time allow this slightly out-of-phase, imperfect component to be part of the musical experience.[22-14]

Blues musicians refer to the groove as what breathes life into the musical experience, and what animates it. The groove makes the musicians—as well as the audience—move with the music. The moves might be subtle or more demonstrative, but it is difficult to remain motionless when "it" happens. The groove unites rhythm and melody, and occurs spontaneously when musicians are "tuned in" to one another, and by extension, to the "field" of co-creation provided by the audience's collective attention or energy. Fans referred to this quality as happening mainly when the musicians and audience "click," are "in sync," or "tune in." Most however, struggled to describe it. The groove is crucial to an experience of blues music. Without it, the music becomes mechanical and contrived. It is similar to having our thoughts and actions disconnected from our emotions; others pick up on the fact that our levels of awareness (thoughts, feelings, and actions) are not coherent or in sync. The groove cannot be willed or forced.

When I asked musicians whether they groove when they play by themselves, they stated that it can happen. When it does happen, it is as a result of involvement with the music in the moment; the music then almost becomes an entity with which they communicate. Some musicians and fans stated that the groove can "become a spiritual experience of sorts." All struggle to fully define it, but they are in agreement that it is something that they recognize as either present or absent in a musical performance. Musicians however, uniformly stated that it is easier to "groove" when playing with other "good musicians." What constitutes a "good musician" in this sense is less technical know-how, and more an ability to "get in the pocket"—to find that common state where all work together to infuse the music with a felt quality of vibrancy. The musicianship, however, has to be experienced and solid enough that the musicians can detach from the *act* of playing, and allow an immersion into the *experience* of playing it. Defining "the groove" is challenging. Based on this study, my own experience, and input from various musicians and literary sources, here is an attempt:

*The groove happens when the rhythm section (bassist and drummer), or other musicians playing percussively, tap into a reciprocal and shared "feel" rather than being preoccupied with **controlling** components of the musical experience. The groove is not a tangible product, but rather a fluid process of sharing musical life force, expressed in intuitive musical communication **and** individual involvement. Groove happens as a "flow" that is precognitive—if it is scrutinized and analyzed, or even thought about, it disappears. Groove is not "perfect," but, in fact, is created by slight imperfections in time that breathe life into the music in order for it to become its own entity—larger than the sum of its parts—and it is experienced as vibrant, engaging and momentarily all-encompassing.*

The groove is what turns the music into artistic expression. It is the equivalent of what makes language poignant when expressed in poetry, where rules of punctuation and strict grammar are bent, so that words—in a few syllables and in rhythmic synthesis—speak volumes. It is a manifestation of hard-to-describe experiential qualities that make life worth living. "It"—not the photographic perfection of the rendering—is what makes a simple drawing, or painting, capture the vibrant essence of its motif. The groove is a humble and mysterious artistic creation that, by its slight imperfections, captures flawlessness in ways we cannot grasp with our analytical faculties alone. When we groove together in blues music, we connect to an accessible, primal, complex, and difficult-to-describe artistic expression that is found in the meeting place between emotional connection to self, others, and something beyond the rational framework of the mind. It is quite possibly an expression of a meeting of the divine and the essence of humanity made manifest.

The Eternal Timekeeper

De Pretto found that when we are given "regular and irregular sensorimotor synchronization tasks," an internal sense of rhythm activates with the regular rhythmical beats, but not with the irregular ones.[22-15] In other words, when given regular cues, with which we can start relating to a rhythm by tapping our fingers to a beat, we find an internal "clock" that automatically indicates when the next beat is supposed to happen. De Pretto finds that musicians often state that they feel the beat in their bodies, or their "soul," and not in their brain. They point to their gut rather than their head when asked to locate it. De Pretto finds that "the beat might be in our minds, but it is also in our bodies . . . and that this at least should remind us that the brain IS part of the body."[22-16] De Pretto states that "beat processing" is a process of automation. Test subjects first depended on external cues to stay "in time," then varying degrees of automation took over, requiring less brain activity. However, when subjects were left without external cues, most would veer off and either slow down or speed up. When test subjects were given intermittent reminders of the rhythm, most would stay "in time" without much activation in certain areas of the brain. De Pretto concluded that time-processing happens as a function of both internal and external cues.[22-17]

Our bodies are regulated by rhythmical cycles. We breathe in and out, the heart pumps steadily, reproduction is made possible through rhythmical moves of intercourse, and our brain waves are measured in EEG frequencies. De Pretto's work show that we depend on external cues combined with a sense of inner automation (an internal time keeper), to stay in sync rhythmically to self and entrain with others. Oliver Sacks points out that we have used rhythm to entrain to one another in various ways throughout human history. Workers find rhythm and collective strength in the repetitive beat and synchronized efforts of work songs. In religious rites, communal singing and chanting is often part of the experience, which in some cultures also includes dancing and total body experiences capable of bringing on trance states. In military marches, soldiers move as one collective, and possibly gather joint courage from the endeavor.[22-18]

Rhythm is part of humanity's social nature—or, according to biologist, naturalist, and author Edward O. Wilson, "eusocial" nature.[22-19] Eusociality is the highest form of organization within animal groups. Eusociality is characterized by cooperative care of offspring, division of work according to ability within a group, and overlapping generational interaction. Wilson sees humans as eusocial in a unique way in that cooperation and bonding within a group brings out altruistic and selfless behavior. Conversely, the need to defend the group makes them protective. This protectiveness and need to confront others who are deemed different than us, ultimately, according to Wilson, is also the foundation of wars—cultural tribalism: the "us versus them" mindset.[22-20] This is, I believe, at the core of our innate human paradoxical nature; we want to protect those who—at any given time, and by any given definition—are seen as being "like us," and fight those who are not.

Animals might have other ways of synching up with their fellow kin, but music—and rhythm particularly—is a way for humans to find resonance, to be aligned, and together feel the pulsation of our commonality. When we engage in rhythmical activity, it is partially from a desire to synchronize rhythmically to those around us (as women's menstrual cycles synchronize to each other's when in close proximity over time). Although Harvard psychology professor, Steven Pinker, refers to music as evolutionary "auditory cheesecake with no survival advantage,"[22-21] evidence points to the contrary: rhythmic musical expression might in fact have been extremely important for the survival of our species. It allows us to synchronize with one another, to feel united and connected.

Wilson observes that music serves similar functions in the oldest and most isolated tribes that are still observable today; music rites are "typically communal, and they address an impressive array of life issues. . . . The music of modern hunter-gatherers generally serves basically as tools that invigorate their lives." [22-22] Elsewhere Wilson writes about the role of rhythm and music in such cultures: "Singing and dancing serve to draw groups together, direct the emotions of the people, and prepare them for joint action."[22-23]

Evolutionarily, we have banded together in eusocial clans against outside forces to survive and protect our young, work together, and further intergenerational cooperation. Music, beat, and particularly rhythm—the groove—acted as a magical force field that helped our ancestors sync with the unseen "field of being" that resonated among them. There are many indications that this field of togetherness and courage—carried by the rhythm, dance, and singing (or flute playing)—was a uniting, preverbal force, whether spoken language was also used or not. In places where rhythm plays a role today, we can observe that communication attained in the field of the groove binds us together emotionally in powerful ways that are difficult to describe. It seems plausible that these effects of rhythm go back to our origin as a species, and thusly, when we tap into the groove, we tap into parts of ancient communication that foster bonding and a sense of belonging. Those who dance and play rhythms together stay together. Whether modern blues fans tap their foot to the beat or dance freely in front of the stage, they feel connected in ways that are similar to those of our ancient ancestors. The groove becomes a bond that rhythmically connects people with themselves and to others emotionally, and potentially adds a dimension of contact that we cannot see, talk about, or hear, but that we know without question is there.

In the realm of neuroleadership, David Rock explains that we can sense if someone attempts to portray loving and kind energy but is really frustrated and angry underneath: we can learn to trust our intuition (or internal BS meters) and pick up this dissonance, this lack of authenticity. There is an internal connectedness that is experienced by the individual when we are in sync: when we have integrated dialogue between our thoughts, feelings, and actions and there is an external connectedness shared with others, as when we groove musically. In the blues, these synchronization loops are components of what blues boomers described as connection to self, connection to others, and connection to "spirit."

We can certainly observe that there is an experiential field, a mysterious, preverbal sense of connectedness that is experienced also in blues music today. Such authentic communication is restorative to many of us who experience our Western culture as superficial, fake, and disingenuous. Our faith in humanity, or sense of connectedness, is restored when we entrain with this experiential field generated individually and collectively. Blues speaks an honest and sincere language of the heart, and a simple shift in perception from one that is mental to one that is more heart-centered can add a healing perspective (and possibly one that is more inclusive of those perceived as "different from ourselves") to our busy, fragmented, 21st century lives. This kind of communal shift "to the heart" can also partially explain why we emerge from a blues concert—or a personal listening experience at home—restored.

To entrain with ourselves and find coherence of thought and feeling helps us consciously take action. To entrain with others in rhythm, music, dance, and song is a preverbal mode of communication that is inherent in our human potential. The blues is one possible gateway to rediscovery of other aspects of our humanity. We can feel relief from a sense of isolation and disappointment through authentically felt connection. We can once again feel our bodies thump to the beat without fear of repercussions for acting upon bodily impulses as a gateway to discovery. We can get carried away into light (or more pronounced) states of trance, states of being that are as old as mankind.[22-24]

Blues the Healer

In 1989, John Lee Hooker released an album called "The Healer." The album featured many collaborative tracks with other musicians, such as Bonnie Raitt, George Thorogood, Robert Cray, Canned Heat and others. The title track is co-written with, and features, Carlos Santana.[22-25] The song contains many repetitive elements that are almost hypnotic. The lyrics, other than stating that the blues can heal people no matter who, and where, they are, concludes by stating that the blues will heal you *if you let it in.* This is consistent with what contemporary blues fans stated. Blues music, and blues experiences, offer access to a reciprocal process of letting in the experience of the music by going where it leads. By one's willingness to allow such immersion, one also impacts the manifestation of the blues indirectly or directly. It does not work as deeply for the uninitiated, and it works itself progressively deeper into one's soul the more one acquaints oneself with its history, lineage, and potential. It does not have life-altering potential for those who are not open to it, who have not connected to the "stories of the blues," who have not yet discovered its soul, or who are unwilling to let go and let the blues take over; for them, blues music is, at best, just nice, albeit simple, uncomplicated, or maybe even a bit boring or monotonous, music to listen to.

Bradford Keeney is an anthropologist and a scholar of cultural studies who has studied first-hand with the Bushmen of the Kalahari Desert. He finds that our "linear" (reasoned, fragmented, disconnected) world is missing many of the more "circular" (whole, cyclical, connected) aspects of humanity. In New Orleans in 2004, as part of a spoken song he delivered with "first lady of jazz, gospel, and blues" Kim Prevost, he said:

> *First let me tell you who the shamans are. They may not be who you expect. I'm not talking about magic or superpowers, or hidden secrets. I'm talking about something far more mysterious and wonderful. The shamans are the people who get broken, and at their lowest moment, they desperately and sincerely reach up, asking for help. They appeal to a mind that is greater than any single human personality, or group know-how. They ask a Greater Power, a Greater Mind to come upon them, to touch them and make them whole again . . . . Yes, I'm saying that a song can be put in your heart in your greatest time of need. Yes, I'm saying a song is delivered, when nothing else will help. Yes, I am saying that the shamans bring down the songs. The shamans bring down the music. . . . The shamans are the song catchers. They snare the songs that hold the power to heal our broken hearts and anguished souls.[22-26]*

Just as a "civilized" member of Western society, according to Bolton and Newbold, might not be able to experience trance, so might the uninitiated, unmotivated, skeptical, overly-analytical or self-conscious audience member (or the friend or family member whom we invited to join us at a blues concert and who just doesn't connect to it) not experience the full power of the blues. Conversely, it might not always be the right circumstances for us to experience any benefits of blues music, no matter how motivated, enthused, initiated and uninhibited we may be.

But blues music is at its core a manifestation of continually evolving syntheses of influences that can help heal our hearts and souls. If we let it.

Chapter 23:

What will Be the Future Relevance of Blues?

Engaging with the blues serves as an antidote to a world that continually pushes us to perform, perfect, and pretend. Blues fans stated that the blues helps them to take a break: it offers a musical landscape in which they can dance, play, and let go. When faced with difficulties, blues music inspires them to hold on and not give up, knowing that they are not alone. Blues fans stated that their lives were enhanced knowing that the blues offered a safe environment (actual or figurative) to simply be who they are. It allows moments in which they musically, metaphorically, and literally experience life more fully. Blues music can be a vessel that furthers authentic connection to others, to oneself, and to something that inspires and lifts. Experiences with blues music "disarm the baggage," as Joe Louis Walker so beautifully stated – breaking down barriers between people. For fans, the blues also offers a bridge of understanding to those who do not look or sound like them. Whether this is the case when whites play the blues and African Americans listen is unexplored territory. Since only a few handfuls of African American/black blues fans responded to the anonymous survey I posted, and over one thousand were white, I regrettably cannot speak with any sort of insight about the broader African American experience in blues today.

Who will be the blues fans of the future? Will the blues die out as an active, continuing phenomenon and simply have historical relevance, or will new generations and other ethnic groups discover (or re-discover) it? Will there once again be a vibrant blues scene in the African American community, or can the blues reach more broadly and help us simply see human beings and not color of skin once we gradually and continually work to offload the baggage? Of course nobody has the answers to these questions. The insights provided by blues fans through the study do, however, reveal what has hooked current fans on the blues, and this might thus offer a few clues about what might work to expand love of blues music to others:

- First and foremost, the blues shows up today in a culture that is often experienced by current fans as hollow, uncaring, and superficial: to look great, be the best, go it alone, and to appear successful. Blues music and the blues community offer opportunities for communication from heart to heart. Blues interaction offers another way of relating in which non-competitive qualities are front and center. Instead of "nail the test, perform, perfect, pretend" – the message is "be yourself, be authentic, connect."

- The blues cannot be forced on someone. Becoming open to blues music often happens at a time in someone's life when they are at a crossroads: something has happened that closes one path and they are not sure which to take next, or they are fed up with certain circumstances of what has been before. Or it simply is discovered as having new and invigorating possibilities for experience that were previously unknown.

- There are elements of blues that are revelatory in nature. Becoming a blues fan has an initiatory element to it, and this is something that cannot be taught or proselytized. It either happens or it doesn't. What evades attention one day, might "hook" a prospective new fan the next under slightly different circumstances. It is dependent on what is going on around us and in us. Blues works inside-out as a personal discovery that can turn into a quest, a treasure hunt, and a mission.

- The element of personal ownership is crucial to many blues fans whether they play blues themselves or not: they state that they find themselves in it. The blues is less about living up to expectations and more about tapping into something that is not measurable. It is something they embrace because it simply feels good, restorative and/or genuine.

- At the same time, the collective experience of finding authentic connection in the blues is equally important: the notion that it connects fans to others in a fun and entertaining setting, to blues ancestors, to an experience of fellowship in making/hearing the notes and feeling the subtle communication beyond words, and/or experiencing emotional resonance.

- Blues offers a possibility for apprenticeship – no matter the age of the acolyte. There is a well of wisdom that is taught by blues masters: how to make the notes speak and communicate a language of "heart and soul," powerful stories of blues history told from the precipice of existential cliffs, the ability of blues masters to tell it like it is, how to build a song from inspiration, how to rest in the moment, how to be spontaneous, how to stay cool under fire, how to allow meaningful connection to happen without pretense, how to learn to immerse oneself into an experience that connects body and soul, how to first learn from imitation and then find a personal sound or expression, and many other subtle but all-encompassing such "lessons." Throughout time, blues masters have offered an alternative education that is not achievement based, but instead based on willingness to dig deeper and dare to be bold. They teach that we can find the groove, find connection, be alive in the blues— and these lessons somehow translate beyond the musicians. These lessons are not about what can be weighed and measured; instead they offer something that cannot be taught via textbooks or tutorials. When Walter gives seminars, workshops, or talks to young musicians about the blues, it often centers on how to play music with feeling and be less concerned with scales and more concerned with what you "say," also nonverbally. It typically also touches on learning to forego the temptations of drugs and alcohol as they hinder rather than further authentic expression (as well as tend to be long-term overall life-and sanity destroying). He passes on hard-learned lessons from his own life, but certainly also the lessons he received from blues masters who taught him to "find himself in the blues." These lessons of blues masters are powerful when modeled and facilitated in person and through story-telling and lived example.

- Young musicians may enter into the field of playing music partially intrigued with musical gear: various amplifiers and guitar makes and models. As they discover blues, the fascination with elaborate gear and "costume" outfits may step to the side and other elements of the musical experience, as we have covered previously, step to the front.

- Because the blues is such a simple format, it is broadly accessible. Most can learn to play it, or at least tap along to it. I believe it is no coincidence that so many blues fans refer to the fact that they themselves play the blues "for fun," semi-professionally, or professionally. They take part, they feel it, and they want to express it. And at the same time, there is no doubt that even as the blues is accessible, it is *simultaneously* very difficult to play. It takes a level of mastery to do it well which requires years of deep apprenticeship and willingness to go where the blues leads. To achieve blues mastery is to once again cross over yet another intangible, initiatory line; it is to discover that the *playing* aspect steps to the background, and instead simply *being* a vessel for the music comes to the fore. The communication *comes through* musicians, it is not of them. It is not unlike spiritual mastery: it takes devotion, practice, self-sacrifice, immersion, and time. Young blues artists watch blues masters and blues ancestors reach a kind of musical transcendence that speaks beyond words, and it reels them in.

Will a Younger Generation Discover the Blues?

Blues fans expressed that music can make history come alive. And that blues has the potential to teach it in new ways as it offers possibilities for personal discovery along the way. In a sense, the best way to "teach" the blues might be to get our opinions about what it "is" out of the way and let the blues speak through what it "does." The blues speaks through the people who have lived it, and those who have been touched by it. The music becomes relevant as it tells someone's story, and when we suddenly realize that we know that feeling too, it then links their story to ours. Then musical enjoyment, understanding, appreciation, compassion, and even gratitude follow. Ultimately, blues fans stated that the music connects us beyond ourselves when we find ourselves in groups of people, and we look around and see that others feel what we feel too—whether it is moving around, standing in awe, or feeling a collective "lift" as the music takes us on a journey.

Our three sons did not discover the blues because we taught it to them. It has certainly been available for them to find, but we did not "preach" the blues to them. It was first and foremost a serious crisis that brought them into relationship with the blues. When Walter became deathly ill, our boys, started delving into blues history and found ways to connect to it as something that had relevance for them. It became a link to their father, but also a link beyond—to blues ancestors who taught how to walk through the blues, expressing it while engaging in the healing vibrational field of musical immersion.

It is important to note that where the current main audience of the blues had a certain social and cultural backdrop upon which the blues came to fill certain needs, young people today have a different one. They are the internet generation. YouTubers or vloggers like Casey Neistat, Joey Graceffa, The Shaytards, or Roman Atwoodvlogs tell it like it is. In some ways they take reality TV and bypass big, elaborate, and staged productions, and make it (at least appear) "raw," unpolished, real, and in some cases even brutally honest, like the daily vlog CTFXC as it follows a cancer survivor through diagnosis, treatment, and aftermath. Rap music and hip-hop often utilize very direct method of tellin' it like it is, and are certainly not veiled or indirect. Younger generations may not be wired like baby boomers to appreciate the blues' more subtle possibilities for emotional recognition, resonance, ritual and catharsis. In fact, younger people, no matter their ethnicity, often view the blues as music "for old-timers." Many young people also spend a good amount of time expressing themselves (and watching others do the same) on social networks such as Tumblr, Instagram and Snapchat. In some ways, this is where they get some of the immediate relief from self-censorship and self-constraint that they otherwise need to apply to succeed academically or professionally.

If and when young people discover the blues today, there is likely an element of personal discovery mixed with a sense of mystique that bowls them over. In the case of African American young people who embrace the blues, there is likely also a strong connection to a shared, direct historical background and lineage. From my personal experience with young blues guitar players, it often starts by meeting or hearing a blues master, who somehow "gets to them." He or she might encourage, awaken, or "see" something in them, or exemplify a way of communicating that is within their reach, but that hasn't been explored by anyone else in their lives. And this connection opens up new ways of communication that are exciting, direct, and offer potential for a new kind of self-expression that feels comforting, direct, and honest, and not about having to conform to standards set by others. This blues master offers a new kind of emotionally transparent role model and maybe even a possibility for (direct or indirect) apprenticeship. This initiatory meeting may coincide with the initiate experiencing addiction, illness, being a misfit, parents' divorce, danger, or other kinds of emotional turmoil that the young person somehow can address properly distanced through playing or hearing blues music. Once they are over the initiatory experiential threshold and the blues speaks to them personally, they engage in the treasure hunt and they get just as hooked on it as older generations of blues fans.

But many of these young blues musicians do not broadly attract younger audiences. The blues community does a good job embracing them, but at the same time, until young blues audiences get their own activities, their own types of events, their own community of similarly aged peers, the blues will probably not effectively transcend the age barrier. Blues music will not connect more broadly to young people if they look around the room and mainly see people that are their grandparents' ages. It is beyond my research and experience to talk about how it feels, for instance, to be a young black person who goes to see a blues band and finds him or herself in a room full of white baby boomers. But I can certainly imagine what that must be like. And no matter the color of their skin, when such new, younger blues fans attend a concert, seeing older people "float away" on the music might actually turn them off rather than help them become blues fans. Likewise, new potential blues fans will likely walk through existing museums with displays of the old blues masters and find little there that feels relevant to them.

If we are to teach blues to younger generations, beyond the study of its mere musical elements, it might be helpful to make the blues relevant to students as a personal vehicle of expression—one that is not aggressive, threatening, and in your face, but simply transparent, "real," and possibly with elements of self-deprecating humor. It may also be an offering that music therapists, or other helping professionals can consider making available to young people who struggle with depression, addiction, anxiety, etc.

It is possible to "teach" the blues, or rather somehow help (younger) people connect to it, by facilitating opportunities for making it a personal discovery. In seminars, sessions, or classes, such can be facilitated by asking questions for individuals to consider and groups to discuss along these lines:

- Which blues character are you? A quiz offering an introduction to blues ancestors by drawing an imaginary link to one's own situation or personality.
- How do you Snapchat the blues? How do you make a blues Instagram posting? In short: how do you combine these new,

electronic modes of self-expression with the subtle, and ultimately powerful, indirectness that is a big part of the blues?

- Student loan blues: a look at how sharecropping and feelings of being stuck financially in student debt share similar, yet also immense historical differences.

- How do you write your personal blues song? This would include listening to blues music—how do blues musicians accomplish the transfer of emotion lyrically? Elements of repetition, word-rhythm, non-sensical "deeper" modes of expression, indirectness, signifyin', etc.

- What would your day be like if you were a blues man or woman in 1930's Mississippi?

- Students can listen to a blues instrumental from an artist like Blind Willie Johnson and draw a picture of what they associate with the music or write a few phrases—or a poem—that captures the feelings in the music.

- What does it mean that there is "feeling" in a song?

- How can we listen to other people's interpretation of music and allow it to broaden our own understanding of it, of other people and of ourselves, rather than to tell them that their interpretations are "wrong"?

There are many potential avenues to tailor a study of the blues to a younger generation, but it might be important to find a way to first make a connection, so we don't communicate past each other. Again, when a new initiate discovers the blues and starts the treasure hunt, the many lessons of the blues, of history, and of immersion in musical (emotional) engagement follow. And then new creation might also follow—new expressions that are recognizable as blues, but also are new amalgamations and mergers of influences that continue the vibrancy of expression within the format.

The study indicates that blues fans do not need to be poor or of any particular ethnicity to play or enjoy the blues: living life and dealing with the adversities, joys, and tensions inherent in the human experience is what wires us for it. And to study where the blues came from enriches our understanding of much more than the music; it broadens our ability to understand the flipside of our culture in a historical context beyond the text books. Here blues fans stated that the musical exploration helped them understand and appreciate that others are both completely different from themselves, that other people's trials can be much worse than their own, and that all human beings at the same time are made of the same building blocks linking us across geography, ethnicity and time. It also opens up an acceptance that even privileged folks can have trauma, have suffered abuse, dealt with life-threatening illnesses, lost loved ones, etc. And that it is through acknowledgement and willingness to deal forthrightly with one's troubles rather than ignoring them that connection, healing, and ultimately understanding and gratitude can be found.

In order to broaden the blues fan base, it might be beneficial to look at two kinds of equally important factors:

1. The current core group of blues fans is largely a very homogenous group. It is, whether we like it or not, largely (white) baby boomers, and the current blues scene fills many needs specifically for this group of people. This core group is a sustaining force of the blues community today, so it is paramount to continue to offer plenty of opportunities for this group of blues fans to enjoy music and come together.

2. At the same time, it is equally important to embrace and support artists, educational incentives, community groups, blues societies, and industry professionals that take the blues in new directions. When they connect with fans outside the current blues community and reach different age groups and groups with a higher degree of ethnic diversity, it leads to new growth along the blues timeline continuum. Here of course it is important to support the creation of new, or modification of old, environments where blues can find fellowship beyond the already initiated. These new expressions or community forums will likely provoke a sense of discomfort (and

maybe even feelings of betrayal) for those who are today's hard core fans.

It is certainly possible to do both simultaneously, particularly if we are aware of the innate power of blues music beyond simply that it is "great music," to which uninitiated fans might simply shake their heads. Blues fans expressed a definite need to convey the depth of enjoyment they find in the music to others, and often a very lackluster sense of accomplishment around succeeding at it. It will typically take multiple levels of repeated exposure coupled with an inner and outer readiness before a new blues fans "gets it." And then they get it on their own terms. No two blues fans connect to the blues the same way, no matter how homogenous the fan base may be. Each of us has our own blues story, and every new fan will create his or hers as well.

Blues is musical enjoyment first and foremost, but the place where we really connect to it, sits beyond chords, musical equipment, and gig reports. The power of the blues exists in how it impacts us. It has the potential to reach deeply and further connection, understanding, and a sense of commonality. And talking about what the blues does to us— how it impacts our lives—might inspire others in more profound ways than our opinions about why it is good music, who is allowed to play it, and how they "should" play it.

Blues continues to grow each time we reach back and understand its history better, because we connect to it through the study of those who lived it. Blues grows each time bands manage to "click" and have the audience click with them. Blues grows when new bands synthesize it in new ways while connecting back to tradition. Blues grows each time we experience the lift of coming home from a concert feeling lighter than before. Most importantly, blues grows when the music thrives—when fans brave the weather, forego the comfort of the sofa, and head out to clubs and concert venues to experience it.

Chapter 24:

What Is the Relevance of the Blues
to its Current Audience? (A Summary)

In a rapidly changing world, the blues invites us to connect. It is like a good friend that doesn't let you down. Whether we turn the car radio to a blues station, put on an album by a favorite artist, or go out to hear a blues band live, the blues is comforting and always accessible. It allows us to connect to ourselves, each other, to those who came before, and to restorative forays into the experiential. The blues doesn't inspire revolution or protest. It helps us find our equilibrium when the world turns upside down. The blues helps us find cohesion. Artists build continuing blues traditions cumulatively on styles from the past, adapting them through imitation until they eventually claim new blues expressions as their own by merging influences with inspiration.

Befriending the blues invites us to be real and show up as we are. Many blues boomers feel disengaged with—and disconnected from—a world around them that they perceive as filled with phoniness, misunderstood political correctness, superficiality, disingenuousness, and diffuse power structures. For them, blues music serves as an antidote, providing something real, in an environment that is unproblematic, safe, enjoyable and fun. Blues music connects the dots between an inner, often opaque universe of sensations, and an outer shared experience. Engagement and empathy are possible when blues fans feel safe enough to connect with others. The blues is such a safe place. In the 21st century, blues music thus plays a powerful role in the lives of its fans, although the makeup of its core audience has changed.

In the 1960s, when the main audience for the blues shifted from African Americans to whites, the role of the blues partially shifted with it. In the black community, the blues had been an escape valve, an essential vessel for emotional release. Through "signifyin'," it provided a safe way to state one's feelings, while delivering an implicitly understood stab at those in power. The blues form afforded a repetitive, rhythmical, and lyrical structure that helped to induce light, trance-like, or mildly hypnotic states in which one could escape the troubles of the day, at least momentarily. After the Civil Rights Movement, blues music was largely left behind by African Americans who continually brought new styles of music into being, styles that were often more efficient in communicating the direct language of expression that was necessary as the African American community determinedly climbed toward the mountaintop of equality. Blues music was broadly shunned by younger generations of blacks, maybe because it was a reminder of a painful past when the chokehold of racial oppression was an inescapable reality.

Some elements of the blues are adept in capturing and expressing universally felt emotions and this partially explains why this art form has had—and continues to have—such depth of influence in our culture. Blues is well suited to tell it like it is: to express joy, elation, celebration, frustration, confusion, a sense of being stuck, etc., in an uncomplicated and accessible musical form. Blues boomers grew up in times of rapid social change, when the ideal was to be strong, silent, self-contained, and hard-working. Such ideals, however, soon confronted the breakdown of social conventions in the late 1960s. For baby boomers, old morals often conflicted with new ideals. Fear of an individual as well as a collective show of vulnerability, doubt, or weakness in the postwar psyche was ubiquitous. Blues, and many genres built on blues influences, offered a musical language that was able to express the complex emotions that accompanied growing up in a repressed, suspicious, and bottled-up culture, and offered access to a more spontaneous mode of self-expression. Musicians became role models for the new "cool:" a way of being real. Blues musicians showed their courage through emotional straightforwardness and authentic connectedness, both in their musical performances as well as in their personal appearances. On many 1960s college campuses, and for suburban youths growing up with contact with the blues scene, blues music also offered visceral learning opportunities about social injustice thanks to the ability of the music to deliver emotionally poignant lessons through emotional identification with the plight of bluesmen and women.

In the second decade of the 21st Century, blues fans are overwhelmingly white and middle-aged. They use blues music to relax, have fun, and be entertained. Blues offers them access to an inner universe of immediacy, authentic connection to others—as well as dreamy states of being that open them to realms *slightly* outside normal, everyday awareness. Blues boomers find emotional healing in blues music. Musicians and fans playing the blues help continue a tradition of simple yet sincere, deep, and honest music that requires deep levels of immersion to master. Engaging with blues music creates possibilities for loosely and individually designed, yet collectively celebrated, rituals, which include an experiential inner initiation, a way to work through stress and anxiety, an opportunity for catharsis, and an experience of connection to emotionally connected ancestors.

The blues is dependent on a reciprocal relationship between those who play it and those who listen. It does not "do" anything by itself. It is not therapy although it contains therapeutic elements. It is not merely entertainment, although it is certainly often entertaining. It is not a drug, although it can alter perceptions and offer mood enhancements. It is not a museum piece, although it can connect us to a visceral knowledge about the past. Such study of blues history provides insights into the commonality of human beings through time. It is not a spiritual practice, although the blues can offer access into realms of the experiential. The blues is apolitical, although resonating with the field of other people's joys, concerns, suffering, and misdeeds can bring about feelings of compassion and resolve that inspire a desire to bring about change. The blues is not a cure for anything, although it can act as a healer of both emotional and mental anguish.

One can speculate that playing and listening to blues music that concerns itself with difficult aspects of human life, could potentially contribute to a process of self-destruction: that musical immersion through reliving traumatic, sad, or desperate topics could bring about a permanent sense of victimhood, where painful past experiences were reprogrammed into a continuing "story" through repeated exposure to the blues. Here blues music could theoretically aid in the perpetuation of drug addiction, alcoholism, loneliness, and continuing emotional re-injury. One might speculate that this could have been a contributing factor to the early demise of the members of the "27 club"—artists who lived hard and died young. It is important to note however, that these artists didn't die from feeling and expressing difficult emotions. They died from trying to self-medicate with drugs and alcohol to *prevent* themselves from feeling, or to embellish on what they thought they wanted to feel. They can be seen as examples of what happens when we forget that we do not get to choose only one side of the coin: the road to joy opens more fully when we also dare to boldly walk through our blues. Living a life in wholeness of experience cannot be short cut through a quest for pleasure and comfort, at least not long-term.

This component of blues music aiding in self-destructive patterns was not a discernible factor among blues fans today. Instead, they categorically and enthusiastically talked about benefits they receive from their love of the music. Listeners' mental benefits were dependent on the blues performers' musical transparency, honesty of expression, and ability to invite listeners in. The benefits were just as dependent, however, on listeners' ability to let go, their level of initiation, who they were accompanied by, and where the concert or listening experience took place. Among modern blues fans, the access to something "real"—even if it was around difficult or painful emotions—felt subtly cathartic and was experienced as a relief. This transparency was often referred to as an indirect or subtle way to move *through* emotions rather than getting stuck in them.

The language of blues is both universal and context-specific. It holds the potential to speak the language of the heart universally. It thus helps to further understanding, connection, and a sense of compassion across time, as well as to overcome socially constructed barriers between people. It can also have a specific relevance and meaning to certain demographic groups when viewed through the interpretive lens of a specific era, ethnic, social, and/or cultural background. Each generation of blues musicians merges influences, inspiration, trends, sounds, musical equipment choices, and lyrical topics with what is going on around them. Fans resonate because the music strikes a chord within them—they perceive it as relevant to their situation beyond obviously enjoying how it sounds.

Blues boomers stated that the blues is fun—helping them connect to a communal experience in which they felt entertained, set free, validated, and accepted. They expressed that their inner landscape was resonated in an outer community, one in which they felt accepted in spite of—or maybe because of—more readily shared imperfections. They talked about the blues milieu as refreshingly unpretentious and supportive. They also wanted to pass on the gift of the blues to others, and to honor those who helped synthesize the genre.

Blues facilitates contact with a language of the heart. In making that contact, fans experience emotions without fear of judgment that otherwise might be opaque or out of reach. Listening to blues music helped them feel that the lowest lows, as well as the highest highs, are part of the human experience that can be shared in the blues. Blues music, and its history, inspired fans to not run away from their own fear, pain, or sorrow, but to find comfort in the fact that others had felt that way too, and that by this realization, feelings of stress and anxiety were often lessened in their lives. Learning about blues ancestors certainly helped them put their own worries and anxieties in perspective. Blues helps those who love it accept that our shared humanity is not easily grasped in sound bites. It is paradoxical and complex, but ultimately it also holds the potential for deep connectedness and authentic beingness including experiences that are spiritual.

Blues boomers use blues music as a vessel in which it is possible to connect to, and integrate, ancient knowledge, as rhythms sync up and the groove carries them through the night. The sound, lyrics, and repetitive rhythm seem deceptively simple, yet are in fact subtly and passionately complex, musical components that require deep immersion to master. One can speculate that the repetitive and simple—or polyrhythmic and complex—rhythms that have been practiced in indigenous cultures' rituals and ceremonies for thousands of years, in fact, have been crucial in our survival as a species, because it enabled us to feel united and therefore stronger. Might this sonic and experiential field have connected us internally, as well as to everything around us, as we expressed emotional energy in a shared container that held us, resonated with our deepest feelings, and gave us reason to celebrate, as well as courage to move through our fears, in community? We can only speculate about this evolutionary aspect of grooving together.

But we do know that this is indeed a part of the relevance of blues music for those who love it today. For blues fans, the ancient knowledge and wisdom that survived in this music combine with the potential inherent in modern civilization. And in this combination, modern blues fans have access to an integration of powerful potentiality. The study of blues fans in the 21st century hints that Steven Pinker's claim might be woefully incomplete, when he states that music, evolutionarily speaking, is merely auditory cheesecake. Blues fans agree en masse that blues is, as Iglauer stated, "the most emotionally fulfilling music ever." And as the music evolves along the blues evolution timeline, it continues to connect us to our roots, our feelings, and to those who play, partake, and listen.

Epilogue:

The End of All Our Exploring

Should the Voyager spacecraft ever bring Blind Willie Johnson's voice into contact with extraterrestrial life forms, they might feel drawn to encounter Homo sapiens, who seemingly have such a sincere desire to communicate. Were such foreign life forms to enter earth's atmosphere accepting our invitation for mutual discovery, however, they might find themselves under fire: attacked by humans who want to defend themselves against the unknown. The dual nature of humanity would likely be as confounding to alien life forms as it is to us.

In our journey through life, the blues is one possible vessel that can take us out of ourselves, effortlessly joining Blind Willie, no matter how far out in space the Voyager reaches. The blues also offers to take us further and further into ourselves. Every time we listen, it is as if we know ourselves better, and, implicitly, we feel more compassion for those who played it and those who, like us, listen and "get it." We stand united with them in an understanding beyond words. The blues can move us—no matter the color of our skin, our social standing, or our political persuasion. One of the legendary bluesmen of today, Deacon Jones, said in a recent documentary, "You can be green and step off a space ship and play in the band—as long as you know how to play the blues."[23-1] Blues appreciation is a colorblind activity, yet in the same breath it is important to remember that the blues emerged in the African American community out of a very specific historical set of circumstances. Our appreciation of blues history is a constant reminder for us to learn from the hard lessons of the past. Digging into the history of the blues helps us realize that just because we want the wounds of racism to heal, they still haven't.

It is up to us to continue the quest for social justice through conscious and deliberate action. I believe it is a misconception to say that we, in order to heal such wounds of the past, should disregard new kinds of expression of the blues. It is counterproductive to claim that it can only be played by (certain) African Americans. People in China, Europe, Japan, India, and in all corners of the world now love and play the blues. And as young people find the art form, including young African Americans who are starting to emerge on the blues scene once again, they claim it for themselves when they merge it with the sounds, topics, and sensibilities of their current realties as well as their particular heritage. No matter who plays the blues today, or where they are, they must reach within, as well as back to tradition, to synthesize and merge influences to reach an authentic blues expression. And when they send it into their community, connecting also to the field of experience all around them and their audiences respond, the blues continues its synthesis of evolutionary developments that keeps it fresh, authentic, relevant, and alive.

Through this research, I have learned much about myself. I have resonated with others and felt my being move through collective space. My concurrent inner journey has opened my eyes to why I am so in love with blues music, but more significantly, it has helped me be more aware of what it is that makes life worth living. Bluesmen and women have taught me much about the potential of human existence. It is a personal journey that will continue. My love of the blues opens up the doors to exploration of a sense of limitless wonder. And here I join other blues fans, Blind Willie, and all the bluesmen and women through time, on a journey that may ultimately help me hold the inner tension of my own paradoxical nature with a bit more grace, a bit more patience, and a bit more understanding.

And as the blues helps those—who let it—tell it like it is, we find that we are more alike than we are different. The blues reminds us that we are all made from the same cosmic dust, the same basic elements—even if we were to step off a spaceship. As in T.S. Eliot's poem "Little Gidding," one can say that the blues helps us explore internal places: familiar places that we—

through continuous communal exploration—encounter again as for the first time. May this exploration help us make peace—not just with ourselves— but with each other.

SANKOFA

References

Chapter 1

1-1 NASA. (n.d.). *Voyager - The Interstellar Mission*. From NASA Jet
Propulsion Laboratory:
http://voyager.jpl.nasa.gov/spacecraft/music.html

Chapter 2

2-1 Pipher, Mary (2008). *The Shelter of Each Other – Rebuilding Our Families*.
New York, NY: Riverhead Books, p. 23.

2-2 Turkle, S. (Director). (2012). *TED talk: Connected but Alone?* [Motion
Picture].

2-3 Turkle, S. (2011). *Alone Together - Why we Expect More from Technology and
Less from Each Other*. Philadelphia, PA: Perseus Books Group, p. 1.

Chapter 3

(No endnotes)

Chapter 4

4-1 Oliver, P. (1960). *Blues Fell This Morning*. New York, NY: Cambridge
University Press, p. 150.

4-2 Steinberg, J. R., & Fairweather, A. (2012). *Blues Philosophy for Everyone*.
Chichester, UK: Wiley & Sons, Inc., p. xiv.

4-3 Steinberg, J. R., & Fairweather, A. (2012). *Blues Philosophy for Everyone.* Chichester, UK: Wiley & Sons, Inc., p. xiv.

4-4 King, D. (1997). *Separate and Unequal: Black Americans and the US Federal Government.* Oxford: Clarendon Press.

4-5 Jones, L. (1963). *Blues People - The Negro Experience in White America and the Music that Developed from It.* New York, NY: William Morrow and Company, p. 86.

4-6 Brown, B. (2013). *The Power of Vulnerability - Teachings on Authenticity, Connection, and Courage.* Sounds True Presents - Self-Guided Video Course. Sounds True, Session I part 3.

4-7 Brown, S. (2009). *Play: How it Shapes the Brain, Opens the Imagination, and Invigorates the Soul.* Penguin, pp. 3-32.

4-8 Brown, S. (2009). *Play: How it Shapes the Brain, Opens the Imagination, and Invigorates the Soul.* Penguin, p. 15.

4-9 Alcoff, L. (1991-1992, Winter). *The Problem of Speaking for Others.* Cultural Critique, pp. 5-32.

4-10 Brown, S. (2009). *Play: How it Shapes the Brain, Opens the Imagination, and Invigorates the Soul.* Penguin, p. 59.

Chapter 5

5-1 Storr, A. (1992). *Music and the Mind.* New York, NY: Random House, Inc., pp. 3-4.

Chapter 6

6-1 Winborn, M. (2011). *Deep Blues.* Carmel, CA: Fisher King Press., p. 69.

6-2 Ruiz, D. M. (1997). *The Four Agreements.* San Rafael, CA: Amber-Allen Publishing, Inc., pp. 1-21.

Ms. Anna Bennett

Ekphrasis or ecphrasis, from the Greek description of a work of art, possibly imaginary, produced as a rhetorical exercise, often used in adjectival form, ekphrastic. A graphic, often dramatic, description of a visual work of art.

A376180

6-3 Davidson, R. (2012). *The Emotional Life of Your Brain*. New York, NY: Penguin Group, p. 89.

6-4 Davidson, R. (2012). *The Emotional Life of Your Brain*. New York, NY: Penguin Group, p. 89.

6-5 Brown, B. (2007*). I Thought It Was Just Me (But It Isn't) - Making the Journey from "What will people think?" to "I am enough"*. New York: Gotham Books, p. 155.

6-6 Tart, C. T. (1983, 2000). *States of Consciousness*. Lincoln, NE: iUniverse.com, inc., p. 34.

6-7 Davidson, R. J. (2012). *The Emotional Life of Your Brain*. New York, NY: Hudson Street Press, p. 11.

6-8 Hari, J. (2015). *Chasing the Scream - The First and Last Days of the War on Drugs*. New York, NY: Bloomsbury, p. 271.

6-9 AFSP. (2014). *Suicide Statistics* . Retrieved from American Foundation for Suicide Prevention: https://afsp.org/about-suicide/suicide-statistics/

6-10 Hu, G., Wilcox, H., Wissow, L., & Baker. (December, 2008). *PubMed.gov*. From US National Library of Medicine, National Institutes of Health: http://www.ncbi.nlm.nih.gov/pubmed/19000847/

6-11 CDC. (2010, July). *Unintentional Drug Poisoning in the United States*. From www.cdc.gov: http://www.cdc.gov/homeandrecreationalsafety/pdf/poison-issue-brief.pdf, p. 1.

6-12 CDC. (2010, July). *Unintentional Drug Poisoning in the United States*. From www.cdc.gov: http://www.cdc.gov/homeandrecreationalsafety/pdf/poison-issue-brief.pdf, p. 2.

6-13 Dvorsky, G. (2012, 19-June). *Prescription Painkillers Now the Leading Cause of Accidental Deaths*. From io9:

http://io9.com/5919434/prescription-painkillers-now-the-leading-cause-of-accidental-deaths

6-14 Rose A. Rudd, M., Noah Aleshire, J., Jon E. Zibbell, P., & R. Matthew
      Gladden, P. (2016, 1 16). *Increases in Drug and Opioid Overdose Deaths
      — United States, 2000–2014.* Retrieved from Centers for Disease
      Control and
      Prevention: http://www.cdc.gov/mmwr/preview/mmwrhtml/m
      m6450a3.htm

6-15 Steven M. Frenk, P., Kathryn S. Porter, M. M., & and Leonard J.
      Paulozzi, M. M. (2015, February). *Prescription Opioid Analgesic Use
      Among Adults: United States, 1999–2012.* Retrieved from NCHS
      Data Brief,No. 189:
      http://www.cdc.gov/nchs/data/databriefs/db189.pdf

6-16 https://www.drugabuse.gov/publications/drugfacts/nationwide-trends

6-17 Judith Weissman, P., Laura A. Pratt, P., Eric A. Miller, P., & and
      Jennifer D. Parker, P. (2015, May). *Serious Psychological Distress Among
      Adults: United States, 2009–2013.* Centers for Disease Control and
      Prevention, National Center for Health Statistics. Retrieved from
      http://www.cdc.gov/nchs/products/databriefs/db203.htm

6-18 Fairchild, C. (2014, 3-June). *Number of Fortune 500 Women CEOs Reaches
      Historic High.* From Fortune:
      http://fortune.com/2014/06/03/number-of-fortune-500-women-
      ceos-reaches-historic-high/

6-19 Zillman, C. (2014, 3-February). *Microsoft's New CEO: One minority exec in a
      sea of white.* From Fortune:
      http://fortune.com/2014/02/04/microsofts-new-ceo-one-
      minority-exec-in-a-sea-of-white/

6-20 Ante, S. E., & Lubin, J. S. (2012, 7-February). *Young CEOs: Are They Up
      to the Job?* From Wall Street Journal:
      http://www.wsj.com/articles/SB100014240529702033158045772073
      1063501196

6-21 Palmer, B. (2013, 2-January). *Democracy or Gerontocracy.* From Slate.com:
      http://www.slate.com/articles/news_and_politics/explainer/2013

/01/average_age_of_members_of_u_s_congress_are_our_senator
s_and_representatives.html

6-22 Brown, B. (2010). *The Gifts of Imperfection - Let Go of Who You Think You're
Supposed to Be and Embrace Who You Are*. Center City, MN:
Hazelden, p. 20.

6-23 Eastman, R. (1988). *Country Blues Performance and the Oral Tradition*. Black
Music Research Journal, 161-176., p. 164.

Chapter 7

7-1 Goldstein, R. L. (1971). *Black Life and Culture in the United States*. New
York, NY: Thomas Y. Crowell Company, p. 84.

7-2 Davidson, R. (2012). *The Emotional Life of Your Brain*. New York, NY:
Penguin Group, pp. 78-81.

7-3 Lafferty, C. L. (Vol. 75, No. 3, Summer 2010). *Neuroleadership, Sustaining
Research Relevance into the 21st Century*. SAM Advanced Management
Journal, 32 - 42.

7-4 Rock, D. (2009, December 2nd). *Google Tech Talks*. Retrieved from
Youtube: http://www.youtube.com/watch?v=XeJSXfXep4M

7-5 Hecht, M. L., & Jackson, R. L. (2003). *African American Communication:
Exploring Identity and Culture*. Marwah, NJ: Lawrence Erlbaum
Associates, Inc., Publishers.

7-6 Rainwater, L. (1967). *Crucible of Identity: The Negro Lower-Class Family*.
Boston, p. 174.

7-7 Most, S., Chun, M., & Widders, D. (2005, 4-December). *Attentional
Rubbernecking: Cognitive Control and Personality in Emotion-induced
Blindness*. Pscychonomic Bulletin and Review, pp. 654-661.

7-8 Rock, D. (2009, December 2nd). *Google Tech Talks*. Retrieved from
Youtube: http://www.youtube.com/watch?v=XeJSXfXep4M

7-9 Braun, J. (1995). *The Nature and Psychology of Civil Society*. Social Pathology in Comparative Perspective, Westport, CT: Praeger Publishers, p. 77.

7-10 Petersen, H. (2011). *Talking Music*. London, ON: Insomniac Press, pp. 111-112.

7-11 Arndt, M., & Smith, S. W. (2013, 13-March). *Michael Arndt on Theme*. From Screenwriting from Iowa - and other unlikely places: http://screenwritingfromiowa.wordpress.com/2013/03/29/micha el-arndt-on-theme/

7-12 Brown, B. (2010). *The Gifts of Imperfection - Let Go of Who You Think You're Supposed to Be and Embrace Who You Are*. Center City, MN: Hazelden, p. 56

7-13 Rock, D. (2009). *Your Brain at Work*. New York, NY: HarperCollins Publishers, p. 99.

Chapter 8

8-1 Petersen, H. (2011*). Talking Music*. London, ON: Insomniac Press, p 98.

8-2 Wolkin, J. M., & Keenom, B. (2000). *Michael Bloomfield, If You Love These Blues - An Oral History*. San Francisco: Miller Freeman Books, p. 18.

8-3 Sauter, Eisner, Ekman, & Scott, (2010, 9-Feb) *Cross-cultural recognition of basic emotions through nonverbal emotional vocalizations*. Proceedings of the National Academy of the Sciences of the United States of America, p. 2408–2412

8-4 Wolkin, J. M., & Keenom, B. (2000). *Michael Bloomfield, If You Love These Blues - An Oral History*. San Francisco: Miller Freeman Books, pp. 8-11

8-5 Brown, S. (2009). Play: *How it Shapes the Brain, Opens the Imagination, and Invigorates the Soul*. Penguin, p. 62.

8-6 Cook, B. (1973). *Listen to the Blues*. New York, NY: Charles Scribner's Sons, p. 144.

8-7 Brown, B. (2010). *The Gifts of Imperfection - Let Go of Who You Think You're Supposed to Be and Embrace Who You Are*. Center City, MN: Hazelden, p. 9.

Chapter 9

9-1 Petersen, H. (2011). *Talking Music*. London, ON: Insomniac Press, p. 84.

9-2 Hamlin, J. K., Neha Mahajan, Z. L., & Wynn, K. (2013). *Not Like Me = Bad: Infants Prefer Those Who Harm Dissimilar Others*. Sage Publications (APS), 589-594.

Chapter 10

10-1 Jackson, K. T. (1985). *Crabgrass Frontier*. New York: Oxford University Press, p. 232.

10-2 Jackson, K. T. (1985). *Crabgrass Frontier*. New York: Oxford University Press, p. 232.

10-3 Roosevelt, F. D. (1938). *Housing Files*. Roosevelt Library, Hyde Park, NY. New York, NY.

10-4 Stilgoe, J. R. (1988). *Borderland: Origins of the American Suburb*. Yale University.

10-5 Tillitt, M. H. (1944, 24-April). *Barron's National Business and Financial Weekly*. From American Merchant Marine at War: http://www.usmm.org/barrons.html

10-6 Elder, G. H. (1999). *Children of the Great Depression: Social Change in Life Experience*. Boulder, CO: Westview Press, p. 282.

10-7 Friedan, B. (1963). *The Feminine Mystique*. New York: W.W. Norton & Company, Inc., p. 213.

[10-8] Jackson, K. T. (1985). *Crabgrass Frontier.* New York: Oxford University Press, p. 419.

[10-9] Friedan, B. (1963). *The Feminine Mystique.* New York: W.W. Norton & Company, Inc., p. 15.

[10-10] Friedan, B. (1963). *The Feminine Mystique.* New York: W.W. Norton & Company, Inc., p. 243.

[10-11] Friedan, B. (1963). *The Feminine Mystique.* New York: W.W. Norton & Company, Inc., p. 244.

[10-12] Bush, G. W. (2001, 20-September). *Text: President Bush Addresses the Nation.* From Washington Post: http://www.washingtonpost.com/wp-srv/nation/specials/attacked/transcripts/bushaddress_092001.html

[10-13] N. I. H. (2010, October). *Post-Traumatic Stress Disorder (PTSD).* From NIH Fact Sheets: http://report.nih.gov/nihfactsheets/ViewFactSheet.aspx?csid=58

[10-14] Rostker, B. (2013). *Providing for the Casualties of War.* Santa Monica, CA: Rand, p. 230.

[10-15] ADAA. (n.d.). *PTSD Symptoms.* From Anxiety and Depression Association of America: http://www.adaa.org/understanding-anxiety/posttraumatic-stress-disorder-ptsd/symptoms

[10-16] Galovski, T., & Lyons, J. A. (2002*). Psychological Sequelae of Combat Violence: A Review of PTSD on the Veteran's Family and Possible Interventions.* Jackson, MS: Pergamon, p. 20.

[10-17] Vento, C. S., & Childers, T. (2011). *The Hidden Legacy of World War II: A Daughter's Journey of Discovery* . Camp Hill, PA: Sunbury Press, p. 14.

[10-18] Moorhead, J. (2012, 28-December). *The Railway Man's Forgotten Family: 'We were victims of torture too'.* Article in The Guardian,http://www.theguardian.com/lifeandstyle/2013/dec/28/railway-mans-forgotten-family

10-19 Pew, R. (2010, 8-March). *The Return of the Multi-Generational Family Household.* From Pew Research Social and Demographic Trends: http://www.pewsocialtrends.org/2010/03/18/the-return-of-the-multi-generational-family-household/

10-20 Balswick, J. O., & Peek, C. W. (1971, Vol. 20, No. 4-Oct). *The Inexpressive Male: A Tragedy of American Society.* The Family Coordinator, p. 365.10-21 Balswick, J. O., & Peek, C. W. (1971, Vol. 20, No. 4-Oct). *The Inexpressive Male: A Tragedy of American Society.* The Family Coordinator, p. 365.

10-22 Balswick, J. O., & Peek, C. W. (1971, Vol. 20, No. 4-Oct). *The Inexpressive Male: A Tragedy of American Society.* The Family Coordinator, p. 368.

10-23 Balswick, J. O., & Peek, C. W. (1971, Vol. 20, No. 4-Oct). *The Inexpressive Male: A Tragedy of American Society.* The Family Coordinator, p. 367.

10-24 Library of Congress, (2010, 23-August) *Everyday Mysteries – Fun Facts from the Library of Congress.* http://www.loc.gov/rr/scitech/mysteries/tvdinner.html

10-25 Duany, A., Plater-Zyberk, E., & Speck, J. (2000). *Suburban Nation.* New York, NY: North Point Press, pp. 4-11.

10-26 Duany, A., Plater-Zyberk, E., & Speck, J. (2000). *Suburban Nation.* New York, NY: North Point Press., p. 4.

10-27 Duany, A., Plater-Zyberk, E., & Speck, J. (2000). *Suburban Nation.* New York, NY: North Point Press, pp. 4-5.

Chapter 11

11-1 Davies, A., & Sinfield, A. (2000). *An Introduction to Literature and Society 1945-1999.* New York: Routledge, p. 1.

11-2 Long, J. B., & Eichengreen, B. (1991). *The Marshall Plan - History's Most Successful Structural Adjustment Program*. Cambridge, MA: National Bureau of Economic Research., pp. 3-4.

11-3 Bargielowska, I. Z. (2002). *Austerity in Britain, Rationing, Controls, and Consumption 1939 - 1955*. Oxford: Oxford University Press., pp. 9 – 26.

11-4 Shepherd, J., & Shepherd, J. (2014). *1950's Childhood: Growing up in Post-war Britain*. Shire Library.

11-5 Shepherd, J., & Shepherd, J. (2014). *1950's Childhood: Growing up in Post-war Britain*. Shire Library.

11-6 Williams, S. (2013). *Politics Is for People*. Harvard University Press., p. 17.

11-7 Shepherd, J., & Shepherd, J. (2014). *1950's Childhood: Growing up in Post-war Britain*. Shire Library.

11-8 Shepherd, J., & Shepherd, J. (2014). *1950's Childhood: Growing up in Post-war Britain*. Shire Library.

11-9 Davies, A., & Sinfield, A. (2000). *An Introduction to Literature and Society 1945-1999*. New York: Routledge, p. 3.

11-10 MacDonald, I. S. (1974). *Anglo-American Relations Since the Second World War*. London: David and Charles., pp. 181-182.

11-11 Davies, A., & Sinfield, A. (2000). *An Introduction to Literature and Society 1945-1999*. New York: Routledge, p. 2.

11-12 Ward, B. (1998). *Just My Soul Responding - Rhythm and Blues, Black Consciousness, and Race Relations*. Berkeley, CA: University of California Press., p. 91.

11-13 Find the Data, t. w. (2015). *British Empire 1603 - 1949*. From Find the Data: http://empires.findthedata.com/l/1/British-Empire.

11-14 Ward, P. (2004). *Britishness Since 1870*. London: Routledge., p. 91.

11-15 Clarke, J., Hall, S., Jefferson, T., & Roberts, B. (1975). *Resistance Through Rituals: Youth Subcultures in Post-War Britain*. Birmingham: Routledge, Taylor & Francis Group, pp. 9-10

11-16 Braun, J. (1995). *The Nature and Psychology of Civil Society*. Social Pathology in Comparative Perspective, Westport, CT: Praeger Publishers, p. 328.

11-17 Barber, C. (2013, 19th-December). (M. Trout, Interviewer)

11-18 Barber, C. (2013, 19th-December). (M. Trout, Interviewer)

11-19 Barber, C. (2013, 19th-December). (M. Trout, Interviewer)

Chapter 12

12-1 Mezzrow, M. & Wolfe, B. (1990). *Really the Blues*. New York: A Citadel Press Book published by Carol Publishing Group, p. 5.

12-2 Mezzrow, M. & Wolfe, B. (1990). *Really the Blues*. New York: A Citadel Press Book published by Carol Publishing Group, p. 18.

12-3 Mezzrow, M. & Wolfe, B. (1990). *Really the Blues*. New York: A Citadel Press Book published by Carol Publishing Group, p. 18.

12-4 Mezzrow, M. & Wolfe, B. (1990). *Really the Blues*. New York: A Citadel Press Book published by Carol Publishing Group, p. 323.

12-5 Wolkin, J. M., & Keenom, B. (2000). *Michael Bloomfield, If You Love These Blues - An Oral History*. San Francisco: Miller Freeman Books, p. 11.

12-6 Wolkin, J. M., & Keenom, B. (2000). *Michael Bloomfield, If You Love These Blues - An Oral History*. San Francisco: Miller Freeman Books, p. 27

12-7 Wolkin, J. M., & Keenom, B. (2000). *Michael Bloomfield, If You Love These Blues - An Oral History*. San Francisco: Miller Freeman Books, p. 17.

12-8 Wolkin, J. M., & Keenom, B. (2000). *Michael Bloomfield, If You Love These Blues - An Oral History*. San Francisco: Miller Freeman Books, p. 30.

12-9 Wolkin, J. M., & Keenom, B. (2000). *Michael Bloomfield, If You Love These Blues - An Oral History.* San Francisco: Miller Freeman Books, p. 30.

12-10 Smith, W. (2012). *The Pied Pipers of Rock 'n' Roll - Radio DeeJays of the '50s and '60s.* Iconoclassic Books, p. 14.

12-11 Mayberry, C. E. (2011). *Sam Phillips, Elvis, & Rock N' Roll: A Cultural Revolution. Explorations, Humanities and Fine Arts, Vol. VI*, p. 100.

12-12 Smith, W. (2012). *The Pied Pipers of Rock 'n' Roll - Radio DeeJays of the '50s and '60s.* Iconoclassic Books, p. 64.

12-13 Hari, J. (2015). *Chasing the Scream - The First and Last Days of the War on Drugs.* New York, NY: Bloomsbury., p. 18.

Chapter 13

13-1 Jourdain, R. (1997). *Music, the Brain and Ecstacy.* New York, NY: Avon Books, p.258

13-2 Keil, C. (1966, 1991). *Urban Blues.* Chicago, IL: The University of Chicago Press, pp. 58-58.

13-3 Keil, C. (1966, 1991). *Urban Blues.* Chicago, IL: The University of Chicago Press, pp. 232-233.

13-4 Dvořák, A. (1895, February). *Music in America.* Harper's New Monthly Magazine, pp. 429-434.

13-5 Pleasants, H. (1955). *The Agony of Modern Music.* New York: Simon and Schuster.

13-6 Russell, T. (2010). *A Renegade History of the United States.* New York, NY: Free Press - Simon and Schuster, Inc., p. 39.

13-7 Riggs, Marlon (1987) *Ethnic Notions.* Documentary.

13-8 Merry, P. (2013). *How Blues Evolved - Volume I.* Kindle e-book, p. 1127.

13-9 Browne, R. B. (1980). *Rituals and Ceremonies in Popular Culture.* Bowling Green, OH: Bowling Green State University Press., p. 151.

13-10 Jordan, W. (1968). *White Over Black, American Attitudes Toward the Negro, 1550-1812.* Durham: University of North Carolina Press, pp. 238-239.

13-11 Jordan, W. (1968). *White Over Black, American Attitudes Toward the Negro, 1550-1812.* Durham: University of North Carolina Press, p. 491.

13-12 Lott, E. (1992, Summer). *Love and Theft: The Racial Unconscious of Blackface Minstrelsy.* Representations, pp. 23-50, p. 23.

13-13 Browne, R. B. (1980*). Rituals and Ceremonies in Popular Culture.* Bowling Green, OH: Bowling Green State University Press, pp. 153-154.

13-14 Russell, T. (2010). *A Renegade History of the United States.* New York, NY: Free Press - Simon and Schuster, Inc., p. 41.

13-15 Kellogg, J. H. (1881). *Plain Facts for Young and Old .* Burlington, IA: Segner and Condit, pp. 294-296.

13-16 Kellogg, J. H. (1881). *Plain Facts for Young and Old .* Burlington, IA: Segner and Condit, p. 382.

13-17 Kellogg, J. H. (1881). *Plain Facts for Young and Old .* Burlington, IA: Segner and Condit, p. 402.

13-18 Rainwater, L. (1967). *Crucible of Identity: The Negro Lower-Class Family.* Boston., p. 173.

13-19 D'Emilio, J., & Freedman, E. B. (1997*). Intimate Matters: A History of Sexuality in America - Second Edition.* London, UK: University of Chicago Press, pp. 95-96.

13-20 Lott, E. (1992, Summer). *Love and Theft: The Racial Unconscious of Blackface Minstrelsy.* Representations, pp. 23-50, p. 30.

13-21 Lomax, A. (1993*). The Land Where the Blues Began.* New York, NY: Dell Publishing, p. 83.

[13-22] Lomax, A. (1993). *The Land Where the Blues Began*. New York, NY: Dell Publishing, p. 84.

[13-23] Stevenson, B. E. (1996). *Life in Black and White - Family and Community in the Slave South*. New York, NY: Oxford University Press, p. 238.

[13-24] Stevenson, B. E. (1996*). Life in Black and White - Family and Community in the Slave South*. New York, NY: Oxford University Press, p. 238.

[13-25] Stevenson, B. E. (1996). *Life in Black and White - Family and Community in the Slave South*. New York, NY: Oxford University Press, p. 237.

[13-26] Russell, T. (2010). A *Renegade History of the United States*. New York, NY: Free Press - Simon and Schuster, Inc., p. 55.

[13-27] Russell, T. (2010). *A Renegade History of the United States*. New York, NY: Free Press - Simon and Schuster, Inc., pp. 54-55.

[13-28] Bolton, Charles C. (2004) *Farmers without Land – the Plight of White Tenant Farmers and Sharecroppers*.

[13-29] Phillips, Kenneth E. (2015) *Sharecropping and Tenant Farming in Alabama*. Encyclopedia of Alabama

[13-30] (Carter, Dan T. 2000, p. 27) *The Politics of Rage: George Wallace, the Origins of the New Conservatism, and the Transformation of American Politics*. Baton Rouge, Louisiana, LSU Press. p. 27.

[13-31] Mailer, N. (1957). *The White Negro* . Dissent Publishing Associates, p. II.

[13-32] Mailer, N. (1957). *The White Negro* . Dissent Publishing Associates, Part III.

[13-33] Mailer, N. (1957). *The White Negro* . Dissent Publishing Associates, Section II.

[13-34] Mailer, N. (1957). *The White Negro* . Dissent Publishing Associates, Section III.

[13-35] Mailer, N. (1957). *The White Negro* . Dissent Publishing Associates, Section III.

13-36 Mailer, N. (1957). *The White Negro* . Dissent Publishing Associates, Polsky Rebuttal.

13-37 Lund, J., & Denisoff, R. S. (1971). *The Folk Music Revival and the Counter Culture: Contributions and Contradictions.* American Folklore Society, pp. 395-396.

13-38 Lund, J., & Denisoff, R. S. (1971). *The Folk Music Revival and the Counter Culture: Contributions and Contradictions.* American Folklore Society, 394-405, pp. 395-397.

13-39 Lund, J., & Denisoff, R. S. (1971). *The Folk Music Revival and the Counter Culture: Contributions and Contradictions.* American Folklore Society, p. 398.

13-40 Lund, J., & Denisoff, R. S. (1971). *The Folk Music Revival and the Counter Culture: Contributions and Contradictions.* American Folklore Society, p. 402.

13-41 Lund, J., & Denisoff, R. S. (1971). *The Folk Music Revival and the Counter Culture: Contributions and Contradictions.* American Folklore Society, p. 394.

13-42 Lund, J., & Denisoff, R. S. (1971). *The Folk Music Revival and the Counter Culture: Contributions and Contradictions.* American Folklore Society, p. 402.

13-43 Leland, J. (2004). *Hip: The History.* New York, NY: HarperCollins, p. 24.

13-44 Leland, J. (2004). *Hip: The History.* New York, NY: HarperCollins, p. 59.

13-45 McClary, S., & Walser, R. (1994). *Theorizing the Body in African-American Music.* Black Music Research Journal, pp. 76-77.

13-46 Keil, C. (1966, 1991). *Urban Blues.* Chicago, IL: The University of Chicago Press, p. 233.

13-47 Adelt, U. (2010). *Blues Music in the Sixties.* New Brunswick, NJ: Rutgers University Press, p. 61.

13-48 Orforlea, A. N. (2012). *[Un] veiling the White Gaze: Revealing Self and Other in The Land Where the Blues Began.* The Western Journal of Black Studies, p. 297.

13-49 Levitin, D. J. (2006). *This is Your Brain on Music - The Science of a Human Obsession.* New York, NY: Penguin Group, p. 258.

13-50 Levitin, D. J. (2006). *This is Your Brain on Music - The Science of a Human Obsession.* New York, NY: Penguin Group, p. 257.

13-51 Blacking, J. (1974). *How Musical is Man?* Seattle, WA: University of Washington Press, p. 111.

13-52 Lomax, A. (1993). *The Land Where the Blues Began.* New York, NY: Dell Publishing, pp. 262-263.

13-53 Orforlea, A. N. (2012). *[Un] veiling the White Gaze: Revealing Self and Other in The Land Where the Blues Began.* The Western Journal of Black Studies, pp. 297-298.

13-54 Lomax, A. (1993). *The Land Where the Blues Began.* New York, NY: Dell Publishing, pp. 85-86.

Chapter 14

14-1 Berish, A. (2012). *Lonesome Roads and Streets of Dreams - Place, Mobility, and Race in Jazz of the 1930's and '40's.* Chicago, IL: University of Chicago Press, p. 1.

Chapter 15

15-1 Spencer, J. M. (1993). *Blues and Evil.* Knoxville, TN: The University of Tennessee Press, p. 39.

15-2 Watkins, R. B. (2011). *Hip-Hop Redemption: Finding God in the Rhythm and the Rhyme.* Ada, MI: Baker Academic, p. 59.

15-3 Winborn, M. (2011). *Deep Blues.* Carmel, CA: Fisher King Press, p. 67.

15-4 Scheff, T. (1979). *Catharsis in Healing, Ritual, and Drama.* Berkeley and Los Angeles, CA: University of California Press, p. 14.

15-5 Winborn, M. (2011). *Deep Blues.* Carmel, CA: Fisher King Press, p. 69.

15-6 Keil, C. (1966, 1991). *Urban Blues.* Chicago, IL: The University of Chicago Press, p. 164.

Chapter 16

16-1 Block, R. (2006). *Robert Johnson's Family - and the Down at the Crossroads Blues meets Gospel Tours.* From Rory Block's Official Website: http://www.roryblock.com/Pages/Page%20Links/Johnson%20Family.htm

16-2 Lincoln, B. (1977). *Two Notes on Modern Rituals.* Journal of the American Academy of Religion, 147-160, pp. 147-160.

16-3 Shlain, L. (1998). *The Alphabet and the Goddess - The Conflict Between Word and Image.* New York, NY: Penguin Group, p. 418.

16-4 Bargh, G. (2012). *100 Social Networking Facts for 2012.* From Visually: http://visual.ly/100-social-networking-statistics-facts-2012

16-5 Nørretranders, T. (1991). *The User Illusion.* New York, NY: Penguin Group, p. 126.

16-6 Grof, C. (1993). *The Thirst for Wholeness, Attachment, Addiction and the Spiritual Path.* New York, NY: Harper Collins Publishers, p.1.

16-7 Scheff, T. (1979). *Catharsis in Healing, Ritual, and Drama.* Berkeley and Los Angeles, CA: University of California Press, p. 14.

16-8 Browne, R. B. (1980). *Rituals and Ceremonies in Popular Culture.* Bowling Green, OH: Bowling Green State University Press, p. TOC.

16-9 Lincoln, B. (1977). *Two Notes on Modern Rituals.* Journal of the American Academy of Religion, 147-160, p. 149.

16-10 Bird, F. (1980). *The Nature and Function of Ritual Forms: A sociological Discussion*. Studies in Religion/Sciences Religieuses, 387-402(Fall 1980), p. 387.

Chapter 17

17-1 Steinberg, J. R., & Fairweather, A. (2012). *Blues Philosophy for Everyone*. Chichester, UK: Wiley & Sons, Inc, p. 47.

17-2 Steinberg, J. R., & Fairweather, A. (2012). *Blues Philosophy for Everyone*. Chichester, UK: Wiley & Sons, Inc, p. 47.

17-3 Jones, L. (1963). *Blues People - The Negro Experience in White America and the Music that Developed from it*. New York, NY: William Morrow and Company, pp. 147-148.

17-4 Nelson, P., & Hedin, B. (2004). *Studio A - The Bob Dylan Reader*. New York, NY: W.W. Norton and Company.

17-5 Wilber, K. (2000). *Integral Psychology - Consciousness, Spirit, Pshychology, Therapy*. Boston, MA: Shambhala Publications, Inc, p.5.

17-6 Keil, C. (1966, 1991). *Urban Blues*. Chicago, IL: The University of Chicago Press, pp. 69-70.

17-7 Rehding, A. (2000). *The Quest for the Origins of Music in Germany Circa 1900*. The Journal of the American Musicological Society, p. 379.

17-8 Rehding, A. (2000). *The Quest for the Origins of Music in Germany Circa 1900*. The Journal of the American Musicological Society, p. 378.

17-9 Rehding, A. (2000). *The Quest for the Origins of Music in Germany Circa 1900*. The Journal of the American Musicological Society, pp. 377-378.

17-10 Drescher, S., & Engerman, S. L. (1998). *A Historical Guide to World Slavery*. New York: Oxford University Press, p. 32.

17-11 Merry, P. (2013). *How Blues Evolved - Volume I*. Kindle e-book, p. location 202.

17-12 Oliver, P. (1970). *Savannah Syncopators African Retention in the Blues*. New York: Stein and Day, p. 75.

Chapter 18

18-1 Ambrose, S. E. (1994). D-*Day: June 6, 1944--the Climactic Battle of WWII*. New York: Simon and Schuster, Inc, p. 147.

18-2 Krause, L. (2001, 15-February). *Black Soldiers in WW II: Fighting Enemies at Home and Abroad*. National Geographic News, p. http://news.nationalgeographic.com/news/2001/02/0215_tuskeg ee.html.

18-3 Sklaroff, L. R. (2004). *The Jubilee Show and the Paradox of Racializing Radio during World War II*. Project Muse - Johns Hopkins University Press, p. 945-973.

18-4 Ambrose, S. E. (1994). D-*Day: June 6, 1944--the Climactic Battle of WWII*. New York: Simon and Schuster, Inc, p. 147.

18-5 Sklaroff, L. R. (2004). *The Jubilee Show and the Paradox of Racializing Radio during World War II*. Project Muse - Johns Hopkins University Press, p. 946.

18-6 Sklaroff, L. R. (2004). *The Jubilee Show and the Paradox of Racializing Radio during World War II*. Project Muse - Johns Hopkins University Press, p. 946.

18-7 Ambrose, S. E. (1994). D-*Day: June 6, 1944--the Climactic Battle of WWII*. New York: Simon and Schuster, Inc., p. 148.

18-8 Ambrose, S. E. (1994). *D-Day: June 6, 1944--the Climactic Battle of WWII*. New York: Simon and Schuster, Inc., p. 148.

18-9 Krause, L. (2001, 15-February). *Black Soldiers in WW II: Fighting Enemies at Home and Abroad*. National Geographic News, p. http://news.nationalgeographic.com/news/2001/02/0215_tuskeg ee.html.

18-10 Ambrose, S. E. (1994). *D-Day: June 6, 1944--the Climactic Battle of WWII*. New York: Simon and Schuster, Inc., pp. 148-149.

18-11 Ambrose, S. E. (1994). D-*Day: June 6, 1944--the Climactic Battle of WWII*. New York: Simon and Schuster, Inc., p. 149.

18-12 Mullen, R. W. (1973). *Blacks in America's Wars*. Pathfinder Press, p. 55.

18-13 Woodland, J. (2011). *How Did Participation in America's Wars Affect Black Americans?* From Liverpool John Moores University - American Studies Today: http://www.americansc.org.uk/Online/Woodland.htm#15

18-14 King, D. (1997). *Separate and Unequal: Black Americans and the US Federal Government*. Oxford: Clarendon Press, p. 183.

18-15 King, D. (1997). *Separate and Unequal: Black Americans and the US Federal Government*. Oxford: Clarendon Press, p. 189.

18-16 Boustan, L. P. (2010). *Was Postwar Suburbanization "White Flight" Evidence from the Black Migration*. The Quarterly Journal of Economics - Oxford Journal, pp. 417-443.

18-17 Halpern, Stephen C. (1995). *On the Limits of the Law: The Ironic Legacy of Title VI of the 1964 Civil Rights Act*. John Hopkins University Press p. 10

18-18 Abrams, Charles (1955) *Forbidden Neighbors: A Study of Prejudice in Housing*. New York, NY: Harper Collins Publishers, p. ix

18-19 Halpern, Stephen C. (1995). *On the Limits of the Law: The Ironic Legacy of Title VI of the 1964 Civil Rights Act*. John Hopkins University Press

18-20 Wiese, A. (2004). *Places of Their Own: African American Suburbanization in the Twentieth Century*. Chicago: University of Chicago Press, p. 100.

18-21 Halpern, Stephen C. (1995). *On the Limits of the Law: The Ironic Legacy of Title VI of the 1964 Civil Rights Act*. John Hopkins University Press p. 229)

18-22 Kochhar, Rakesh & Fry, Richard (2014 12-December). *Wealth inequality has widened along racial, ethnic lines since end of Great Recession.* Factank, Pew Research Center

18-23 Weissman, D. (2005). *Blues: The Basics.* New York, NY: Routledge, p. 121.

18-24 Rainwater, L. (1967). *Crucible of Identity: The Negro Lower-Class Family.* Boston, pp. 194-195.

18-25 Springer, R. (1976 - Vol. 4, no. 3). *The Regulatory Function of the Blues.* The Black Perspective in Music, p. 281.

18-26 Springer, R. (1976 - Vol. 4, no. 3). *The Regulatory Function of the Blues.* The Black Perspective in Music, p. 283.

18-27 Oliver, P. (1968). *Screening the Blues: Aspects of the Blues Tradition.* New York, NY: Da Capo Press, Inc., p. 12.

18-28 Springer, R. (1976 - Vol. 4, no. 3). *The Regulatory Function of the Blues.* The Black Perspective in Music, p. 286.

18-29 Springer, R. (1976 - Vol. 4, no. 3). *The Regulatory Function of the Blues.* The Black Perspective in Music, p. 279.

18-30 Springer, R. (1976 - Vol. 4, no. 3). *The Regulatory Function of the Blues.* The Black Perspective in Music, p. 286.

18-31 Steinberg, J. R.. & Fairweather, A. (2012). *Blues Philosophy for Everyone.* Chichester, UK: Wiley & Sons, Inc., pp. xiii – xiv.

18-32 King, A & Vaughan, S (1983, 6-December). *In Session.* CHCH-TV Ontario, Canada.

18-33 Ellison, R. (1953). *Shadow and Act.* New York: Random House, p. 286.

18-34 Martino, Pat; Milkowski, Bill (2011). *Here and Now! The Autobiography of Pat Martino.* Milwaukee, WI. Backbeat Books - Hal Leonard Corporation, p. 73.

Chapter 19

[19-35] Rouget, G. (1985). *Music and Trance - A Theory of the Relations Between Music and Possession.* Chicago: The University of Chicago Press, pp. 325-326.

[19-36] Grof, S. (2000). *Psychology of the Future, Lessons from Modern Consciousness Research.* Albany, NY: State University of New York Press, pp. 7-11.

[19-37] Rouget, G. (1985). *Music and Trance - A Theory of the Relations Between Music and Possession.* Chicago: The University of Chicago Press, p. 10.

[19-38] Aldridge, D., & Fachner, J. (2006). *Music and Altered States - Consciousness, Transcendence, Therapy and Addictions.* Philadelphia, PA: Jessica Kingsley Publishers, p. 18.

[19-39] Jourdain, R. (1997). *Music, the Brain and Ecstacy.* New York, NY: Avon Books., pp. 327-328.

[19-1] Moody, R. (2010). *The Secret World of Nonsense.* Unpublished mss. Anniston: AL, p. 205.

[19-2] Tart, C. T. (1983, 2000). *States of Consciousness.* Lincoln, NE: iUniverse.com, inc., p. 33-34.

[19-3] Moody, R. (2010). *The Secret World of Nonsense.* Unpublished mss. Anniston: AL, p. 137.

[19-4] Moody, R. (2010). *The Secret World of Nonsense.* Unpublished mss. Anniston: AL, p. 142.

[19-5] Moody, R. (2010). *The Secret World of Nonsense.* Unpublished mss. Anniston: AL, p. 168.

[19-6] Smiley, Tavis & King, B.B. *PBS interview.* (2013, 10-September)

[19-7] Moody, R. (2010). *The Secret World of Nonsense.* Unpublished mss. Anniston: AL, p. 182.

[19-8] Johnson, R. (1937). *Hellhound on my Trail.*

19-9 Ledbetter, H. (1939)

19-10 Elliottt, M & Timbaland, M. (2002) From the album: Under Construction.

19-11 Hendrix, J. (1967)

Chapter 20

19-12 Eastman, R. (1988). *Country Blues Performance and the Oral Tradition.* Black Music Research Journal, p. 166.

20-1 Pretto, M. D. (2001). *In Quest of an Internal Timekeeper: Contribution to the Understanding of How the Brain Deals with Rhythmical Behaviours.* Geneve: University of Geneva, pp. 8-9.

20-2 Mezzrow, M., & Wolfe, B. (1990). *Really the Blues.* New York: A Citadel Press Book published by Carol Publishing Group, 1990, p. 322.

20-3 Sloman, L. (1998). *Reefer Madness: A History of Marijuana.* New York, NY: St. Martin's Press, pp. 146-147.

Chapter 21

21-1 Tart, C. T. (1983, 2000). *States of Consciousness.* Lincoln, NE: iUniverse.com, inc., p. 250.

21-2 Berry, E. L. (1984). *Shakespeare's Comic Rites.* Cambridge, United Kingdom: Cambridge University Press, p. 8.

21-3 Hanson, R. P. (2009). *Buddha's Brain - Happiness, Love & Wisdom.* Oakland, CA: New Harbinger Publications, Inc., p. 68.

21-4 Hanson, R. P. (2009). *Buddha's Brain - Happiness, Love & Wisdom.* Oakland, CA: New Harbinger Publications, Inc., p. 68-74.

21-5 Hanson, R. P. (2009). *Buddha's Brain - Happiness, Love & Wisdom.* Oakland, CA: New Harbinger Publications, Inc., p. 75.

21-6 Scheff, T. (1979). *Catharsis in Healing, Ritual, and Drama.* Berkeley and Los Angeles, CA: University of California Press, p. 51.

21-7 Jourdain, R. (1997). *Music, the Brain and Ecstacy.* New York, NY: Avon Books, p. 330.

21-8 Johnson, R. (1937). *Hellhound on My Trail.*

21-9 Jourdain, R. (1997). *Music, the Brain and Ecstacy.* New York, NY: Avon Books, p. 327.

21-10 Petersen, H. (2011*). Talking Music.* London, ON: Insomniac Press, p. 100

21-11 Arewa, O. (2012). *Copyright and Borrowing.* Intellectual Property and Information Wealth: Issues and Practices in the Digital Age, *Vol. 1, Chapter 2, Praeger Publishers, 20*, pp. 34-36.

21-12 Arewa, O. (2012). *Copyright and Borrowing.* Intellectual Property and Information Wealth: Issues and Practices in the Digital Age, *Vol. 1, Chapter 2, Praeger Publishers, 20*, p. 41.

21-13 Pleasants, H. (1955) *The Agony of Modern Music.* New York, NY: Simon and Schuster, p. 173

21-14 Zald, D., & Zatore, R. (2011). *Neurobiology of Sensation and Reward.* Boca Raton, FL, http://www.ncbi.nlm.nih.gov/books/NBK92781/?report=printable: Proceedings of the Ntional Academy of Sciences of the United States of America, p. 19.4.8.

21-15 Zald, D., & Zatore, R. (2011). *Neurobiology of Sensation and Reward.* Boca Raton, FL, http://www.ncbi.nlm.nih.gov/books/NBK92781/?report=printable: Proceedings of the Ntional Academy of Sciences of the United States of America, p. 19.4.5.

Chapter 22

22-1 Keil, C. (2010). Defining "Groove". *PopScriptum*, p. 1.

22-2 Jourdain, R. (1997). *Music, the Brain and Ecstacy*. New York, NY: Avon Books, pp. 120-154.

22-3 Grof, S. (2000). *Psychology of the Future, Lessons from Modern Consciousness Research*. Albany, NY: State University of New York Press., p. 5.

22-4 Grof, S. (1992). *The Holotropic Mind*. New York, NY: HarperCollins Publishers, p. 190.

22-5 Grof, S. (2000). *Psychology of the Future, Lessons from Modern Consciousness Research*. Albany, NY: State University of New York Press, p. 186-187.

22-6 Pretto, M. D. (2001). *In Quest of an Internal Timekeeper: Contribution to the Understanding of How the Brain Deals with Rhythmical Behaviours*. Geneve: University of Geneva, p. 8.

22-7 Newbold, W. (1895). *Psychology*. The American Naturalist, p. 505.

22-8 Newbold, W. (1895). *Psychology*. The American Naturalist, p. 507.

22-9 Sacks, O. (2008). *Musicophilia, Tales of Music and the Brain*. New York, NY: Vintage - Random House, p. 266.

22-10 Rouget, G. (1985). *Music and Trance - A Theory of the Relations Between Music and Possession*. Chicago: The University of Chicago Press, pp. 119-121.

22-11 Rouget, G. (1985). *Music and Trance - A Theory of the Relations Between Music and Possession*. Chicago: The University of Chicago Press, pp. 120-121.

22-12 Owsinsky, B. (2009). *How to Make Your Band Sound Great: Music pro guides*. Hal Leonard Corporation, p. 87.

22-13 Keil, C. (2010). *Defining "Groove"*. PopScriptum, 1-4, p. 2.

22-14 Keil, C. (2010). *Defining "Groove".* PopScriptum, 1-4, p. 2.

22-15 Pretto, M. D. (2011). *In Quest of an Internal Timekeeper: Contribution to the Understanding of How the Brain Deals with Rhythmical Behaviours. (Doctoral Thesis).* Geneva: University of Geneva, http://archiveouverte.unige.ch, p. v.

22-16 Pretto, M. D. (2011). *In Quest of an Internal Timekeeper: Contribution to the Understanding of How the Brain Deals with Rhythmical Behaviours. (Doctoral Thesis).* Geneva: University of Geneva, http://archiveouverte.unige.ch, p. 110.

22-17 Pretto, M. D. (2011). *In Quest of an Internal Timekeeper: Contribution to the Understanding of How the Brain Deals with Rhythmical Behaviours. (Doctoral Thesis).* Geneva: University of Geneva, http://archiveouverte.unige.ch, p. 109.

22-18 Sacks, O. (2008). *Musicophilia, Tales of Music and the Brain.* New York, NY: Vintage - Random House, pp. 267-268.

22-19 Wilson, E. O. (2012). *The Social Conquest of Earth.* New York, NY: Liveright Publishing Corporation.

22-20 Wilson, E. O. (2012). *The Social Conquest of Earth.* New York, NY: Liveright Publishing Corporation, pp. 289-297.

22-21 Pinker, S. (2009). *How the Mind Works.* W.W. Norton and Company, p. 534.

22-22 Wilson, E. O. (2012). *The Social Conquest of Earth.* New York, NY: Liveright Publishing Corporation., p. 282.

22-23 Wilson, E. O. (1975). *Sociobiology.* Cambridge, UK: Cambridge University Press, p. 564.

22-24 Rouget, G. (1985). *Music and Trance - A Theory of the Relations Between Music and Possession.* Chicago: The University of Chicago Press, pp. 139 -147.

22-25 Rogers, R., Santana, C., Thompson, C., & Hooker, J. L. (Directors). (1989). *The Healer* [Motion Picture].

22-26 Keeney, B. (2005). *Bushman Shaman, Awakening the Spirit through Ecstatic Dance*. Rochester, VT: Destiny Books., p. 218.

Chapter 23

23-1 Duijnisveld, F. (Director). (2014). *The Blues Came Callin'* [Motion Picture].